Engaging Biblical Authority

Engaging Biblical Authority

Perspectives on the Bible as Scripture

EDITED BY
WILLIAM P. BROWN

Westminster John Knox Press
LOUISVILLE • LONDON

Scripture quotations, unless otherwise indicated, are from the New Revised Standard Version of the Bible, copyright © 1989 by the Division of Christian Education of the National Council of the Churches of Christ in the U.S.A., and used by permission.

Scripture quotations from *The Tanakh: The New JPS Translation according to the Traditional Hebrew Text.* Copyright 1985 by the Jewish Publication Society. Used by permission.

Book design by Sharon Adams
Cover design by Night & Day Design

First edition
Published by Westminster John Knox Press
Louisville, Kentucky

This book is printed on acid-free paper that meets the American National Standards Institute Z39.48 standard. ⊗

PRINTED IN THE UNITED STATES OF AMERICA

07 08 09 10 11 12 13 14 15 16 — 10 9 8 7 6 5 4 3 2 1

Library of Congress Cataloging-in-Publication Data

Engaging biblical authority : perspectives on the Bible as Scripture / William P. Brown, editor.
    p. cm.
  ISBN 978-0-664-23057-9 (alk. paper)
  1. Bible—Evidences, authority, etc.   I. Brown, William P.
  BS480.E54   2007
  220.1'3—dc22   2007006717

Contents

Acknowledgments   vii

Abbreviations   viii

Introduction   ix
  William P. Brown

1. Biblical Authority: A Jewish Pluralistic View   1
  Marc Zvi Brettler

2. Hearing the Master's Voice   10
  Michael Joseph Brown

3. The Biblical Mainstay of Liberation   18
  Katie G. Cannon

4. "Lámpara es a mis pies tu palabra": Biblical Authority
   at the Crossroads   27
  Carlos F. Cardoza-Orlandi

5. The Soil That Is Scripture   36
  Ellen F. Davis

6. The Authority of the Bible and the Imaging of God   45
  Terence E. Fretheim

7. On the Authorities of Scripture   53
  Robert W. Jenson

8. The Bible's Authority for and in the Church   62
  Luke Timothy Johnson

 9. Inhabiting Scripture, Dreaming Bible   73
    Serene Jones

10. Authority and Narrative   81
    Sarah Heaner Lancaster

11. Alternative Worlds: Reading the Bible as Scripture   90
    Jacqueline E. Lapsley

12. Biblical Authority and the Scandal of the Incarnation   98
    Frank J. Matera

13. The Charter of Christian Faith and Practice   106
    S. Dean McBride Jr.

14. The Bible's Wounded Authority   113
    Peter Ochs

15. Authority and the Practice of Reading Scripture   122
    Allen Verhey

16. The Word of Creative Love, Peace, and Justice   132
    Seung Ai Yang

Notes   141

Contributors   155

Acknowledgments

As editor I want to express my appreciation to the sixteen authors who contributed to this worthy project. Together they made the resulting volume an accessible and stimulating resource for the church and the classroom. Editing and presenting the essays for a wide readership was a gratifying experience from beginning to end.

This volume is dedicated to the many students whom I have had the honor of teaching (and learning from) at the two institutions I have been called to serve during my teaching career: Union Theological Seminary and Presbyterian School of Christian Education in Richmond, Virginia, and Columbia Theological Seminary in Decatur, Georgia. Without their questions, concerns, and occasional confrontations the idea for this volume would never have developed.

Abbreviations

AB	Anchor Bible
ABD	*Anchor Bible Dictionary.* Edited by D. N. Freedman. 6 vols. New York: Doubleday, 1992.
ABRL	Anchor Bible Reference Library
BC	*Book of Confessions*
CBQ	*Catholic Biblical Quarterly*
DBI	*Dictionary of Biblical Interpretation.* Edited by John H. Hayes. 2 vols. Nashville: Abingdon, 1999.
IDB	*The Interpreter's Dictionary of the Bible.* Edited by G. A. Buttrick. 4 vols. Nashville: Abingdon, 1962.
JBL	*Journal of Biblical Literature*
KJV	King James Version
NJPS	*Tanakh: The Holy Scriptures: The New JPS Translation according to the Traditional Hebrew Text*
NRSV	New Revised Standard Version
NT	New Testament
OT	Old Testament
OTS	Old Testament Studies

Introduction

William P. Brown

It is claimed that as W. C. Fields was on his deathbed reading the Bible, his physician asked him, "What are you doing?" He answered, "I'm looking for loopholes." This apocryphal anecdote points to a serious topic. The rubric of authority as applied to the Bible has been and continues to be a divisive issue for people of faith. For some, the term "authority" smacks of legalism, forcing one to look for loopholes, and reflects the painful history of the church's abuse of the Bible. Others regard "authority" as an essential feature of Scripture that promotes life-sustaining obedience. Biblical authority, in short, means different things to different people from different contexts, *especially* among people of faith, for whom the rubric of authority is inescapable. The authority of Scripture remains a given, but its import and extent within the life of faith is a matter of significant debate.

The roots of the debate run deep. The formation of the Christian canon was met with its detractors almost at the outset, from the gnostic Marcion of Pontus of the second century CE, who considered the Old Testament and some of the New Testament Scriptures to be theologically and morally objectionable, to the pagan philosopher Celsus (also of the second century), who wrote extensively on the Bible's internal contradictions and dependencies on popular myths. Propelled by the development of scientific and historical inquiry, the Enlightenment of seventeenth-century Europe directly challenged the veracity of biblical revelation while, at the same time, setting the stage for the "scientific" study of the Bible. A mixed blessing by any measure, the rise of rationalism in Western history resulted, as coined by Hans Frei, in the "eclipse of biblical narrative."[1]

More recently, the claim of biblical authority has suffered both the rise of biblical illiteracy within the church and the profusion of pluralistic claims to truth entering the popular mainstream, all vying for attention. And there is, of course, the long history of abuse and exploitation committed by individuals, faith communities, and governments under the aegis of Scripture. In the face of such developments, many have found the rubric of authority no longer useful for appreciating the significance of Scripture and its life-shaping power. The aim of this volume is to offer constructive ways of speaking about biblical authority.

Although a number of recent works have developed particular views on biblical authority, this volume is markedly different. First, it is multi-authored and, as such, covers a spectrum of perspectives articulated by serious readers and teachers of Scripture. Each essay finds the rubric of authority to be useful, but in varying degrees and in diverse ways. Second, it is designed specifically as a resource for students who are encountering, perhaps for the first time, the critical study of Scripture at a seminary or divinity school. For many, an introductory course to the Old Testament in the first semester of theological study presents nothing short of a culture shock, if not a theological crisis, from first-time exposure to pentateuchal sources, literary genres, settings in life, historical contexts, and contextual hermeneutics, including perspectives informed by race, class, and gender. Together they present a bewildering array of approaches to the biblical text that any student would find confusing at best, and at worst deeply threatening. Consequently, the notion of biblical authority is either seriously called into question by students or staunchly (and defensively) defended. All too often, students fall into fierce resistance or intractable despair when it comes to biblical studies.

This volume is designed to mitigate the "shock" and help readers articulate an understanding of biblical authority in relation to the critical study of Scripture. Featured are contributions from those who have not only survived the passage of theological education but gained much from it (though not without some struggle), and now teach in a theological context. Moreover, they continue to find Scripture foundational to their lives, finding it inconceivable to think otherwise. In this volume, many share how their view of biblical authority has changed over the years while teaching (and learning) within their theological disciplines (e.g., Bible, theology, church history, philosophy, missions). On one level, each essay is a case study: behind each contribution stands someone firmly rooted in her or his faith community who has seriously struggled with this issue. One can simply read these essays as personal reflections. But they are more than that; they are offerings that articulate something of the Bible's efficacy and depth for persons of faith.

The offerings are diverse. Various Christian denominations are "represented." In addition, two Jewish scholars have generously formulated their reflections for this volume. The contributors "represent" a variety of cultural and ecclesial contexts: some are white males or females; others are African American, Asian, and Latino. I use the term "represent," however, with great reservation. The contributors were not asked to represent anything other than themselves as they discussed the promise and challenge of biblical authority. Specifically, each was asked to address three interrelated matters:

1. The author's personal engagement with the issue of biblical authority within his or her ecclesial and cultural context;
2. A view of biblical authority that proposes a statement, model, or metaphor (or combination thereof) of biblical authority that indicates how the author engages the Bible as Scripture;
3. Hermeneutical implications that demonstrate how the author's view of biblical authority works in practice.

It was left to each contributor to determine how much weight to be given for each part. Some gravitated toward the first, while others focused predominantly on the second or third.

Diverse as they are, the essays contained in this volume do not represent every possible position. They were not chosen to cover the entire theological spectrum. There is, for example, no essay that champions the inerrantist or fundamentalist position. Conversely, there is no essay that proposes doing away with the rubric of authority altogether (despite the opening of one essay). Most find themselves somewhere in the middle. But such a comparison is egregiously reductive, as if they could all be plotted on a horizontal axis in relation to some central point. The essays are simply different, some complementing and some conflicting with each other. Some are highly theological in orientation; others plumb the complexities of the biblical text. Some contributors speak from experiences of pain over how the Bible has been used oppressively; others have consistently found great comfort and empowerment from Scripture. All indicate sincere struggle with the issue of biblical authority. As the Bible, according to 2 Timothy 3:16–17 (see below), exercises authority specifically within the context of teaching, so it is only appropriate that the contributors invited for this volume are themselves experienced teachers.[2]

PROLEGOMENA TO BIBLICAL AUTHORITY

While the following essays speak for themselves, a brief preliminary orientation to biblical authority and to the issues raised by the essays is in order. First, the word "authority." Excerpts from two dictionary definitions are given below:

the power and a right to command, act, enforce obedience, or make
final decisions; jurisdiction . . . authorization . . . the power derived
from opinion, respect or esteem; influence of character or office.[3]

power to influence or command thought, opinion, or behavior . . .
freedom granted . . . convincing force . . . grounds, warrant.[4]

One notes the wide semantic range spanned by the word "authority," but
essential is the notion of *power*. Etymologically, the term is even more richly
nuanced. The Latin origin connotes a creative sense. "Authority" comes from
auctoritas, meaning "origination," from which also the word "author" derives.
The word is also related to the verb *auctorare*, "to bind." But such richness is
easily depleted in the most common uses of "authority" in contemporary discourse. The word frequently has its home in legal or academic discourse, particularly when a specific decision is sought. People, for example, seek an
authoritative precedent or reason that results in a binding decision in a legal
case. Journalists seek an authoritative or credible source for their research and
reporting. Certain individuals assume authoritative status because they have
become experts in their respective disciplines. Authority is domain specific.

When "authority" is applied to the Bible, certain questions naturally emerge:
To what domain(s) does the Bible's authority pertain? Does it apply to scientific and legal matters as it does to matters of faith and moral conduct? That
may be easy to answer, but what about murkier matters such as sexuality, cli-
mate change, and stem-cell research, where ethical and theological reflection
needs to engage the natural and social sciences? To complicate matters further,
whereas the recourse to authority frequently involves seeking specific decisions
or answers for a specific issue, how does one seek such things from biblical storytelling or the lament psalms? How does one "squeeze" authority out of the
love poetry of Canticles? Or is only the legal or instructive material of the Bible
to be deemed authoritative? As a whole, the Bible is an altogether unique source
of wisdom, quite different from things we usually regard as authoritative, such
as legal texts and scientific reports.

Perhaps the best point of departure is to acknowledge first and foremost that
Scripture is authoritative primarily with respect to its theological subject, God,
who lies beyond the purview of scientific and historical inquiry. Nevertheless,
because God is the creator of all things, respect for the authority of Scripture
does not exclude but in fact requires respect for the authorities of the sciences.
On the one hand, the Bible does not reveal everything about the world in which
we live and move, and what it does reveal can be misleading. Is infertility a sign
of divine affliction? Must we adopt a geocentric worldview because the sun
"stood still" at Gibeon when Joshua defeated the Amorites (Josh. 10:12–13)?
The so-called skydome model of the waters above and below separated by a

celestial firmament (Gen. 1:6–8) finds little correspondence with the structure of the cosmos as discerned by science. On the other hand, the Bible fully acknowledges that there are many aspects about our world that can be discerned only through empirical observation and that there are realities that remain unexplained. This is indeed the premise of the Old Testament's wisdom tradition, as represented by Proverbs, Job, and Ecclesiastes.

"Authority" in the biblical sense takes on a different nuance from its normal usage in contemporary legal discourse, for example. Solomon's decree to cut the infant in half was not in itself the right *legal* decision—indeed it would have been horrifically wrong had it been *literally* carried out (1 Kgs. 3:25)! Rather, it served to provoke a response from the contesting parties to resolve a particular conflict. The Bible's "authority" is, thus, more at home with the original sense of the term, one that connotes a generative, provocative power that elicits a response and, in so doing, shapes the conduct, indeed identity, of the reader or reading community. Simply put, biblical authority is reader responsive: through our genuine engagement of Scripture, God "authors" us. Scripture's authority is dynamic and life shaping; it provokes a response that carries with it the acknowledgment, if not the conferral, of the Bible's authority. Authority, after all, must be acknowledged in order to be authoritative.

One of the few places in which the Bible directly speaks about itself is found in 2 Timothy 3:16–17.

> All Scripture is inspired by God and is useful for teaching, for reproof, for correction, and for training in righteousness, so that everyone who belongs to God may be proficient, equipped for every good work.

On the face of it, this passage makes a modest claim. Simply put, Scripture is a gift from God that functions to teach and equip the community of faith. Its inspiration is defined in terms of what it can do for the body of Christ ("everyone"). The Bible's authority is demonstrated by its usefulness, by Scripture's capacity to edify and sustain, to teach and equip people for the life of faith.

According to this brief epistle, the Bible's authority is fundamentally a *functional* authority or, more accurately, a *formative* authority. What makes the Bible the Word of God does not depend on any particular theory of inspiration so much as to testify to what the Bible has done and continues to do in people's lives. To talk about the Bible as a normative document is to say a lot about what is formative about the Bible, of what it can *do* for "training in righteousness" and equipping the community "for every good work." Put in contemporary terms, Scripture's authority denotes the Bible's capacity to shape and transform people into mature communities of faith, to command as well as to edify, to commission as well as to sustain. Biblical authority is evidenced in practice as it is lived out by readers of Scripture. It is not something that adheres to the printed words of the text, like font size or the color of its letters (even if it is red).

As many of the essays point out, biblical authority does not entail blind submission. The difference between being authoritative and authoritarian is deep. The Bible gives reasons or warrants for its claims, for proper authority is *freely* acknowledged; it is not forced. This does not imply, however, that the Bible must be renegotiated on a day-to-day basis. The Bible is more than a friendly persuader; it mediates God's living presence.

To speak of biblical authority in a certain way is to view the nature of Scripture in a certain way. Of human and divine words, the Bible is complex and, as such, so is its authority. The Bible is not a systematic book of definitions and diagnoses, complete with a handy index. It is a book filled with narrative and polity, reflective musings and context-specific letters, songs of praise and protest as well as of love. More an anthology than a monograph, the Bible is a thoroughly mixed corpus by any measure: historically, literarily, and theologically. The literature spans nearly a millennium and a half of historical struggle and theological inquiry. The Bible does not claim kinship with the Book of Mormon, dropped from heaven on gold plates. Nor does it bear much resemblance to the Qur'an, transmitted to an illiterate prophet within a mere twenty-two years. The Bible, rather, reflects centuries upon centuries of communal struggle and theological discernment. It speaks in many voices, some harmonious, some dissonant.

Discerning the many voices of Scripture, cast in various rhetorical forms and rooted in diverse historical contexts, is the challenging task of interpretation. The Bible's authority is intimately wedded to its interpretation. Indeed, one cannot discuss the one without the other: the authority of the Bible is realized in its interpretation, and interpretation gives concrete expression to the Bible's authority. Because Scripture interprets itself as earlier traditions are reformulated for new generations and contexts, it corrects and counters itself dynamically. Scripture is dialogical; the Bible *debates* itself! "Do not answer fools according to their folly, or you will be a fool yourself" is an admonition in Proverbs that is followed immediately by opposing counsel: "Answer fools according to their folly, or they will be wise in their own eyes" (Prov. 26:4–5). To respond or not to respond, that is the question with regard to fools, and there is no one mind on the issue. Or take the example of John the Baptist's declaration, (mis)quoted from Isaiah: "The voice of one crying out in the wilderness: 'Prepare the way of the Lord, make his paths straight'" (Matt. 3:3). Ecclesiastes, however, observes: "Consider the work of God; who can make straight what he has made crooked?" (Eccl. 7:13).

An authentic articulation of biblical authority must engage the complexities of biblical interpretation. The dialogical, self-interpretive quality of Scripture complexifies the issue of biblical authority, for the task of interpretation requires the reader to find ways to mediate the contesting voices and claims about God and God's way in the world. Is there a center or focal point to the Bible, a coherence, an overarching framework or narrative, or at least certain theological highlights that should be privileged over other perspectives contained in the Bible? And, then, what about the voices and perspectives muted by Scripture that cry out for a hearing: the voice of the alien, that of the Canaanite slated for destruction, the cry of Hagar and other women marginalized by the patriarchal household? Every interpreter must mediate the plethora of voices that make up the great extended family called Scripture.

The contributions that shape this volume explore in greater depth the issues raised above, and then some. As a guide for the reader, I suggest the following interrelated questions to bear in mind for the purpose of formulating one's own understanding of biblical authority.

1. What is the author's concept of authority? What misconceptions about authority or abuses of authority does the author identify with respect to the Bible? How does the author's own ecclesial and cultural context shape his or her understanding of authority?
2. What is the extent of the Bible's authority? In what domains of life does the Bible speak most authoritatively and directly? How and when is it appropriate to rely on other authorities in conjunction with Scripture to resolve particular issues or questions?
3. How is the author's view of biblical authority reflected in her or his view of the Bible itself? How does the Bible, consisting of both Testaments, cohere theologically? Does a view of biblical authority rest on some notion of the Bible's coherence, and how is that coherence to be defined (e.g., through narrative, confessional statements about God, or underlying rhetorical structures)? What is the author's selective canon or "canon within the canon"?
4. What is the role of the faith community in relation to the Bible's authority? What is the role of the Holy Spirit in acknowledging Scripture's authority?
5. How are authority and interpretation to be related? Does a common view of the Bible's authority among readers necessarily result in identical interpretations? Conversely, to what extent do different interpretations of Scripture reflect differing views of biblical authority?
6. Does the Bible express timeless truths or timely truths? If both, how does one distinguish the two?
7. Where is the Bible's authority to be primarily found: in what the Bible *says* (e.g., about God and world); what the Bible *is* (e.g., holy, sacred, a place for encountering God); or what the Bible *does* (e.g., sanctify, shape character, form community)?

8. What reading strategies does the author stress? What role do the critical tools of exegesis play in ascertaining the biblical text's meaning and significance?

Such questions raise issues treated in this volume that every interpreter of Scripture must deal with to some degree, if only provisionally.

1

Biblical Authority

A Jewish Pluralistic View

Marc Zvi Brettler

I am an observant Jew: I pray each weekday morning while donning tefillin (phylacteries), abstain from work from Friday evening through Saturday night, and refrain from eating pork products or mixing milk and meat.[1] A mezuzah adorns each door of my house. I grew up in a traditional Conservative home, and through high school attended an Orthodox Jewish day school, where I learned traditional Jewish texts in their original Hebrew and Aramaic. Jewish observance has always been an important part of my life. Although currently a member of a modern Orthodox synagogue, I do not label myself as Orthodox, especially in terms of belief or opinion (*doxa*). Because different aspects of various Jewish denominations speak to me, I am in many ways postdenominational. I am not ordained and have never seriously considered ordination.

I began the academic study of biblical texts at age seventeen as a first-year student at Brandeis University, studying Psalms with Professor Nahum Sarna. It was a deeply enriching but somewhat traumatic experience, as I quickly realized that the traditional Jewish ascription of Psalms to David was wrong, that the Torah was not authoritative for the authors of Psalms, and that modern philology was often far superior to the insights of the classical rabbis and medieval exegetes such as Rashi. But by the time the course was over, I was convinced of the validity and conclusions of much of the historical-critical method, and I continued to study that method and ancient Near Eastern languages and literatures at Brandeis University and the Hebrew University at Jerusalem. As a student, I struggled to understand how I might reconcile the historical-critical method and my Jewish commitments, discussing such issues with friends and costudents. There was very little written on the topic.[2]

My post–high school education was not confessional; it differed little from that of my contemporaries who studied for their PhD's, for example, at the Near Eastern Languages and Civilizations Department at Harvard. I encountered biblical theology only when Professor Moshe Goshen-Gottstein taught a course on that subject at Brandeis University, but even there he did not develop his nascent ideas on Jewish biblical theology.[3] My teacher Nahum Sarna mentioned several times that the editors of the standard Hebrew biblical encyclopedia, *Encyclopedia Miqra'it*,[4] had a great deal of trouble finding biblical scholars to write articles on most theological topics, and often used scholars of later periods of Jewish studies for this purpose. The reluctance of Jewish scholars to engage in such studies has been explained cogently by Jon Levenson.[5]

I am one of a small number of scholars who have become interested in Jewish biblical theology.[6] My interest in some sense originated when I tried, as a student, to understand how Judaism and the historical-critical method fit together. Over the last fifteen years, outside of my university teaching, I have taught in adult Jewish education classes, served as a scholar in residence at synagogues and other Jewish venues, talked about teaching the Bible[7] to Jewish educators, and preached in synagogues. This has encouraged me to ask how my academic understanding of the Bible connects with my commitment to enhance the Jewish life of others and has served as an impetus for me to begin to write on these issues. Coediting *The Jewish Study Bible*[8] and authoring *How to Read the Bible*,[9] a Jewishly sensitive introduction to the Bible, reflect my commitment to bridging academic scholarship and the Jewish community.[10]

BIBLICAL AUTHORITY?

I find the phrase "biblical authority" confusing and foreign—it is not part of my vocabulary either as a practicing Jew or as a biblical scholar who happens to be Jewish. Although I consider myself relatively well read in biblical studies and in religion, I have read very few of the books cited in the seven articles on biblical authority that cover forty double columns in the *Anchor Bible Dictionary*.[11] Moreover, I find the content of many of these articles as foreign to me as studies of the medieval scientific notions of ether. The opening of Goshen-Gottstein's essay on "Biblical Authority in Judaism" suggests that my reaction as a Jewish scholar is typical. He observes: "The issue of biblical authority has never been a question which bothered Jews."[12]

I can venture some guesses on why this is so. Biblical authority is a different problem for Christians than for Jews because Christian tradition understands the Old Testament plus the New Testament to be Scripture, and biblical authority to some extent deals with how these two very different corpora fit together as Bible. There is no comparable problem in Judaism. Though classical Jewish tradition may speak of the written law (e.g., the Hebrew Bible or Tanakh, or often just the Pentateuch or Five Books of Moses) and the oral law (e.g., the rabbinic interpretation of the Bible as found in the Mishnah and the Talmud)[13] as a package, they are not a unity in the same way that the Old and New Testaments are in Christian tradition. They do not constitute a single work, and the oral law is recognized as a type of (subservient) interpretation of the written law in a way that is fundamentally different from how the NT is traditionally connected to the OT. In addition, much of the discussion of biblical authority in Christian circles focuses on the role of Jesus as the central figure of Scripture. There is nothing comparable to this core issue in Jewish tradition.

In my recent work, I have discussed issues that fall under the purview of biblical authority.[14] Simply put, the Bible for me "is a sourcebook that I—within my community—make into a textbook. I do so by selecting, revaluing, and interpreting the texts that I call sacred."[15] I will clarify this statement by focusing on and expanding on some of its core phrases. My ideas should not be generalized to Judaism or even to some segment of Judaism—they only reflect the thinking of one observant Jewish biblical scholar.

To my mind, the entire Hebrew Bible is sacred—this is reflected in one of the rabbinic titles for the Bible: *kitvei qodesh* or "holy writings."[16] The holiness of the Bible is connected to its canonization, though I am not prepared to say whether it was canonized because it was holy or became holy because it was canonized.[17] But authoritative and holy are not identical ideas: authoritativeness, at least etymologically, is connected to authorship, which to my mind has nothing to do with sanctity. In addition, many Jews treat the Bible as holy—they will kiss a copy of the Bible that falls to the ground and rise when a Torah scroll is raised—but not treat the contents of the text as authoritative.

I remain perplexed on whether or not parts of the biblical text are more sacred than others, and what this might mean. Many would consider the Torah more sacred than the other two parts of the Bible, the Prophets and the Writings.[18] Jewish law suggests this distinction in various ways. For example, only the Torah is read in its complete form in the synagogue; there are special laws concerning the writing of the Torah on scrolls; and halachic (Jewish legal) decisions are typically made only from the Torah. However, the Prophets and Writings are just as much a part of the tripartite Tanakh, or Hebrew Bible, and it is unclear what it might mean to call them "less sacred" Scripture.

Certain postbiblical texts from the classical rabbinic period (the Talmud and various early midrashic works from the same period) are sacred as well, though they are not on a par with the Bible. Movements have developed within Judaism at various times that have rejected the authority of postbiblical Jewish law. Karaism, which continues to have a small number of adherents, is the best known of these.[19] Part of my being a Jew rather than a Karaite means by definition that rabbinic literature has some type of sacred status for me, albeit a secondary sacred status.[20] But only certain postbiblical books have this status. I conform, by and large, to rabbinic norms rather than the type of norms found in the Dead Sea Scrolls or in the early Jewish pseudepigraphic Book of Jubilees. I find the Scrolls and Jubilees fascinating as a scholar; they help me understand the development of Judaism, but I do not consider them sacred.

In discussing biblical authority, I insist on *interpreting* biblical texts. On one level, biblical texts must be interpreted just as all literary texts must be interpreted—there is no such thing as a transparent, perfectly clear literary text. But I would go significantly beyond that claim. As a historical-critical scholar, I believe that the Bible is an anthology. Diverse, even contradictory traditions are often juxtaposed in the Bible, and this demands that the reader, using the tools of interpretation, must both discern the more original texts[21] and, with this awareness, interpret the final highly edited product. Thus, both atomistic and holistic interpretations are important to me.[22] Finally, as a Jew, I am well aware of the rich Jewish legacy of biblical interpretation, a legacy that had already begun in the biblical period and continues to this very day.[23] As Simon Rawidowicz observed in his classic essay "On Interpretation," postbiblical Jewry "has become a people of commentators, all postbiblical Jewish literature being a chain of commentaries on the 'text' and commentaries to the commentaries."[24] There never has been, and likely will never be, *the* authoritative Jewish biblical interpretation. Even modern interpretations may be seen as potentially authoritative, following the tradition articulated most clearly in rabbinic literature: "indeed even the comments that some bright student will one day make to his teacher—were already given to Moses on Mount Sinai."[25] Thus, insisting that the Bible must be interpreted, rather than simply read, is a very Jewish act.

On the one hand, as a critical Bible scholar I am quite insistent on historical-critical or, better, contextual methods of interpretation,[26] which ask what the Bible *meant* in its earliest context(s). On the other hand, as a Jew connecting the Bible to my life, I am quite open to using a wide variety of interpretive methods, even when they do violence to the "original" contextual meaning of the text. Here I follow traditional rabbinic interpretation, which was extremely open to a wide variety of interpretations and interpretive methods—almost nothing was seen as beyond the pale.[27]

According to my view of biblical authority, it is within my rights to "select" particular biblical texts as more important than others. To paraphrase American jurisprudence, not all texts are created equal. I perform this selection out of an awareness that the Bible is a contradictory anthology, and thus speaks in many voices, and if I want it to be authoritative for me (within my community), I must decide which voice is authoritative. For example, if I am going to celebrate Sukkot, the fall harvest festival, I need to decide if I should "hold the Feast of Booths for seven days" (Deut. 16:13) or if I should append to it "a complete rest on the eighth day" (Lev. 23:39). Similarly, I would have to decide whether the prohibition against eating nonslaughtered meat applies to me (Deut. 14:21) or only to priests, and whether as a nonpriest I may eat a cow found dead by the side of the road (see Lev. 17:15). These texts are to my mind irreconcilable, and along with many other examples, offer clear proof of the validity of the documentary hypothesis, the theory that the Torah is a composite document, written by different authors at different times and reflecting different interests.[28] But how can each of these texts be equally authoritative, given the existence of other, contradictory texts?

Let me complicate this issue further: How should I treat a law or norm when it is represented only in one strand of the tradition while absent in other strands? May I select the silent strand over the explicit law? For example, the prohibition against male homosexual intercourse is found in Lev. 18:22 and 20:13, in one of the Torah's law collections, the Holiness Code or Collection. The two other great pentateuchal law collections, in Exodus (the Covenant Collection) and Deuteronomy, have no such prohibition. Perhaps I can choose their silence over the direct, repeated prohibition in Leviticus? Can the silence of two sources be more authoritative than the prohibition of one?

Biblical texts must be "revalued." Helpful is the well-known distinction made by Krister Stendahl between what a text meant and what it means.[29] Though this notion has been criticized,[30] it remains valuable. Similar to my approach, it takes seriously the notion that the Bible should have a core role in the religious community. At the same time, however, it acknowledges that the Bible is an ancient text, formed in (and by) a distant community, and thus cannot be seen as timeless in a simplistic fashion.

What do I mean by creating a "textbook" from a "sourcebook"? Sourcebooks are multiperspectival, and thus offer a suitable image for the Bible as a complex anthology, reflecting different interests, time periods, geographical settings, classes, and perhaps genders.[31] But it is very hard to give a sourcebook authority, precisely because it is multivocal rather than univocal. Thus, I suggest that, whether people realize it or not, by ignoring certain passages and highlighting others they create a textbook Bible out of the sourcebook Bible. Most people do not go about "whiting out" large sections of the text. Instead, they *effectively* white out passages by treating them as if they were written in a miniscule, impossible-to-read 3-point font while others are written in a large, 36-point bold type. Thus, nothing is excised from the sourcebook—it is still all there, since the Bible cannot be changed[32]—but only certain parts are readable, and thus intelligible and truly authoritative.[33]

Let me offer an example of how this is done already in early rabbinic culture. As the historical-critical perspective on the Bible has pointed out, there is a clear contradiction in the Hebrew slave laws between Exodus 21:6 (see also Deut. 15:17), which says that a slave who loves his master may become a slave in perpetuity, and Leviticus 25:40, which insists that such slaves are released at the jubilee year. The early rabbinic midrash, the Mekhilta, resolves this contradiction by engaging in "creative philology,"[34] glossing the word "forever" in Exodus with "until the jubilee year."[35] This method is often characterized as "reconciling" the two texts, but I do not believe that this description is quite correct, for a reconciliation would involve hearing the voices of *both* texts. In this case, the voice of Exodus and Deuteronomy, which stipulates that Hebrew slaves may be slaves for perpetuity, disappears and is replaced by the voice that claims that all such slaves or servants are to be released at the jubilee year. In essence, the word "forever" disappears, but it cannot *really* disappear, since the rabbis do not literally excise difficult or contradictory texts. Instead, we should view the word "forever" not only as a continued part of the text in Exodus and Deuteronomy but also as written in such a small font that it can scarcely be read: it *virtually* disappears.

To facilitate the move from the Bible as sourcebook to the Bible as textbook, some texts must be treated as more important than others. Of course, they are not physically marked as such. For example, the opening words of the Shema ("Hear, O Israel! The LORD is our God, the LORD alone") in Deuteronomy 6:4, a key verse for Judaism, is not printed entirely in a larger[36] or special font or in a special color ink.

The decision of what texts are "more authoritative" than others, and which may be deselected, or revalued or reinterpreted to mean something fundamentally different, is a complex phenomenon that has no obvious guidelines. Perhaps within the Bible, Torah texts are more authoritative—after all, the Torah within Judaism is considered first among equals. Possibly the number of times a particular idea is mentioned should be considered. Maybe the number of different authors who mention an idea expresses that idea's relative importance. Perhaps the number of times a verse is cited in rabbinic literature, or alternatively, in liturgical texts, is of importance.[37] I cannot suggest one clear principle that makes one text more authoritative than another.

HERMENEUTICAL IMPLICATIONS

Let me conclude with some brief observations of the implications of my understanding of biblical authority for how I view and interpret biblical texts as a

Jew. I will look at Exodus 20:5 (=Deut. 5:9) from the Decalogue.[38] In choosing a text from the Decalogue, and ultimately suggesting that it should *not* be seen as authoritative, I am being intentionally provocative.

The text reads: "You shall not bow down to them or serve them. For I the LORD your God am an impassioned God, visiting the guilt of the parents upon the children, upon the third and upon the fourth generations of those who reject Me" (NJPS). To what extent should I view vicarious intergenerational punishment as authoritative biblical doctrine and as an authoritative Jewish idea?

The problem is quite simple: elsewhere the Bible blatantly disagrees with this doctrine. For example, Deuteronomy 7:9–10, a mere two chapters after Deuteronomy's version of the Decalogue, states:

> Know, therefore, that only the LORD your God is God, the steadfast God who keeps His covenant faithfully to the thousandth generation of those who love Him and keep His commandments, but who instantly requites with destruction those who reject Him—never slow with those who reject Him, but requiting them instantly. (NJPS)

Michael Fishbane has shown that this is an explicit polemic against, indeed a rejection of, Exodus 20:5–6.[39] In Deuteronomy 7, which has many verbal similarities to this section of the Decalogue and is clearly citing it, there is no vicarious intergenerational punishment. God requites sinners "instantly." As is well known, Ezekiel 18, which insists that "the person who sins, only he shall die" (vv. 4, 20 NJPS), agrees with Deuteronomy 7 rather than with the Decalogue.

As an observant Jew who takes both the Bible and the historical-critical method seriously, I see the theological difference between these texts and perhaps could even find a historical explanation that explains this difference. I begin to wonder which is *more* authoritative or, as suggested earlier, which should be cast in larger font size. I would prefer to see Deuteronomy 7 and Ezekiel 18 as the more authoritative texts, in part because they comport better with the God in which I would like to believe and in part because postbiblical rabbinic tradition has deemed those texts as by and large the "winners,"[40] with the idea of personal responsibility "trumping" intergenerational punishment. Thus, I prefer to see Deuteronomy 7 and Ezekiel 18 as correcting the Decalogue, as being more authoritative, as having been written, as it were, in a 36-point font.

I mentioned earlier that "interpreting the texts that I call sacred" helps to facilitate the move from sourcebook to authoritative textbook. In this case, I might use interpretation to make the "simple" meaning of Exodus 20:5 "go away," just as the rabbis undid the simple meaning of "forever" in Exodus 21 and Deuteronomy 15. I would start by calling attention to the rendition of this verse in the Aramaic Targum Onkelos, the "standard" Aramaic translation of the Bible: "for I the Lord your God am a jealous God, avenging the sins of the fathers upon the *rebellious* children, upon the third *generation* and upon the fourth *generation* of those who hate Me, when the children follow their *fathers in sinning*."[41] This understanding is also sanctioned in the commentary of Rashi, the great medieval exegete (1040–1105) and other classical sources.[42] This interpretation, however, is not acceptable in terms of the rules of Hebrew grammar and is contravened by Exodus 34:7, which reads, ". . . but visits the iniquity of parents upon children and children's children, upon the third and fourth generations," without the final words "of those who reject me" found in chapter 20. When I am interested in exploring issues of biblical authority as a Jew, I first use the historical-critical method in order to discern the variety of traditions and beliefs and, using a variety of criteria, find one of these traditions (as reflected in Deuteronomy 9 and Ezekiel 18) to be more authoritative. One factor in deciding which text is more authoritative is the manner in which rabbinic interpretation has already made the simple meaning of the intergenerational punishment phrases in the Decalogue disappear. Thus, I use both critical and traditional interpretation to make the judgment that the end of Exodus 20:5 should be written in a 3-point font.

The use or lack of use of a particular biblical text in the Jewish liturgy might also influence how authoritatively that text should be viewed. Though the Decalogue is no longer part of the Jewish liturgy,[43] the attributes of God found in Exodus 34:6–7 are recited on a variety of occasions, including as part of the Torah reading on public fast days and as part of the penitential prayers (*selichot*) recited from before Rosh Hashanah through Yom Kippur. However, when these attributes are recited, the section concerning intergenerational punishment is left out. For example, on public fasts, the congregation recites aloud the section about God's "positive" attributes but not those concerning vicarious punishment. The reader still recites them—the text cannot be "whited out"—but it is relegated to a secondary role through these liturgical practices, which support the notion that not all biblical texts are equally authoritative.

To summarize: Biblical authority is a foreign term to me as a Jewish biblical interpreter, and I suspect that the manner in which I have developed it is quite foreign to what it means as a technical term in Christian theology. Yet I believe that those interpreting biblical passages as authoritative within Christian tradition may still benefit from some of these "Jewish" observations, especially on how the historical-critical method may be used in conjunction with other methods in a constructive fashion within the believing community and how modern biblical scholarship might force believers to make choices both in the texts that we choose to value and in the interpretive methods we choose to adopt.

POSTSCRIPT

Several readers of an earlier draft of this essay pointed out that I hardly talk about God, either generally or as a locus of authority. This is not accidental. First of all, I see the main locus of sacredness of the biblical text to be connected to the Jewish community and not to God.[44] Additionally, though I am a theist, I do not claim to have a good understanding of God and the workings of the divine. Several texts that discuss God or the divine actions as "unfathomable" (Isa. 40:29; Ps. 145:3; Job 5:9; 9:10) resonate deeply with me, and I cannot begin to imagine how God is involved in the revelation of Scripture. Many liberal Jews speak of "divine inspiration" for Torah or for the entire Bible, but I find this concept fuzzy at best.

Other readers may be surprised that I do not view early texts as more authoritative than late biblical texts. In part, along with many biblical scholars, I am no longer sure how to date many texts. More significantly, however, I do not find a direct association between antiquity and authority. To my mind, even texts that are clearly secondary or editorial editions, or from late sources, are sacred. After all, sacredness comes from the community, and the Jewish community does not make value judgments about biblical texts based on scholarly understandings of their antiquity or lateness. Furthermore, to the extent that Jews might evaluate biblical texts in relation to rabbinic texts, the later biblical texts, which are more proximate chronologically and more similar to rabbinic texts and norms, might be viewed as more authoritative.[45]

2

Hearing the Master's Voice

Michael Joseph Brown

From 1991 to 1999, a very formative time in my life, I lived in Chicago. In the center of that city is a place that continues to influence me. Across from the Water Tower Mall, in the area dubbed "The Magnificent Mile," there stands a church. Striking because of its distinctive Gothic structure set off by the numerous shops and offices surrounding it, this church stands squarely in the heart of the "City of Big Shoulders."

Walk into Fourth Presbyterian Church and you will see inscribed over the door of the vestibule an elegant, if archaic, translation from the Gospel of John: "The Master is here, and he calleth for thee" (based on John 11:28). This statement in many ways shapes my reading and understanding of Scripture. "The Master is here." That is, outside of the physical presence of Jesus, which is no longer accessible, and in addition to the Spirit's continuing presence in the life of the church, the Bible provides us with a number of powerful presentations and interpretations of the God we deem worthy of worship. By reading the Bible, we come into the presence of the holy. And "he calleth for thee." It is through the various Gospels, letters, homilies, apocalypses, and other biblical writings that the holy makes a claim on us. I believe as a fundamental principle—as that without which there can be no true, objective knowledge of God—that Scripture, although perspectival, makes a claim on us and forms us as human beings replete with divine potential, as children of the living God.

MY PERSPECTIVE AND WHY IT MATTERS

Like many practitioners, I used to believe that my own life situation mattered little when it came to the interpretation of Scripture. I have come to realize,

10

however, that my context influences much of my scholarship and interpretive practice. If nothing else, my life situation shapes the kinds of questions that I raise and pursue.

I grew up in a family tradition shaped by ministry. I am the son of a father who was an African Methodist Episcopal Church minister and of a mother who was the daughter of a pastor and schoolteacher. In fact, I can trace a commitment to ministry in my family back five generations. I entered the ministry at an early age myself. At fourteen, I felt and accepted my call to ministry. I am truly a child of the church. I was ordained an African Methodist and have served as pastor or associate pastor of several AME churches.

My interest in the discipline of biblical studies came as a consequence of a series of serendipitous events. My intention on entering college was to pursue a major in political science. I had planned to follow up with law school and seminary. My vision was to practice law and pastor a small, maybe a medium-size, church. However, I found the study of political science to be as boring as watching grass grow. (This is not to say that it is not and should not be exciting to others. It just did not interest me.) At the same time, I was taking a course on the New Testament and one on Greek history. These interested me. The instructor of my New Testament course took an interest in me and offered to mentor me. He helped me explore further my interests in the Bible and the Greco-Roman world. This started me on my trajectory in New Testament studies.

After college I attended graduate school. By that time I had already decided to pursue a doctorate. I decided to get a master of divinity rather than a master of arts because part of me still wanted to serve the church. In fact, I saw my teaching and scholarship as a form of ministerial service. It is within this historical particularity that I read the Bible, guided and influenced by questions that arise from the multiple experiences that constitute my life. Whatever knowledge I gain is, by necessity, filtered through the lens of my experience. In short, my interpretation of the Bible and understanding of its authority is by necessity perspectival—much like the Bible itself. This does not mean that my practice of interpretation is arbitrary. Quite the contrary. All forms of biblical interpretation are in dialogue with the general modes of thought prevailing at the time.

My understanding of the Bible's authority is rooted in my belief that it is the means by which we connect to the core of the apostolic witness. This witness is not identical to the literal words on the page. It is more like hearing the voice behind the words, the Word behind the words. To say it another way, the Bible would have no authority if it did not serve as the instrument by which we come to experience God. As a consequence, any attempt we make to exercise the Bible's authority must undergo careful scrutiny, because we can easily misunderstand what the Bible is saying, apply this authority inappropriately, and miss hearing the Master's voice.

HISTORY, RATIONALITY, AND COMMUNITY

My first interest in the Bible is historical. I believe that the primary ground on which any endeavor involving the Bible should rest is a rich understanding of its context—as in our modern world, where we run the risk of misunderstanding a person if we do not take into account the context in which she spoke. Of course, there are some scriptural passages that are powerful in themselves. Paul writes, "If God is for us, who is against us?" (Rom. 8:31). This is a passionate claim that reaches across the ages and takes hold of us as believers. There may appear to be no need in our minds to dig any deeper into the context of the claim. Yet if we did, we would find that the apostle is making a statement about the nature of salvation. The apostle is saying that even though we do not at present experience the fullness of what it means to be in Christ, we do experience some of it, and we also have the rock-solid assurance that God is faithful to this covenant, despite any difficulties we may encounter along the way. This belief expressed by the apostle was one articulated in a context where he found himself in the minority. Paul writes Romans because he has to explain his theological perspective to other Christians and convince them that his understanding of the gospel is just as valid as others that are better known. In other words, his statement is already compelling, but it is greatly enhanced when read in the context of Paul's confidence about the validity of his ministry. The fact that we revere Paul today can overshadow the fact that in his own day the apostle represented a minority Christian view.

Let me provide a more pointed example of the fundamental importance of context. Ever since I was a child I had heard the story of the widow's mite and that she was a shining example of how we should sacrifice our financial resources for the sake of the gospel. Although I never questioned it explicitly, something did not seem right about that understanding to me. The story is presented in two Gospel accounts, Mark 12:41–44 and Luke 21:1–4. Jesus is sitting across from the Temple treasury when he begins to notice the giving habits of various wealthy individuals. As he is watching the scene, a "poor widow came and put in two small copper coins, which are worth a penny" (Mark 12:42). In response, Jesus calls over his disciples and comments on the widow's gift. He says, "For all of them have contributed out of their abundance; but she out of her poverty has put in everything she had, all she had to live on" (12:44). Unfortunately, many modern Christians believe that Jesus is praising the poor widow.

He is not praising her; he pities her. Just a few verses earlier in Mark and Luke, Jesus tells the listening crowd that the scribes—one group of religious leaders—"devour widows' houses and for the sake of appearance say long prayers." He then says, "They will receive the greater condemnation" (Mark 12:40). In short, Jesus is saying that the scribes exploit those who are socially vulnerable. The widow's religious devotion, expressed by giving all of her financial resources to the Temple, is an illustration of how religious institutions can "devour" those who truly cannot afford to give. The two copper coins that the widow gave were insignificant, but it was everything she had.

In the Old Testament we are told time and again that strangers, widows, and orphans are to be protected. Deuteronomy states, "For the LORD your God is God of gods and Lord of lords, the great God, mighty and awesome, who is not partial and takes no bribe, who executes justice for the orphan and the widow, and who loves the strangers, providing them food and clothing" (Deut. 10:17–18). Later in 14:29, we read that a tithe shall be brought to provide for the widows, among others, so that they "may come and eat their fill so that the LORD your God may bless you in all the work that you undertake." In other words, widows were supposed to be protected. They were expected not to give but to receive. Yet we find repeatedly in the Old Testament individuals and institutions that exploit them (see Exod. 22:22–23; Job 22:9; 24:3; 31:16; Ps. 94:6; Isa. 1:23; 10:2; Mal. 3:5). This poor widow was vulnerable, and Jesus makes it clear that the religious leaders exploited her vulnerability.

In Luke the widow is described more graciously as "needy" (Greek *penichran*, Luke 21:2). In Mark she is called "destitute" (Greek *ptōchē*, Mark 12:42, 43). In either case, she was not in a position to give anything to the Temple. The Hebrew word for widow connotes someone who is unable to speak. Without a son or male protector, she had no one to represent her interests. As in the case of Naomi and Ruth, a widow might be forced to seek out even distant family members for protection. The early church understood the plight of these women and took care of them if they were not able to remarry (1 Tim. 5:1–13). In short, the story of the widow's mite is really one of religious exploitation. She gave what she could not afford to give, "all she had to live on." In my mind, this is a shining example of why understanding context is important. When we neglect to put such actions as the widow's in their proper context, we run the risk of misunderstanding the message we are to derive from the text.

Because we live in a world where people want to make normative claims (i.e., assertions about how we should conduct our lives) from Scripture, my second interest or concern with biblical interpretation is rationality. Does this make sense when it comes to how we should conduct our lives before God? Although this is properly a theological question, it is extremely important when it comes to determining when, where, and how the Bible's authority should be applied and measured. This is where we must distinguish between the words of Scripture and the Word of God. Christian theology, at least until recently, has never maintained that simply because something was written in the Bible it must be true, and that we must assent to it or else suffer damnation. To put it simply, the Bible is not a reference manual. What we seek, rather, is the Word behind the words. In the case of the New Testament it would be the "apostolic witness"—to borrow a phrase from Schubert Ogden—from which the various documents of the New Testament originated and to which we are ultimately accountable. Let me explain.

The reformer Martin Luther saw justification as a central element running through the New Testament, particularly in Paul's letter to the Romans, and thus part of that apostolic witness to which it points. The outcome of Luther's struggle to understand this witness was the Protestant Reformation itself. Others have read Romans and gleaned other important aspects of this witness as well. In modern times, the first major writing of the Swiss theologian Karl Barth was a commentary on Romans (1918). In this writing he argues passionately that the righteousness of God is a central element of the apostolic witness. John Calvin obtained his doctrine of double predestination from Romans 9–11. Finally, John Wesley developed his distinctive teaching on sanctification from Romans 6 and 8. What all of these theologians were trying to accomplish was to hear the Master's voice through the various and sometimes contradictory statements found in the Bible. The same is true for us. We seek not just the plain words of the text, but more importantly the profound witness to which it points. We must be careful not to conflate the two.

Yet recovering what we believe to be the apostolic witness does not end our quest. We must also raise the question of credibility. Maybe an example will illustrate what I mean. Recently in our culture we have been struggling with how we should understand and structure our common life. One side in this debate has argued that traditional family values constitute the center of the Bible's witness to us, and that we are obliged to maintain those values as Christians. I do not quibble with the idea that society has an interest in supporting and cultivating family life. I believe as well that the church has an obligation to model and promote responsible conduct among human beings. Yet I question the credibility of a narrowly defined model of family—that is, the nuclear family.

First, such an understanding of family does not fit the Bible's context. For example, there is no word in Greek or Hebrew that corresponds to what we understand to be the nuclear family. The ancients simply did not see the world in that manner. They thought and spoke in terms of households, which would be more akin to our idea of the extended family, although it is not quite that either. To illustrate in more detail: In Jesus' day it would have been common for a child to grow up without at least one of her birth parents. Life expectancy was so low that the blended family, or growing up among one's extended family, was more the norm than the exception. A modern understanding of the nuclear family would appear odd to them. Moreover, we simply ignore the fact that the patriarchs often had multiple wives. Our modern idea of the nuclear family derives primarily from the work of Greco-Roman scholars who identified the model family as the one that predominated among the elite. By contrast, what we find throughout the Bible is a variety of family configurations, some close to our idea of family, yet others far from it.

Second, such an understanding of family and its importance does not always correspond to the apostolic witness we find in the Bible. When I was a pastor, I found it difficult to accept the rationale given in the marriage ceremony for the importance of the institution in Christianity. The two examples cited are Jesus and Paul. According to the liturgy, Jesus, who was not married, supported the institution of marriage because he showed up at one (John 2:1–11). To draw this conclusion is ridiculous. The fact that Jesus was an invited guest at a wedding—even if he did perform a miracle—does not prove that he expected his disciples to get married. Something more egregious happens when we invoke Paul. I am at a loss, based on Paul's undisputed writings, as to how one can determine that Paul promoted the institution of marriage. What he does say is this: "So then, he who marries his fiancée does well; and he who refrains from marriage will do better"—hardly a ringing endorsement (1 Cor. 7:38). In truth, it would not be until the second century CE that an explicit rationale for marriage among Christians would be developed. Men and women marry in order to raise children for the church. It may be possible to say that part of the apostolic witness in the New Testament supports the maintenance of marriage obligations (e.g., Jesus' teachings on divorce) and the household (e.g., the household codes), but that is not the same as claiming that these documents promote the institution of marriage. In other words, the New Testament does not propose that disciples have a religious obligation to marry.

Third, is such an understanding of family credible and, thus, worthy of our appropriation? It is probably clear by now that I would say no. The examples provided to us in the Bible are multiple, suggesting that we should be careful not to pick just one understanding of family and exclude all possible others. Further, the invocation of household/family language, particularly in the New Testament, often points to understanding the "family" as a community of mutual support. This is why the language of "church family" is meaningful. Of course, the church does later develop and articulate a rationale for marriage among believers. The question is: Is that rationale credible? I think not. The idea that the purpose of marriage is to raise children does damage to those couples who may not be able to (or want to) produce offspring. Women, in particular, have suffered greatly under the stigma that they cannot be considered worthwhile individuals and believers until they produce children. In fact, the focus on child rearing reduces all the other benefits marriage brings by defining its primary purpose as reproduction. In addition, the attention placed on marriage in many churches marginalizes people who for whatever reason are not married. How can we claim that the church is a community of mutual support and at the same time stigmatize members of that community because their lives do not conform to a narrowly defined understanding of family? In other words, when we invoke the Bible as a normative authority—as a model for how we should construct both our personal lives and our common life—we must carefully sort out the historical and theological issues involved so as not to arrive at a premature conclusion.

The previous discussion of the church as a community leads to my final concern when it comes to biblical interpretation, the pivotal importance of community. Whether we recognize it or not, we all interpret the Bible in community. Some Bible readers interpret within the confines of the scholarly guild. Others interpret within the context of a particular faith community. Still others, like myself, interpret in conversation with both contexts. Regardless, the existence of these various communities influences to a degree the way we approach, interpret, and ultimately apply the Bible. In fact, any interpretation we arrive at and any authority we ascribe to it find their confirmation within our communities. As an African American, for example, I am sensitive to texts that are (potentially) oppressive. I believe that one of the tenets of the apostolic witness that stands behind the Bible is the fulfillment and flourishing of human life. Thus, scriptural passages that promote worldviews that can harm others are difficult for me to accept. In taking this stance, I occasionally find myself at odds with interpretations in my immediate community that I find oppressive. This, however, is to be expected. Being part of a community of interpretation does not mean that we will always agree. Sharing core values with others does not mean that the possibility for disagreement will disappear.

All knowledge, even when it involves shared values, is perspectival, which means that differences in emphasis and sensitivity are bound to arise. Some, however, find this difficult to accept. They prefer absolute claims that remove the risk and ambiguity involved in decision making. By contrast, I believe firmly that relativity and evolution are central components of human existence. This means that I accept the partial character and freedom involved in the act of biblical interpretation. Any act of interpretation not only allows but also requires further expansion and development. In short, I believe that the most we can hope for in any engagement with the Bible is an adequate but not absolute understanding of the Word behind the words.

"The Master is here, and he calleth for thee." These are the words with which I began, and, perhaps surprisingly to some, it is the place to which my understanding of biblical authority finally returns. My fascination with the Bible appears to be endless. This is because I believe that the Bible makes a claim on us as human beings, and that this claim, which began with the creation of the universe itself, works its way through the various documents that constitute the biblical canon. It is because God seeks to be in relationship with creation and desires that all creation realize its divinely ordained fulfillment. At times the claim is explicit. At other times it is barely recognizable, but the Bible remains authoritative for me because I believe that it is possible to hear—if not absolutely, then at least adequately—the Word of God through the words of Scripture.

3

The Biblical Mainstay of Liberation

KATIE G. CANNON

Every year since 1953 I have participated in some type of catechism class, a course of study where detailed religious instruction is given. At Covenant United Presbyterian Church in Kannapolis, North Carolina, my teachers used a variety of means for conveying and reinforcing the primary doctrines of the Christian faith. I recollect from my early childhood how church school educators, without fear or trepidation, presented me with a series of questions and answers. More than just concerned with a literal interpretation, the guiding principle in this type of study was to instill into the core of our beings, drop by drop, that God is Creator, Sustainer, and Redeemer, and that Jesus the Christ is the Word made flesh. Our Bible drill instructors taught us that as the Incarnate Word, Jesus was present from the beginning, when God first spoke creation into existence.

By the time I reached elementary school, my religious instructors, who considered technical skills in exegesis important but not essential for reading the Bible profitably, concentrated on scriptural memorization by repetition. By this I mean that I, and others who participated in this aspect of the black church tradition, were expected to accomplish the phenomenal feat of learning by rote the major stories from Genesis to Revelation. After a suitable amount of time, we had to repeat aloud in roll-call fashion the sixty-six books of the Bible, and then cite chapter and verse regarding the main events, which ran the gamut from Adam and Eve in the Garden of Eden to the revelatory visions of John the Seer, banished to the Island of Patmos. Our teachers were quite frank in declaring that knowing the Bible stories in our heart of hearts would enable us to partake of the power and energy of God's inspired Word.

During my teen years, Sunday school teachers moved away from reliance on the fixed, mechanical, didactic instructions of quoting and repeating.

Instead, they skillfully wove the complex threads of Socratic logic with the cognitive activity of storytelling so that as students we could skip across time and space, connecting the relevance of particular biblical texts to real-life experiences. This group of religious leaders believed wholeheartedly that biblical narrative is holy because it has both divine and human authors. God spoke directly to humans and guided them as they transmitted the story of God's redemptive actions. Hence, these Christian educators presented both intricate and poignant passages that allowed us to recapture the mentality of biblical characters so that we could readily identify and reenact lessons learned from biblical predicaments in the dailiness of life.

For example, our Bible study leaders usually began our course of study by discussing the grace experienced in the exodus event. Deliverance from oppression was presented as a mighty deed of God. This concrete personification of liberation provided the impetus for the unique covenantal relationship between God and the people. At the same time, by directing our attention to the consonance between the nomadic wandering in the wilderness and the collective sojourn of freed African people, we learned how to disentangle the internalized forty-year slave mentality of the Israelites, as well as how to revitalize the significance of becoming God-dependent.

When I moved to the young adult class, all kinds of fortuitous connections continued to spring up around me. Consider this: my grandfather on my mother's side, Emanuel Clayton Lytle, was born a free person on August 21, 1865. In contrast, all his siblings, parents, and the ancestors that we know by name were born in slavery in the United States of America. My foremothers and forefathers were slaves, legally defined as chattel property whose labor could be exploited for land, goods, and services. In turn, each member of the Westminster Fellowship at Covenant Church took turns sharing family faith journeys. As descendants of Africans in America who were enslaved, subjected to racial apartheid, stripped of material possessions, routinely raped, beaten, and degraded as nonpersons, we resonated with the prophetic messages in canonized Scripture, particularly the biblical worlds of Amos, Isaiah, and Jeremiah.

Notably, as Bible students we were encouraged to share the poetic metaphors we inherited from our ancestors, wherein we talked about the concrete realism of God being a "Burden Bearer" and a "Heavy-Load Sharer," God as a "Mountain Mover" and a "Hell-Hound Chaser." The folks in my home church embody unyielding confidence in God's faithfulness despite existential evidence to the contrary. In other words, we knew the realities of exploited fathers, overworked mothers, substandard housing, functional illiteracy, and malnutrition. And yet, even with denial of full citizenship, especially our constitutional right to vote, our daily testimony was "The Lord will provide." There was not one among us who did not understand that this core message of the Bible engendered practices of liberation.

Soon thereafter, I left home in 1971 to begin my seminary training at the Interdenominational Theological Center (ITC) in Atlanta, Georgia. To my mind it seemed providential that my work-study job at ITC was to conduct archival research for Dr. Charles B. Copher, a highly credentialed, eminent African American scholar of the Old Testament.[1] My assignment was to go through the entire catalog of special documentary materials and record on color-coded file cards every annotation that I could glean related to the Nile Valley civilizations such as ancient Egypt and Ethiopia or Nubia (biblical Cush) and to the descendants of Ham listed in the "Tables of Nations" (Gen. 10). Shining a bright light on this African-centered repository of biblical "data" commanded my attention. Dr. Copher's work required me to sharpen my understanding of African identity and black presence in the biblical world. Thus, as I began my formal ministerial training, reading a draft of Copher's seminal work, "Three Thousand Years of Biblical Interpretation with Reference to Black People," decisively influenced my decision to choose biblical studies as my area of concentration.

Now that I have completed twelve years of formal theological education, I can see that my religious formation has come full circle. The impact of my early church school training explains in part why I return repeatedly to liberation as the basic motif for biblical interpretation. With this placed alongside the core of my professional work as a Christian womanist social ethicist, I continue to focus on questions and answers—studious inquiry into verbal inspirations of faith, aimed at meeting the contemporary challenges of prophetic ministry.

A LIBERATIONIST VIEW OF BIBLICAL AUTHORITY

From the vantage point of being a first-generation Christian womanist ethicist, I recognize Scripture as the story of God's continuing self-disclosure as the divine liberator to members of the believing community. It is not surprising that descendants of enslaved women and men by and large find the height of reverence for the Bible to be liberation, the solemnly proclaimed sacrosanct motif that runs consistently as God's revealed will from Genesis 1:1 to Revelation 22:21. Indeed, this basic theme of liberation is presented with substantial evidence in the work of Latta R. Thomas. Thomas makes a powerful case that there are a number of life lessons in Scripture that connect us to generations past and not yet born.

> The Bible is through and through a collective document which grew out of and is about God's liberation of people from human sin and

human oppression. . . . The Bible pictures the real God of heaven and earth and of Jesus Christ as *always* concentrating liberating efforts and concerns where human beings are in need, being mistreated and held down; that God is doing the same here and now where Black people are being held under by racism.[2]

The line of liberative reasoning in this type of ongoing Christian corrective of institutionalized calibrated violence goes like this: for a race of people who have suffered centuries of exploitative oppression and perverse cruelties due to chattel slavery, followed by one hundred tumultuous years of disparaging and derogative laws that enforced the brutality of racial segregation, there is a genuine longing for freedom from statutory social bondage. Championing this interpretation of Holy Scripture, Thomas writes:

[T]he Bible's chief faith-admonition is that men and women, particularly the suffering and enslaved, are called to work with God who frees, empowers, and heals those who venture into a covenant relationship with God.[3]

Thus, the central claim of progressive Christians is that a liberation interpretation of the Bible is beyond dispute because it maintains a consistency with God's character and requirements.

As a collection of sacred documents, the Bible, according to James H. Cone, "is our indispensable witness to God's revelation and is thus a primary source for Christian thinking about God."[4] That is to say, liberation ethicists evaluate Cone as being substantially right in *A Black Theology of Liberation*. The vast majority of parishioners in the black church community, who wrestle with understanding God's decisive acts in history as deep religious truths, assess the Bible as mirroring the essence of our humanness as women, men, and children created in the image of God. With far-reaching certainty, Cone argues that biblical witnesses lay the foundation for freedom being a reality for all people because God's determinative act is liberation. This means that from the earliest of times, my ancestors prayerfully searched the Scriptures for deliverance that embraces the higher demands of the commonwealth of God in this terrestrial sphere. As the lifeblood of civil rights struggles, liberation calls together people who are oppressed and abused and assures us that God's divine righteousness will vindicate our suffering.

The unitive theme of liberation invites African American Christians to live above the waddling and shuffling of mediocrity. Liberation serves as a mandate for eradicating culturally derogatory stereotypes that perpetuate images of inferiority that rape the psyche regarding our God-given sense of somebodiness. In *Disruptive Christian Ethics*, Traci C. West argues convincingly that a liberative ethical method "allows for the consideration of multiple layers of subjugating assumptions related to gender, race/ethnicity, socioeconomic class, and sexuality."[5] The overall significance of this living message possesses the power to transform the nature of black Christian societal embodiment, wherein we strive, morning by morning, to relate rightly to the God of the whole world and to all "livingkind"[6] therein. Being liberated moral agents enables us to experience the essence of *imago Dei*, and in turn we are energized and strengthened to keep moving "with the faith that what we are doing is right," says Martin Luther King Jr., "and with greater faith that God is with us in the struggle."[7]

In an effort to take the world of the Bible seriously, African American Christians read and study canonized texts in order to know the reverence and power of the abundant life of freedom embedded in Scripture. Black congregations with whom I have been affiliated are attracted to canonical readings of eyewitness events that parallel our human condition and verify our destiny before God. In a word, the goal of authentic Christian discipleship is, according to the writings in the Bible, "to let the oppressed go free" (e.g., Luke 4:18; Isa. 61:1). People of faith appreciate the bulk of these mythical stories, fascinating portrayals, and tales of supernatural miracles because they kindle a never-ending passion for freedom.

Cone, in a subsequent book, *God of the Oppressed* (1975), elaborates a doctrinal concept of Christology wherein the promises of God are realized in Jesus Christ as "Liberator."

> [E]xegesis of the Scriptures is a revelation of God in Christ as the Liberator of the oppressed from social oppression and political struggle, wherein the poor recognize that their fight against poverty and injustice is not only consistent with the gospel but is the gospel of Jesus Christ. . . . Any starting point that ignores God in Christ as the Liberator of the oppressed or that makes salvation as liberation secondary is *ipso facto* invalid and thus heretical.[8]

For the most part, this understanding of Jesus the Christ as Liberator enables African Americans to be delivered from material consumerism, freed from the political servitude of second-class citizenship, and redeemed from ignorance and spiritual bondage. Through his life, death, and resurrection, Jesus not only sets things right among nations but also abolishes all stumbling blocks and hindrances to the well-being of creation. In obedience to the present love of God, African Americans, and all who cast their lot with us, must throw off the smothering, suffocating blanket of white supremacy, male superiority, and class elitism.

Most importantly, since our concern here is appreciating the dialogical-dialectical dynamics between biblical texts and the particularities in African American existential, real-life contexts, we must turn our attention to the monumental work by black scholars in *Stony the Road We Trod: African American Biblical Interpretation*, edited by Cain Hope Felder (1991), and *African Americans and the Bible: Sacred Texts and Social Textures,* edited by Vincent L. Wimbush (2000). These first-rate biblicists provide the rudimentary data for members of black congregations in our ongoing struggle for maturity in Jesus Christ. Over a wide range of historical settings and broad array of ever-changing issues in biblical studies, these activist scholars continue to provide the black church community with astute exegesis of the complex warp and woof of Scripture. By directing our thoughts to God's liberation of the oppressed throughout the Bible and by viewing Jesus as a fellow sufferer who understands the trials and tribulations of the disinherited, black biblical scholars offer indispensable commentary and advocate sound praxis for daily Christian living. Departing from the normative operating assumptions in various guilds and learned societies, African American professors bring a radical critique to Eurocentric inherited traditions and kerygmatic assertions that minimize black people's actualization of our God-given authenticity. The epitome of God's dealings in history is emancipatory liberation, the authoritative lens through which we read critically and seriously this unique body of literature recorded in the Hebrew Bible and the Christian Testament.

Hermeneutical Implications

Whenever I facilitate Bible study courses with parishioners in black congregations, I juxtapose the dialogical character of liberation narratives in the Bible with experiential similarities, diversities, and divergences among a range of voices and constituencies in the African American church community. A case in point is that several years ago I conducted a Bible study series on the Joseph narrative in Genesis 37:1–50:26 at the Presbyterian Church of Ascension in New York City and at First African Presbyterian Church in Philadelphia. More recently, I facilitated a revised, updated version of this same Bible study for the parishioners at First United Presbyterian Church in Richmond, Virginia. Each session begins with introductory remarks about Genesis 36, the story of Esau and Jacob that immediately precedes the Joseph narrative. Both texts deal with conflict-ridden sibling rivalries that threaten to destroy domestic tranquillity. Considering multifaceted dynamics in extended families, I point out that in the initial report that Joseph brings to his father, Jacob, Joseph's concern is not with all his brothers but only with the four sons of his father's secondary wives, a continuation of the struggle between Jacob's mistresses and maidservants. Without any hesitancy, the Bible study participants immediately engaged these biblical texts as a body of knowledge out of which we theologize about familial experiences and social realities.

Three large questions dominate the discussion of Genesis 37. First, what responsibility does a parent have in provoking sibling rivalry by showing preferential love for one of the children with a distinct object of affection, such as a sleeved tunic of many colors? Second, what caused Reuben, the eldest brother, to oppose the plot of murder and instead suggest throwing Joseph into an underground water tank? Third, as there is no word of protest or self-defensive action on Joseph's part when he is seized, stripped of the "coat of many colors," and thrown into the empty cistern, what then might be the significance of Joseph's being sold into slavery for twenty pieces of silver?

After a week of daily reading and studying Genesis 38, the Bible study participants eagerly returned to class the following Wednesday, identifying close connections with Tamar as the liberator, because she is the one who wrestles moral legitimacy from inherited traditions that undermine women's well-being. To understand the aptness of this liberationist claim, along with lively congregational discussion about Tamar being a soul sister, one needs to grasp the variety of ethical strategies that people create in order to live with integrity in situations of oppression. Life-denying gender inequality that forcefully compels women to eke out existence from scratch is true in this pericope.

With rare exceptions, parishioners at all three African American Presbyterian churches voiced an understandable solidarity with Tamar when she devised a risky plan that could have cost both her honor and her life. In order to procure her basic human rights, Tamar seized an initiative that is well known in the black church community as "making a way out of no way." The customary levirate family law obligates the surviving brother-in-law to father a son with the widow of his brother. When Onan, Tamar's brother-in-law, goes through the motions but rejects his obligation to his deceased brother, Judah, the father of the husband's family, sends Tamar back to her father's house without a future, saying that his son, Shelah, is still too young to participate in the traditional levirate family law.

Tamar knew that she was doomed if she returned to her home of origin. So, when she played the harlot to her father-in-law, Tamar insisted that Judah compensate her for sexual favors not with the customary payment of a goat kid but with a pledge from Judah of personal items, things that served as his insignia, such as a ring, cord, and staff. In her act of agency against hierarchal patriarchal subordination, Tamar established the paternity of her pregnancy in such a way that Judah had to confess openly his offense. One of the usable truths emerging from the survivalist intentions in the African American community is that when people have their heads in the lion's mouth, they must treat the lion very gently. Likewise, many of the congregants shared testimonies about desperate people in dire situations doing desperate things.

The theological entrance piece that frames the narrative in Genesis 39 regarding Joseph as a newly acquired slave in Egypt is commonly translated as "The LORD was with Joseph" (v. 2a). Thus, we began our third Bible study session by aligning the slave narrative of Joseph in the Bible with the African American experience of the transatlantic slave trade and two-and-a-half centuries of chattel slavery. We revisit blessings we have received in *knowing that God was with us*, especially when things in life are not going our way. The point here is not that God is present only during good times, but that we must stay conscious of our Creator and Sustainer as a very present help in times of trouble.

When it comes to heart-wrenching, visceral connections when interfacing text with context, the story of Joseph as a blameless victim fleeing the desired clutches of his master's wife gives voice to African American Christians whose memories, in countless ways, are fresh with reflections on the nine black youngsters falsely accused of raping two white women on a freight train in Scottsboro, Alabama, in the 1930s and the mutilated corpse of Emmett Till pulled from the Tallahatchie River in Mississippi in 1955. Even though the allotted time for this part of the Bible study (the time when church folks offer uncanny testimony to the evils of lynching from multiple sites in the U.S.) is never long enough,[9] we move on so that we have time to identify the strategies that Joseph as a slave used in staying faithful, refusing to do wrong even when his enemies did not desist from their corrupt purposes.

Dreams, especially the kind that we cannot easily shake off or forget, play a significant role in Genesis 40 and 41. The touted benefits of being a dreamer and possessing the gift of interpretation are recounted by various participants. The claim here is that there are lessons to be learned from every person in the struggle to achieve freedom. Some of the viewpoints and insights focus on the forgetful cupbearer who received a favorable interpretation of his dream but was not able to remember Joseph's request to mention to Pharaoh that he was innocent of the crime for which he was incarcerated. For some, this week's readings present strategies and tactics for coping when our well-founded expectations are followed by disappointment. For others, matters worthy of consideration explore the complexities of reparations, settling overdue debts that power brokers have long forgotten. At the heart of the drama is Joseph's rise from an incarcerated prisoner to the position of grand vizier.

In the following week, much is said about Joseph's reunion with his brothers in Egypt (Gen. 42–44). General weight is given to assessing possible reasons as to why Joseph allowed his brothers to undergo the severe trial of being tested, arrested as spies, and held in custody for three days. Few Bible study students can fathom why Joseph in a position of power did not show mercy. Others redirect the conversation so that attention is paid to the question, "What is this that God has done to us?" (42:28)—the question posed by Joseph's brothers after they are seized by the powerful fear of defenselessness on discovering the money in the top of their sacks. Part of the answer to this soul-searching question can be found in the scene where the brothers were overtaken by guards and charged as thieves. Not surprising are the number of African Americans who readily identify with the biblical characters who fall under the suspicion of theft. Several members describe real and irrefutable experiences of being falsely accused and how they uttered with conviction the certainty of innocence even when forced to bear punishment with the guilty. Inevitably, one or two parishioners suggest a counterbalance to Jacob's instructions to his sons regarding the presents they must take with them when they return to Egypt. To be sure, we do not adjourn until we discuss the crimes of slavery that benefactors, then and now, want to conceal.

The final Bible study class is always a marathon session. As we close out our study of Genesis 45–50, we leave with open-ended, soul-searching questions: Where in our lives do we resonate with what happens when Joseph makes himself known to his brothers and Jacob, once again, recognizes his son? When have deathbed blessings and promises of liberation been actualized in our lives? And, considering the annihilation of African burial sites as a result of "the stigmata of the Middle Passage,"[10] how important is place in the burial of bones of loved ones, for ancestors who exited "the door of no return," never to go home again?

If nothing else, I am utterly convinced that there is an ongoing need "to proclaim liberty to the captives." After three decades of facilitating liberation Bible studies in African American Presbyterian churches, I possess a greater data base of the relentless ways that our society chips away at black people's God-given sense of possibilities. Federal government programs and civil rights movements have had positive impacts on the African American church community, and yet, here in the twenty-first century, when we chart the progress of affirmative action for equal employment and educational opportunities, we move from segregation to desegregation back to resegregation.

The dismantling of systemic oppression in the 1950s through the 1970s has not been able to offset the virulent backlash that began in the 1980s. The negative effects of societal inequities are inextricably tied to systemic racism, sexism, and class oppression that permeate and dictate both our national and ecclesiastical consciousness. The persistent obstacles of white supremacy, misogyny, and poverty continue to enslave the vast majority of black people to hunger, disease, the prison industrial complex, and the highest rate of unemployment since World War II.[11] In essence, sharing the Bible's message of liberation has always been, and will continue to play, a central role in actualizing my vocational call as I walk between church and academy, between town and gown.

4

"Lámpara es a mis pies tu palabra"

Biblical Authority at the Crossroads

Carlos F. Cardoza-Orlandi

THE BIBLE OVERWHELMS MY LIFE

As I left every Sunday evening for my college town in Puerto Rico, my *Papa's* caring voice uttered the opening verses of Psalm 1: "*Bienaventurado el varón que no anduvo en consejo de malos, ni estuvo en caminos de pecadores, ni en silla de escarnecedores se ha sentado; sino que en la ley de Jehová está su delicia, y en su ley medita de día y de noche....*"[1] With this advice my *abuelo* ("grandfather"), who frequently took a father's role, blessed me with the Word. He was Pentecostal. His journey from Roman Catholic to Methodist to Presbyterian to Pentecostal (and, in his last days, to Disciples of Christ) is a common one among many Christians in Puerto Rico. But, it must be said, all these traditions bear little resemblance to those in the United States or Europe. Mainline Protestant traditions in the Latin Caribbean bear a particular charismatic touch of the Spirit—some heavier than others—yet all are shaped by and dependent on the Scriptures.

I grew up and was nourished in this religious mosaic. In my religious biography I discovered multiple Christian and non-Christian traditions interacting with each other. At times, I would inadvertently move easily from one to another. Other times, I was confused as I tried to sort out the various tensions and incongruities. However, in all the traditions I have found a common variable: the use and misuse of Scripture.

It makes sense. Given life's complexity, the Christian Scriptures, though frequently a source of direction and guidance, were and continue to be a partner that I cannot live without! The Bible became a perfect companion when it confirmed what I needed to do, an imperfect partner when it did not provide cleancut answers, an inspirational guide when I was seeking motivation and energy,

an enemy when it served to restrain my freedom, a sustaining friend in difficulty, an annoying voice when it challenged my comfort, a neglected prophet
when "I did not do what I wanted, but I did the very thing I hated,"[2] and
an ultimate authority condemning those who refused to "understand" and
redeeming those who were considered "deficient" but tried to understand.

Yes, Scripture has been for me a full partner: I would quote Psalms before
going to bed when I was in trouble and needed divine intervention and whenever I needed a good excuse to replace a required chore with spiritual examination. I still quote it to my children, trying to emulate my *Papa*, or trying to
persuade my wife to follow my theological insight into an interreligious experience that she strongly questions. As I think about the Scriptures, I see them
all over my life—in church, school, work, family—my daily life.

In my faith journey, I have located myself in the Christian Church (Disciples of Christ) within the Caribbean and Latino/a context. Scriptures are part
of my day-to-day experience, from daily devotion time to preparing sermons
and lectures, and sometimes my "night life" when I try to make sense of a sermon or testimony.

Recently, my family and I were invited to a friend's fiftieth birthday. Typical of Latino parties, the invited families brought guests to the birthday. In this
large gathering of old and new friends, two new Latino couples showed up.
They were visiting Christian groups in the Atlanta area. They identified themselves as apostles in an Apostolic Network.[3]

Just before we prayed and cut the cake, our friend's wife asked our pastor
and the apostles to share some words of testimony. One of the female apostles
referred to the Year of Jubilee in Leviticus 25. With beautiful words, she
blessed our friend with the "fruits of the land" and the "promise of God's good-
will" in his life. Her eloquent and gracious blessing filled the room, and we
gave thanks to God for my friend's life.

I was overjoyed by the blessing, but it also made me uncomfortable. I could
still hear the words: "For it is a jubilee, it shall be holy to you" (Lev. 25:12a).
But I also remembered the biblical affirmations:

> When you make a sale to your neighbor, you shall not cheat one
> another. . . . You shall not cheat one another, but you shall fear your
> God; for I am the LORD your God. . . . If any of your kin fall into dif-
> ficulty and become dependent on you, you shall support them; they
> shall live with you as though resident aliens. . . . Do not . . . make a
> profit from them. . . . As for the male and female slaves whom you may
> have, it is from the nations around you that you may acquire male and
> female slaves. You may also acquire them from among the aliens resid-
> ing with you, and from their families that are with you, who have been
> born in your land; and they may be your property. (Lev. 25:14, 17,
> 35–36, 44–45)

I could not go to sleep that night. The apostle said nothing about the complicated set of affirmations for the Year of Jubilee in Leviticus or for my friend's fiftieth year. She gave him a blessing of fruitful land and property—a blessing of prosperity—with no responsibilities attached, as stipulated in the biblical text. Why could I not go to sleep?

As I stared at the ceiling and wrestled with the text, I found it even more puzzling that the text referred to slavery and human property with language such as "aliens residing with you" and "slaves," distinguishing foreigners from Israelites. I just could not resolve the conflict between the blessing and the text. The apostle gave a blessing of prosperity to a foreigner, a resident alien, whom the text permits to be enslaved and mistreated. Moreover, "alien," a term charged with political, economic, and racial connotations in our national immigration debate, was never mentioned in the blessing, as if the prosperity part were somehow separate from the ethnic/religious political distinctions. And as if this was not enough, I could hear the text in my heart remind me: "Remember that you were a slave in Egypt and the LORD your God redeemed you from there; therefore I command you to do this [to protect the alien and the foreigner]" (Deut. 24:18).[4]

The next morning, I saw my friend in church and invited him to discover the serious responsibilities and difficult incongruities of the Jubilee blessing in Leviticus 25. I also told him that the apostle gave him only one side of the story, severely limiting the story. I said, "It is totally up to you if you want to keep the blessing, or, perhaps, take it easy on its expectations. I am sorry to ruin your fiftieth birthday blessing, but that's how the Word works!"

Why not just let the blessing stand on its own and ignore the rest of the text? Why do the terms "alien" and "slave" evoke such strong, mixed feelings? Why are references to prosperity and cheating so close together in the text and in my imagination? Why is there a level of familiarity and comfort and, at the same time, a level of alienation and discomfort? Why do the privileged Israelites have permission to mistreat the foreigner? Why do I think about other texts in the two Testaments that are both congruent and incongruent with the Leviticus text?

Furthermore, when I read "alien" and "slave," why do I think about my local congregation—most of them immigrants, some with and some without documentation? When I read about prosperity and cheating, why do I think about how the *consumerist imperative* has been magically imposed on many of us who want to fit the American dream? Why do I resist any status of privilege and condemn any justification to mistreat a foreigner, a Muslim, or a Hindu? Why do I resist any attempt to justify the deficiency of "the other"? And finally, *why so many questions?* Bible school did not teach me that this is "how the Word works," but throughout my faith journey I am discovering that this is how the Scriptures and its authority "work" for me.

THE TEMPLATE AND THE MATRIX

I have discovered two metaphors that crystallize my understanding of biblical authority. The first is the template. I see the Christian Scriptures as a template where multiple religious, cultural, economic, and gender forces are actively *present*. This template metaphor acknowledges the *presence* of these factors in the text and in my own social location. *Presence* is crucial because it indicates who or what is (or is not) present in the text and in my social location. I come from Puerto Rico, which is invisible to most of the U.S. public except for its resorts and entertainment. Being recognized beyond the stereotype of a "party animal" is life-giving. To be *present* and *recognized*, as thousands of Latinos and Latinas were during the *marchas* around the nation claiming justice in the recent immigration debate, is to give a face to a debate void of human reality and flooded by political rhetoric. As we look at the Scriptures and seek their authority in our lives, the template metaphor pushes us to ask who and what are or are not present in the text and in our social location.

When I was a pastor in Brooklyn, New York, a young woman in our congregation was sexually assaulted. Her boyfriend had left her in front of her home, and as she entered a gang assaulted her. As she spoke to my wife and me about the incident, she expressed her frustration: "Pastor, my boyfriend and his family blame themselves for the incident. My parents blame themselves for the incident. Family members seek revenge. Everybody either blames themselves or is going to 'do something' about this incident. But *where am I*?" The template metaphor has pushed me to see who or what is present or absent in the text and in my social location.

In the second metaphor, I see the Christian Scriptures within a matrix of religious, cultural, economic, and gender factors. The matrix metaphor points to the *interaction* of these factors in the text and in my own social location. *Interaction* implies energy, synergy, movement, involvement, activity, and passivity. *Interaction* points to the character and dynamics of the relationship(s) between who or what is or is not there. In the face of widespread American ignorance of the U.S. citizenship of Puerto Ricans and of their ambiguous but determined participation in U.S. wars in the twentieth and twenty-first centuries, engagement in the political forum should add a new perspective, if not agency, to the decision-making process in debates over American war policies. Growing awareness of the economic and cultural agency and contributions of Latino/a immigrants for more than twenty years, of the historical fact that inclusion makes better citizens and that exclusion generates criminal action, gives hope during a difficult transitional time in national politics. As we examine Scriptures and seek their authority in our lives, the matrix metaphor pushes us to ask who possesses agency and who lacks agency in the text and in our social location.

As my wife and I continued our conversation with the young woman in our Brooklyn congregation, she began to describe the assault. It was a heartbreaking moment. My wife held the young woman in her arms and both of them cried. Here I was, pastor of the congregation, deeply moved by this young woman's suffering. Because I wanted to say something to bring some peace and hope, I said, "Have hope, my sister, at least you were not raped."

My wife's teary eyes turned fiery. The young woman looked at me with dismay. I thought, "What? Isn't it true? I said it with my best intentions." I truly forgot that "the way to hell is paved with good intentions." My response in this situation bespoke my gender bias, revealing my ignorance about honor and sexuality among Caribbean/Latina women. To this day, I am still figuring out why my agency was so harmful.

My wife stood up and politely asked me to leave the office: "Pastor, I believe it is time for you to leave your office and leave us alone." I left, confused and nervous. What did I do wrong? If I did something wrong, how much damage had I done? (I was also nervous because I knew my wife would confront me when she got the chance. Thankfully, she did, and with a great lesson!) The matrix metaphor has pushed me to consider the character and dynamics of the relationship(s) between who or what was or was not in the text and in my social location.

Template and matrix work together. The template is a temporary, permeable space. One adds, changes, reconfigures, mixes, and deletes. But the template will let you see what you have and do not have in its space. One caution, however, must be considered. When one template works, we become so accustomed to it that we forget how to alter the template when it becomes necessary. If we reify the template, its vitality is lost. Fortunately, new templates emerge from different sources. Hence, as long as there is an interfacing of templates, we will "see more." We will better observe what is or is not in our template. We will better observe who or what is or is not in the text and in our social locations.

The matrix, on the other hand, requires that all its factors interact with each other. One caution, however, must be considered. We can become so used to a particular interaction—to a way of relating the factors—that we reify the interaction, making it arithmetic rather than algorithmic. Fortunately, as new templates influence our existing templates, we discover new agencies between old and new factors. Moreover, the presence of new factors creates new relationships between old factors, between new factors, and, as stated above, between old and new. Hence, as long as there is interaction between the template and matrix metaphors, we will not only "see more," but will discover new relationships between the factors within the matrix. We will discern better the character and dynamics of the relationship(s) among those present or absent in the text and in our social location.

Some brief examples will help capture the meaning of the metaphors.[5] For many years, I read and understood Luke 4:16–30 as the story of the Jews' rejection of Jesus. The text was not about Christians but about the Jews' deficiency, extended to all who reject Jesus. My template was in place, and my matrix characterized the Jews' relationship toward Jesus as one of contempt, particularly after Jesus' words, "Today this scripture has been fulfilled in your hearing" (v. 21). I repeatedly read the text, but its meaning was the same. I preached the text, but fundamentally the meaning did not change: The Jews rejected Jesus, and those who reject Jesus today are deficient and commit violence against our Lord.

People of other faiths and colleagues involved in interfaith dialogue, however, helped me to notice something different in the text. I had been oblivious to the verse that follows Jesus' upsetting statement: "All spoke well of him and were amazed at the gracious words that came from his mouth. They said, 'Is not this Joseph's son?'" (v. 22). The rest of the narrative now made sense (vv. 23–27). The Jews in Luke 4 rejected Jesus not because he claimed that Scripture had been fulfilled but because he included the marginalized and Israel's enemies as heirs to the promises of the reign of God.[6] The "tent has been broadened" and, ironically, I can live in this new tent because of Jesus' courage and understanding of God's reign and Israel's complex history.

In my old template and matrix, I treated the presence and agency of the widow of Zarephath and Naaman the Syrian either as confirmation of my original interpretation or as simply irrelevant (marginal!). In my template, to justify my original interpretation, I would see them as examples of myopic characters who never got God's purpose for salvation. In my matrix, they served two purposes: to prove the character of deficient people who cannot see God's purpose and to depict the quality of the relationship between deficient people and God. Ultimately, Jews and non-Christians have nothing to say about God. Basically, they are angry people because they just do not get it.

However, colleagues from different cultures and friends from other faiths have broadened my template, helping me to examine the text and my social location anew and changing the algorithmic factors of my matrix. They helped me discover new relationships and new agencies of people in the text and in my social location. Consequently, I read and interpret the text differently. Interestingly, I do refer to my old template to note how I see and live differently according to my new template and matrix. Consequently, as I engage with people of other faiths, particularly those whom I am strongly inclined to regard as deficient, the Spirit brings to bear the promise of God's reign to those I see as marginalized and enemies of my community and faith. They too are heirs to the reign I consider to be my inheritance.

John Lemond is a friend and a Lutheran missionary in China. When I was in Hong Kong, he invited me to a Sunday worship service. His reflection was on the death penalty. His template included two very interesting resources: the Analects of Confucius and the reading of the lectionary for that Sunday, Matthew 5:38–45. He juxtaposed contextual resources from another religious tradition and the New Testament text in the following way.

Confucius's disciple said to him, "We have heard people say that you should return good for evil. What do you say?" Confucius answered, "If you return good for evil, what will you return for good? No, do not return good for evil. Return good for good, and return justice for evil."[7] On the other hand, Lemond read from Scriptures, "'But I say to you, Do not resist an evildoer. But if anyone strikes you on the right cheek, turn the other also; . . . But I say to you, Love your enemies and pray for those who persecute you, so that you may be children of your Father in heaven'" (Matt. 5:39, 44–45a).

It is clear that Confucius's definition of justice is compatible with definitions of justice in the rabbinic tradition, in most Western jurisprudence, and with many Christians. Evil is paid with justice, not with good! To repay evil with good messes up the social order and breaks the contract of equity, which characterizes modern democratic societies.

Nevertheless, the gospel postulates something quite different. The new law is an imperative to live differently. The gospel calls us to overcome a law that, by its own nature, postulates equity, and which in many cases evokes a nation's act of violence as a juridical solution for crime: the death penalty. In fact, many Christians claim that it is a Christian solution to criminal problems. Likewise, the declaration of Confucius serves as a mirror to evoke our own principles of justice, those that we have occasionally confused with the Christian gospel. Therefore, one question might be: Are Christians who support the death penalty more Confucian than Christian? One thing is clear: Lemond's template and matrix for his sermon clearly showed that Confucius illuminates and challenges "our" gospel and mission in our context by showing us our own process of domesticating the gospel with the law of the land!

Another example: I find puzzling Paul's allegory of Hagar and Sarah in Galatians 4:21–5:1. As I read the text, I see these two women in my template. The text also evokes in my template the current conflict between Palestinians and Israelis. In my matrix, these women are compared: Hagar is declared deficient, representing the covenant of slavery, and Sarah represents the covenant of freedom. Also, in my matrix, this text frequently brings up contempt toward Muslims. But is this the complete picture?

Delores Williams[8] and certain Latin American feminists[9] remind me of the Genesis narratives of Hagar and Ishmael (Gen. 16 and 21). In both Old Testament passages we see a very different story and discover a different relationship with God. Thus we may ask: Is Hagar's representation of a covenant of slavery, according to Paul, coherent with her presentation in Genesis as a slave woman *seen* by God, who *names* God, and whose life and progeny are *blessed* by God? What would we say to Paul about this other side of the story? What would an Arab Christian say about the story? What would a Muslim say?

In any case, we can see in this broader template and matrix other stories and discover other relationships: God acts in different ways. As the Galatians and Genesis texts and my own complex social location interact, my theological perspectives come into tension with each other, with no clear solution, only a more illuminated path for a very complex journey that offers no easy answers to difficult issues but requires a grounded position in order to live the faith.

The spirit-religious worldview of the Caribbean is strong and grounded. Despite different modern movements—secularism, communism, scientific worldview, and so on—most Caribbean Latino/a Christians are deeply aware of the world of the spirits, yet many harbor hostility toward spiritists[10] and those who mediate spirits. Drawing from an inherited missionary template and matrix, they demonize the spirits by citing 1 Samuel 28:3–25, the story of Saul consulting a medium. A closer look at the text, however, reveals that there is no condemnation of the medium. In fact, the medium is hesitant to provide the service and deeply frustrated when she discovers that Saul has disguised himself to seek her services. Nevertheless, she still offers Saul words of advice and hospitality. Moreover, there is no biblical reference to the downfall of Saul based on his "spiritual consultation." Ironically, in this narrative the spirit of Samuel reminds Saul why the Lord has forgotten him, and it has nothing to do with the medium.

The narratives of the transfiguration (Matt. 17:1–13; Mark 9:2–13; Luke 9:28–36) can be a headache for the Christian who discovers that Spiritualists find in this text an *affirmation* of the spirit world under the dominion of Jesus Christ. Within the inherited missionary and modern matrix, the significance of Elijah's and Moses' relationship with Jesus serves only to affirm Jesus as the culmination of the law and the prophets, while the Caribbean matrix recognizes the participation of the spirits/ancestors in Jesus' ministry. They are not just "symbolic representations" of the law and the prophets. They are transfigured spirits who give witness to Jesus, just as other spirits can give witness to Jesus today.

CONCLUSIONS

I would like to emphasize four principles that speak to my understanding of the authority of Scripture.

1. Though I thought my understanding of the authority of Scripture was propositional, a retrospective reflection shows me that it has been and continues to be incarnational. Biblical authority is embodied as it is tested at the crossroads of daily life experiences.

2. Both the template and the matrix metaphors point to the relational and communal character of biblical authority. It is not individual or private.
3. In the matrix metaphor, the relationship between what is present and what is absent is not dialectic, which requires a one-to-one synthesis. It is rather an algorithmic/polycentric relationship that leads to a "pluritopic hermeneutic."[11]
4. My understanding of biblical authority moves in accord with my own movement and experiences in my social locations.

I love the Scriptures. I have used and misused them, and now that I am aware of my misuse, I can engage them with greater integrity. Biblical authority does not mean that the Scriptures will always provide the answers. But it does mean that as much as I love them, they will continue to keep me up at night and give me the kind of headaches that can only make me grow in the Spirit. In our complex faith journey, all we need is a lamp, and the Scriptures are exactly that.

5

The Soil That Is Scripture

Ellen F. Davis

As an Anglican—a lay member of the Episcopal Church in the U.S.A., to be precise—I belong to a tradition that is not inclined to promulgate statements about the nature of biblical authority, so I am not going to attempt that here. Insofar as I think about authority in the abstract, I view it as a relational phenomenon, one that operates equally from the side of the one "under authority" (Matt. 8:9; Luke 7:8) and from the side of the one exercising authority. In other words, unlike tyranny, authority achieves its desired effects only when it is both recognized and accepted. In this chapter, I focus on the first side of that relationship: What is required of us who *stand under* the authority of Scripture? And, more particularly, what bearing does that have on gaining a deeper *understanding* of Scripture, one of the crucial goals of a theological education?

READING CRITICALLY

Implicitly or explicitly, every seminary or divinity school I know identifies "critical biblical study" as a first step in formal theological study. Yet I have taught for years without trying to define for myself or my students what that means, and I do not think I am unusual in this omission, which now seems to me regrettable. So I begin here with a clarification and even a rough definition: contrary to a common-sense interpretation of the adjective, *critical* study of the Bible is not a matter of identifying which bits I particularly like or do not like and focusing on the former. Indeed, it is almost the opposite, for *the essence of critical reading is grappling with the Bible's inexhaustible complexity.* In

order to do that, we must set aside, or at least subordinate, our own prefer-
ences and try to reckon with Scripture as a whole.

Augustine—surely one of the greatest biblical "critics" of all time, even if
he lived and died entirely innocent of modern historical criticism—had something like that in mind when he spoke of the Bible's "wondrous depth" (*mira
profunditas*). The surface, he says, "may be flattering to the childish"; it might
seem to reflect back the ideas and opinions we bring to it, to confirm just what
we currently think. But if we dare to look in deeply, "*Mira profunditas*, my God,
the wondrous depth! It causes a shudder to peer into it—a shudder of awe, and
a tremor of love."[1] The critical reader of Scripture is encountering something
a lot bigger than the reader, and it is always frightening to feel small, even if
that big thing is genuinely "awesome," genuinely worthy of reverence and
love. So the critical reading of Scripture is ultimately a work of love, as is the
practice of any art—and this is the art on which the church's life depends.

So for Augustine reading Scripture is something like looking into the
Grand Canyon, or whatever is its North African equivalent. The ancient rabbis had another image for what it is to read Scripture critically, a saying I especially like: "*Hafokh bah wehafokh bah.* . . . Turn it over and over; everything is
in it—and in it [or, through it] you will see something."[2] *Hafokh*—it is a verb
one might use of turning a crystal over and over to examine its different facets,
or of turning compost until it is ready for the soil. That latter nuance is especially suggestive of what it is to live productively with Scripture and out of its
richness. Reading Scripture well is like being a master gardener, and the Bible
is like soil; the thoughts of those who study it deeply grow in that medium.
The soil metaphor is not itself biblical, but it works nicely with one of the
Bible's root metaphors: God is light. So our thoughts, planted in the soil that
is Scripture, are growing toward the light of God, and if the soil is well worked,
then they may bear rich fruit.

Habits of Reading Scripture

If we are gardeners, then it is necessary to ask, What are the habits of mind
and heart that a good gardener cultivates? At the least they are humility, love,
and patience. It is not simply that a humble, loving, and patient person is able
to make a garden beautiful; reciprocally, the daily work of gardening seems to
cultivate those qualities in a person. So this is my proposal: *Critical interpretation of the Bible is an essential way that Christians practice the virtues of humility,
charity, and patience in a distinctly intellectual mode.* If the intellectual leaders and
teachers of the church—broadly speaking, those who have a formal theological education—do not practice and model humility, charity, and patience in

reading Scripture, then Christ's ministry of reconciliation through the church will not thrive as it might in our hands. That would be a shame to us and a loss for countless others inside and outside the church.

Humility

I begin with humility, for I follow Augustine in seeing this as the first virtue of Christian biblical interpretation. He compared Scripture to a large room; but its door is very low, so one has to stoop down in order to enter.[3] Our garden metaphor also speaks to the need for humility, because the very word comes from the Latin word for "soil," *humus*. Humility is the quality of being solidly grounded, profoundly "earthed." And what does that mean for the practice of biblical interpretation? If critical Bible study means looking into the inexhaustible complexity of the text, then humility in that work may mean admitting that none of our interpretations is definitive. The very best interpreter is inadequate to the richness of the text. Even those who are most "right" can grasp only part of God's truth as spoken through Scripture. That admission is no liberal or postmodern cop-out from the obligation to stand under the authority of Scripture. On the contrary, it is a matter of ordering all our life, including our intellectual life, in accordance with what George Steiner calls aptly "the immensity of the commonplace . . . the commonplace mystery" of having the Bible in our midst as "a real presence."[4] God's authoritative word "is not in heaven," Moses tells the Israelites at the very end of his life. "No, the word is very near to you; it is in your mouth and in your heart for you to observe." (Deut. 30:12, 14.)

In that position of nearness to God's word, a position both humbling and responsible, it is appropriate to admit the nonfinality of all our interpretations. That admission bespeaks a modesty befitting those who read the Bible knowing that their own sin blinds them—us—to much of the truth of Scripture. And this is true of us not only as individuals but also as members of the church. For we are all deeply embedded in a church that is scandalously divided between East and West, between rich North and exploited South—to name only two ways Christ's body has long suffered at our hands. Precisely because of those acrimonious and sometimes very bloody divisions, it is questionable how much of the wondrous depth of Scripture is visible to any of us.

Charity

A second and closely allied virtue for readers is charity, evidenced first toward the text and second toward those who read it differently from the way I do. But what does it mean to be charitable to a text?[5] In my own Anglican tradition, the liturgy gives us a clue. Immediately after each Scripture lesson is read at Morning and Evening Prayer, the standard congregational response is; "Thanks be to

God." It does not matter how hair-raising any particular passage is; we are still obliged to be grateful. That response is not a whitewashing job; it is a reminder to ourselves that we receive the Bible, day by day, as God's gift to the church. Further, by thanking God, we are expressing our trust that this is a good gift. I think of a preacher who, on the two or three occasions I heard her preach, began with the line, "I hate this text!" She was less subtle than most, but I think her attitude is widespread, and especially with respect to the Old Testament. It is very common to argue, as this preacher did, that much of the Bible in both Testaments represents a moral vision that is deficient, not in accordance with the gospel of Jesus Christ. The implication would seem to be that Scripture has little or nothing to teach about the gospel—a position that lacks humility and logic as well as charity. Anyone who launches into critical biblical study will surely find in both Testaments much that offends; as one of my students said a few years ago, "The Bible doesn't always say what you thought it did—or wish it did." The only way to move through and past that offense is by more study, more probing and questioning. I cannot (and would not) shortcut the process, but I will comment briefly on each of the two directions in which our charity might extend.

First, toward the text: Receiving the Scriptures as God's good gift means opening our minds to be changed by them; it does *not* mean relinquishing the right to disagree with some of what we encounter there—even the necessity of disagreeing on some significant points of faith and practice—since the biblical writers disagree among themselves, even within each Testament. Indeed, the very fact of internal disagreement is crucial for our understanding of scriptural authority and how the Bible itself fosters a critical consciousness. The canon offers us a model for how established religious convictions, even those established by authoritative texts, may be challenged and debated within the community of faith. Every biblical writer who departs from the tradition does so by highlighting other neglected elements of the tradition; every innovation is established on an older foundation.[6] From this precedent I take the principle that if we disagree with a certain text on a given point, then it must be in obedience to what we, in community with other Christians, discern to be the larger or more fundamental message of the Scriptures. In other words, disagreement represents a critical judgment, based on keen awareness of the complexity of Scripture and reached in the context of the church's ongoing worship, prayer, and study. Therefore, it seems to me that members of the church, or the church as a whole, should come to such a judgment slowly and to a degree reluctantly—with the reluctance any of us might feel, as we begin to realize that on a given point we cannot accept the view of a revered elder, a parent, or a beloved mentor. Further, in this matter, self-suspicion is a sign of spiritual maturity. We should continue to study and examine the ramifications of our new position critically, checking to see whether it can indeed be brought into full conversation with Scripture and the Christian tradition. Doing that would be to love the Bible as we love ourselves.

If we aspire to that kind of charity toward the Bible, then it follows that we must also show charity toward those who read the text differently than we do. The currently well publicized fissures in the Anglican communion do not result from disagreement over the issue of homosexuality per se, but rather from lack of humility and charity in our handling of the Bible, on both sides of the issue. I spent several years living, teaching, and worshiping in an international community of Anglicans who have strongly differing views on committed same-sex relations. Yet we persisted in mutual love and cooperation, as well as open disagreement, without any accusing those with whom they disagreed of bibliolatry, on the one hand, or contempt of the Bible, on the other. Despite differing views—and, for many, uncertainty—on this matter, that community still continues in daily prayer, study, and listening for the guidance of the Holy Spirit. In my own limited experience of the church, this is a key instance of how interpretive humility and charity may foster God's work of reconciliation within the church.

Patience

I have saved for last the discussion of patience as an intellectual virtue, and I will treat it at greatest length, for it may be the hardest virtue for us in particular to acquire. North American Christians live in a culture that is rife with impatience, and indeed cultivates it. Road rage might be the most obvious manifestation of our impatience, but isn't that only the flip side of the multiple ways we as a culture cultivate an uncritical admiration for speed? If something is fast, you do not have to say any more to demonstrate that it is good, in everything from automobiles to computers to invasion strategies to reading techniques. I suspect that our infatuation with speed is bad for our souls in any number of ways, but in one area I am sure of it: speed-reading the Bible cancels most benefits of reading it at all. About six weeks into the Old Testament interpretation course, one of my first-year students said, "When I came here, I thought my problem was that I read too slowly. Now I realize I read too fast." Perhaps the first step in acquiring a theological education is learning patience with words, because the biblical writers (and all good theologians who follow them) choose their words with care. Theological meaning unfolds from the way words are put together in phrases, sentences, stories—in the way a biblical book is shaped, or even (as I have suggested) the canon as a whole.

A conversation was reported between the nineteenth-century French poet Stéphane Mallarmé and an unnamed painter, who complained: "I have tried to write poetry, but I cannot do it, even though I have ever so many ideas."

And Mallarmé responded sensibly, "*Chéri*, poems are not written with ideas, but with words." On the whole, it is better to think of the Bible as poetry rather than as prose, at least as we generally distinguish between those two in our reading practices. You cannot skim poetry for plot, and you cannot read it in distraction. That is why poetry is read by poetry lovers: it is a nonutilitarian act, like many other acts of love.[7] Therefore, reading the Bible "as poetry" means slowing down to ponder each phrase, to wonder why *this* word was chosen and not another, how this line or paragraph or story builds on what precedes and leads into what follows.

That kind of reading is in a sense nonutilitarian, and yet it has at least one great practical benefit: dwelling on and thus coming to love the particular words of Scripture may be the best safeguard against empty religious or academic jargon. Dwelling on those complex yet beautiful literary forms just might save us from falling into the pious overgeneralizations or pseudointellectual abstractions that too often make clergy and teachers sound schooled but not educated. And probably the best single way to learn to love those words and forms is to study the biblical languages. That study teaches patience, but a better selling point is this: It will bring you closer to the Word than you ever imagined you could be. It will slow your reading, even in English, for it puts into your mind all sorts of new questions about what these words mean. Language study inevitably generates a certain "productive uncertainty," for almost the first thing any language student sees is that one consistent effect of translation is to reduce ambiguity and make meanings "neat."[8]

I offer one small example of a poetic line that reads quite differently in Hebrew—a verse from Psalm 119, which is especially apt for theological students, as it is written in the voice of one such student, speaking to us from perhaps twenty-five hundred years in the past. One familiar line of this long poem is traditionally rendered thus:

> How shall a young man cleanse his way?
> By keeping to your words.
>   (Ps. 119:9)

That translation is from the *Book of Common Prayer*, and both the King James Version and the NRSV agree on the chief point: the bicolon (the most common form of Hebrew poetry) is to be rendered as a question followed by an answer. But in fact the Hebrew syntax, which is very simple, suggests something quite different. The second colon begins with an infinitive marked with a particle (*lamed*) that normally denotes the start of a purpose clause. So following the grammar more closely, and not yielding to what we have decided in advance the line must mean, we come to this reading:

> How shall a young man cleanse his way,
>   in order to keep to your word(s)?

The crucial difference in this revised translation is that the question mark comes at the end; instead of question-and-answer, the whole bicolon is an open-ended question. Here in the ninth of 176 verses, that is a very significant difference. The translation that follows the Hebrew enables us to see that this poem is written by someone on a quest, an ancient seeker traveling the up-and-down, sometimes poorly marked path of true learning. The traditional rendering, by contrast, suggests the dull didacticism of a smart aleck who's got the map marked in red and is holding it six inches from your nose. Which one of these is the more trustworthy and generous guide for our own study? The revised translation is to be preferred not only on syntactical grounds, but also because it fits the literary context better. The very next line shows that this poet makes no pretense of having it all mapped out:

> With my whole heart I seek you;
>   do not let me stray from your commandments.
>   (Ps. 119:10)

The point of this example is that reading in the original languages freshens the Scriptures. You think you know a passage so well that there is nothing new to discover, and then you read it in Greek or Hebrew and it changes before your eyes. I recently heard one of my own teachers, Professor Moshe Greenberg of the Hebrew University in Jerusalem, say that the real student of Scripture is the one who can read a text a hundred times, and on the hundred-and-first reading see something entirely new. Even better: you read it *with somebody else* in Hebrew or Greek, and it opens up possibilities neither of you ever considered alone. This happens to me over and over in my Hebrew classes, partly because the students have the advantage of reading (in most cases) more slowly and hesitantly than I do—at the outset laboring over every word—and therefore they often read better.

If patience with words is the first thing one must learn in order to interpret the Bible well, then patience with difficulty is probably the second. This seems to me to be a remarkable omission in Christian discourse: it is common to speak as though interpreting the Bible were an easy and forthright thing, regardless of whether people like or do not like what they think it says. But that is simply not the case, and it is past time for the church to be honest about it. Jews are far more perceptive about this. They have a special blessing that is said when one sees a Torah scholar, someone devoted to the study of sacred texts:

> Blessed are you, O Lord, King of the Universe,
>   who has given a portion of his wisdom to those who fear him.

Since ancient times, Jews have known that right understanding of Torah, sacred knowledge, is at once the most consequential and the most difficult of all forms of human inquiry. There is nothing self-serving about that observation: think about our subject matter. We are talking about what Dante rightly called "the Love that moves the sun and the other stars."[9] The Love that—the Love *whom*—we study is considerably more complex than rocket science.

Yet year after year, new theological students are surprised by the fact that making good sense of the Bible and its individual passages is very hard work. My experience is that the tide of impatience rises in the Old Testament interpretation course somewhere around mid to late October, reliable as the annual flooding of the Nile. "When is she going to tell us how to do it, so we can write these exegesis papers the way she wants them—[*subtext*: *and get an A*]?" That impatience gradually subsides, as they, like our young psalmist, realize that there is no simple guide to the interpretation of Scripture and therefore to the life that grows out of Scripture. Certainly there are plenty of "methods" out there. Some of them are good and useful to know, but do not imagine they will or should save you years of hard thinking, real frustration, and lingering uncertainty. The Bible does not explain a lot of things for which we would really like a good explanation: Why did God plant that supremely attractive and forbidden tree right smack in the middle of Eden? Why is Abel's offering preferred over Cain's? What does Leviticus have against eating shrimp, or wearing a nice wool-linen blend? Indeed, Leviticus's idea of a really great explanation is, "I am YHWH" (Lev. 18:5; 19:13, 37; 20:8, etc.). Any questions?

So that is the bad news: no explanations in the Bible, or entirely too few of them to satisfy us and keep us from arguing—in our own minds, among ourselves, and with God. The good news, however, is that once you realize that reading this book well is really hard work, then you are ready to practice the art of interpretation. It seems to me that every art is a matter of reckoning with some difficulty that humans stumble over in the normal course of life. The visual arts reckon with the difficulty of *seeing*, really seeing, the beauty or the tragedy or the intricate design of our world. Musicians reckon with our tone deafness, our frequent inability to *hear*, to discern rhythm and melody in the midst of so much noise. And so on. In every case the true artist labors, with exquisite patience as well as skill, to overcome the negative aspect of difficulty; yet the difficulty itself is neither denied nor dissolved. This is the essential thing in art: when the negative aspect of difficulty has been overcome, what remains is its positive aspect. And the positive aspect of difficulty is always something that has potential for enlarging our humanity. With respect to the sacred arts, including music and iconography, sculpture and architecture, but also exegesis and preaching, the positive aspect of difficulty always leads more deeply into the Divine Mystery.

The young Torah student of Psalm 119 is keenly attuned to that Mystery, and so I conclude with his well-chosen words of prayer:

> Open my eyes that I may behold
>   wondrous things from your Torah/your teaching.
>   (Ps. 119:18, author's translation)

Please, God, even on my hundred-and-first time of reading.

6

The Authority of the Bible
and the Imaging of God

Terence E. Fretheim

In thinking about the authority of the Bible, I reference my upbringing in a Lutheran family rather than cite specific "Lutheran" perspectives, though some of them will become evident along the way.[1] I was raised in a Lutheran parsonage, as was my father. The particular heritage in which we were reared has been called Norwegian Lutheran pietism. The Bible was a centerpiece of our faith and life. I remember well our daily family devotions, with readings from the Bible and personal prayers. My parents prayed as if God were upstairs and the walls were paper thin. Each member of the family was expected to take part, and we learned to think in highly relational terms about the God of the Bible, who received our prayers and responded to them. I think that my professional studies have in part been a long effort to discern the extent to which this heritage was true to the biblical texts.[2]

If pressed, my parents' view of the Bible's authority would have been quite traditional. But, for them, more theoretical understandings of this topic (and others) always took a back seat to religious practice. They were more concerned about whether I *read* the Bible on a regular basis than what I *thought about* the Bible. They assumed that if I read the Bible regularly, I would come to see it as a genuine resource for faith and life and that its authority for me would thereby be established. In other words, if through the use of the Bible I came to see that it "works," that it speaks a word of God to real-life issues, its authority for me would follow as a matter of course. They were right: the authority of the Bible is established for individuals and communities in and through its usage.[3] And so, for example, if persons rarely or never hear preaching/teaching on OT texts, its authority for their faith and life will commonly be diminished over time.

Neglect is probably a basic reason why the authority of the Bible (especially the OT) is no longer a given among many Christian folk, at least in any traditional sense. They are increasingly unfamiliar with the Bible and its often strange vocabulary. The Bible more and more needs to be explained, and that takes more time than many people are willing to give. When you don't "get it," it is easy to ignore the Bible, marginalize it, or dismiss it altogether. For years biblical piety in the churches has not commonly been matched by biblical literacy, a reality that is coming home to roost. Increasingly, we often have neither piety nor literacy.[4]

This reality has been intensified by the remarkably large number of contemporary issues to which the Bible does not speak, at least directly—stem cell research, the Internet, the depletion of the ozone layer, the genome project, euthanasia, space travel, and quantum mechanics, among others. If the Bible offers no particular help on such pressing issues, how can one speak of its authority? At the least, the range of its authority seems to be more and more constricted as life around us develops at ever-increasing speeds. How can the Bible be authoritative in ever-new contexts in which the particularities of people's lives differ so radically from those in biblical times? Such developments suggest that the Bible has authority only with respect to the "constants" of life across time—and what these may be needs much discussion.

My understanding of biblical authority has also been shaped by related factors in American society. We live in a time when many people, both within and without the church, are suspicious of authority or, at least, of authorities that do not agree with them. People have learned that it is right to be suspicious; too many monsters have been let loose in the world in the name of authority, including biblical authority. And so, all claims for authority have to be rethought, and how best to do that is one thing that animates the current discussion. But one way that will not work for most people is to begin with an appeal to special privilege. Except in certain religious enclaves, the Bible does not start with any advantage; special appeals to inspiration or revelation or the Word of God count for less and less. The Bible must often take its place alongside other authorities and demonstrate that it speaks meaningfully to real issues of the day. An important factor here is religious pluralism; the Bible's authority competes with other authorities among our increasingly diverse neighbors. Alternate religious voices are heard in the land and often heeded. Christians are not well prepared to live with or adjudicate among these competing authorities, and, with their Bibles in hand, they are often reduced either to silence or to screaming. In either case, the status of the Bible is diminished still further.

Christians today are faced with an unprecedented challenge to biblical authority. The irony is that discussing the issue of authority in itself will not directly address the problem. Biblical authority will become clear only if we so use the Bible that people can see that it speaks a word of God to their deepest concerns.

VIEW OF BIBLICAL AUTHORITY

I would claim that the Bible is the Word of God, and it has authority because of that. In such a formulation, it becomes clear that the authority of the Bible is derivative. That is, the Bible's authority for readers/hearers is derived from the authority that the God of the Bible has for them. If the God of the Bible is Lord for them, then the Bible has authority because of its witness to that God. If not, then the Bible has no more authority than any other book. The Bible is the basic (but not the only) *vehicle* for God's work among us. We are called to use it in such a way as to bring to the world not a word about the Bible and its authority but a word about God. Indeed, people can use the Bible in such a way as to obscure this word by, say, making the Bible the center of attention. The Bible is used appropriately when it points beyond itself to God.

As the word of God, the Bible may be said to play two roles. Most basically, the Bible has a formational or constitutive role in and through the work of the Holy Spirit. That is, the Bible has a unique capacity to mediate God's word of law and gospel, which can *effect* life and salvation for individuals and communities. When the Bible "does" this, it gains authority. Second, the Bible is the fundamental source for shaping and maintaining Christian self-identity. We turn to these books to discern (a) what the Christian faith essentially was and still properly is, and (b) what the basic shape for Christian life in the world essentially was and continues to be.

Among the words needing discussion in the latter emphasis are "essentially" and "basic." Some interpreters would be more expansive than others in what these words include. For example, the Bible's authority may be understood primarily as a source of information (not unlike the authority of a dictionary or other reference work). In such cases, biblical authority may be defined as "absolute accuracy" with respect to every detail of which the text speaks. If this is not the case, it is claimed, the Bible's authority is compromised (though, generally, that would not be true of other books). In this view, while some texts may *seem* to stand at odds with what we know from other sources (e.g., the age of the earth from geology), this cannot finally be the case, by definition. The effect on the interpretive process, commonly, is a kind of "harmonization syndrome." That is, the interpreter seeks for ways to challenge "knowledge" from sources outside the Bible or to bring the text into conformity with such knowledge (e.g., regarding the days of Genesis 1 as eras rather than actual days). Still others would refine the issue of "accuracy" to speak more narrowly of matters of "faith and life" (and not, say, of science or historiography). And so, for example, what the Bible says about God cannot, finally, be brought into question.

The grounds on which these decisions about "accuracy" are made are often certain understandings of inspiration or revelation, the definition of which varies among interpreters. Basic to them all is a certain understanding of God and the human authors/editors. To put the matter much too simply: God has been able to get what God wants on the pages of the Bible even though the writers are finite and sinful. This claim about God is often assumed and needs closer discussion.[5]

I would claim that there is an inner-biblical warrant to enter into evaluative work regarding biblical texts and to make distinctions among them regarding their more specific authority, even regarding God.[6] That is to say, the Bible itself provides an *internal center* in terms of which the interpreter can begin to sort out matters regarding authority. That is to say, certain texts and/or themes constituting a center *within* the biblical material give some texts a higher value than other texts and constitute an inner-biblical warrant for such a task. Several good reasons exist for making such an evaluative claim.

(1) *Genre or type of literature*. Biblical texts draw certain claims about God into confessional statements. Just by the nature of the genre used, a biblical claim is made about certain matters being central in a way that other matters are not. These formulations are gathered in two primary forms: historical recital (e.g., Deut. 26:5–9) and more abstract confessions such as Exod. 34:6–7, which reads, "The LORD is merciful and gracious, slow to anger, and abounding in steadfast love and faithfulness, . . . forgiving iniquity and transgression and sin, yet by no means clearing the guilty." The God herein confessed is the *kind* of God whom Israel experiences in *every* circumstance. This "core testimony" with respect to God has an authoritative value in helping to sort out the varying theological dimensions of biblical texts yet without shutting down challenges (e.g., Jonah 4:2) or portrayals that stand in tension with this core (e.g., Ps. 77:4–10).[7]

(2) *Pervasiveness*. That this creedal material is a basic theological center for the OT, indeed the Bible,[8] can be seen in the numerous quotations and echoes of these texts throughout the biblical collection, especially in the Pentateuch, Psalms, and Prophets. That these confessional statements cut such a wide swath across biblical traditions makes it clear that they were considered of special theological value on the part of many segments of the biblical community in various times and places.

(3) *NT evaluations of the OT*. Jesus, for example, indicates that some texts are more important than other texts. He speaks of "weightier matters of the law" (Matt. 23:23; cf. Mic. 6:8) and declares the love commandments to be "the greatest" on which "hang all the law and the prophets" (Matt. 22:38–40).[9] Or,

the apostle Paul speaks of Jesus' death and resurrection as "of first importance" (1 Cor. 15:3–4).

These three factors show that the Bible itself contains, indeed commends, an evaluative pattern for making distinctions among texts regarding the nature of their continuing authority.[10] The Bible, thus, is not authoritative equally or independently in all of its parts. In view of this biblical centering, I understand that God's act in Jesus Christ—from within a perspective on God provided by the creedal formulations—constitutes the central word of Scripture in light of which other texts are to be interpreted and evaluated. At the same time, this is only a starting point. The criteria needed to discern *detailed* differences in value are difficult to come by (e.g., biblical laws) and will continue to be an important matter for discussion.

These comments raise the more specific issue of the authority of the OT. I would claim that the OT and NT are equally authoritative on the following grounds:

(1) *NT claims about the OT.* Jesus and the NT authors considered the OT to be authoritative Scripture for themselves, and this prior to the existence of the NT. For the NT authors, the basic issue was not how to use Jesus to help them understand the OT but how to use the OT to understand the Christ.

(2) *NT usage of the OT.* The NT is filled with quotations from and allusions to the OT. By being so integrated into the NT, the OT becomes as new as the NT. (Marcion's truncated NT makes the point.)

(3) *A logical point.* The NT lays the basis for its claims about Jesus on the OT. In the nature of the case, the necessary presupposition of an assertion must be as authoritative as the assertion itself. Importantly, this claim does not mean that Jesus Christ is a fully known reality or that the NT is a more central text than the OT. The NT looks back on Jesus, and the OT looks forward. Both, finally, are equally necessary for claims made about the Christ and the Christian life.

HERMENEUTICAL IMPLICATIONS

I suggest that one's views on biblical authority will have fewer implications for work with specific biblical texts than is commonly imagined. This is evident, for example, in the sharp differences of interpretation on the part of readers committed to a high view of the authority of the Bible (regarding, say, infant baptism or the book of Revelation). Indeed, we know instinctively that the ascription of a high level of authority to the Bible does not guarantee the accuracy of our interpretations (witness the Jehovah's Witnesses!).[11] Even more, individuals who use essentially the same hermeneutic (including, e.g., historical and literary criticism) can sharply disagree with respect to the interpretation of texts. This, in turn, raises still further issues of authority: How can one speak of the authority of the Bible when the meanings of texts among interpreters can vary in such significant ways?

These differences among interpretations are largely due to three factors: the "nature" of the interpreter, the content of the texts, and the medium of the texts.

(1) *The "nature" of the interpreter.* In making interpretive moves, readers cannot finally step outside of themselves or their situation. Hence, something of who they are will be a part of any meaning they claim to see in biblical texts. Only a relative objectivity is possible for readers.

Another way of putting this matter is to say that no interpretation of the Bible is value-free. How we interpret texts will reflect, and even promote, the personal and social values we hold dear. Bible readers through the centuries have always brought their experience and personal convictions to their reading of the Bible. But the interpretive situation at present is quite different in many respects. We now have a much more highly diverse group of Bible scholars and other serious readers than has been the case heretofore in the history of biblical interpretation (e.g., female and third-world interpreters). This reality has complicated these issues immensely, for it means that much more diverse personal experience is at work when the text is being interpreted.

All of us are challenged to become as self-aware as possible regarding how these experiences and convictions affect our interpretations of texts. Whether or not we are fully aware of "who we are," we should stand ready to acknowledge that our feelings, thoughts, actions, and associated experiences with regard to any number of issues are present in *everything* we say about the text.

This point needs no argument. At the same time, a related and often unrecognized issue should be noted: the distinction between the authority of the text and the authority of the *interpretation* of the text. Some interpretations of the Bible seem to take on an authority that approximates that of the Bible itself; if they are challenged, the very authority of the Bible is thought to be called into question (e.g., texts regarding sexuality). Most would say, however, that a text's *interpretation* should not be elevated to a status comparable to the biblical text itself, for whatever we say *about* a Bible passage is never the same as what the Bible itself says. This includes every Bible translation, for every translation is an interpretation. Most Christians *will* want to make some *basic* claims about what the Bible says, especially in view of the scriptural center of which we have spoken, but even those claims are not to be given an authority equal to that of the text itself.

(2) *The content of the texts.* The Bible itself contributes to the problem of its authority, in terms of both content and medium. Many issues of content could be noted; I illustrate the point with respect to the imaging of God presented by the

Bible. In both OT and NT, God is the subject of a remarkably large number of violent actions (e.g., 1 Sam. 15:3; Jer. 13:14; 19:3–9; Rev. 14:9–11). What kind of God does the Bible commend to its readers? Increasing numbers of good Christian folk are raising questions about the amount of violence found in the Bible and the sometimes not-so-subtle implication that its violence can justify our own violence. Reflection about the Bible's violence now approximates the way in which many interpreters earlier came to think about the slavery and patriarchy in the Bible. If the God whom the Bible presents is so violent, and that image of God is rejected, then the rejection or diminishment of the Bible's authority will often follow. How will we speak of the authority of these violent texts?[12]

Influences on the interpretation of the God of the Bible include long-standing ways of churchly thinking about God. An examination of the God-language developed over the centuries includes such words as omnipotence, omniscience, atemporal, and immutable. Though the Bible uses none of these words, their associated ideas have had an immense influence, consciously or unconsciously, on the way in which we interpret the word "God" whenever we encounter it in the text. And what if that traditional language about God, at least in part, skews our reading of texts in some ways or disallows contrary nuances or readings? The biblical center of which we have spoken will guide our way through these waters, but those inner-biblical claims about God are not as wide-ranging as we might like to think.

Despite these issues, the most important question readers can ask of any biblical text is: What is *God* up to according to this text? The God questions are paramount if we are to read the Bible as we ought to and for the greatest profit. But issues of authority regarding the text's imaging of God are with readers at every turn and must not be neglected.

(3) *The medium of the texts.* The way in which the Bible expresses itself raises sharp issues of authority. One thinks of such textual realities as polysemous words, metaphors, gaps in the text, and translation ambiguities. Their presence means that readers will inevitably participate in the making of the meaning of the text. The proliferation of Bible translations in the last half century is a reflection of this textual complexity and shows the openness of the text itself to different readings. Given these textual realities, readings of texts will always be to some extent open-ended rather than fixed and stable. When placed together with the diversity in knowledge and experience of Bible readers, the question is raised again: How can we speak of biblical authority when the meaning of the text can vary, depending in no small measure on the perspective of the reader or hearer?

A further question is thereby raised: Do no constraints on readings exist? A text cannot mean just anything because it can mean many things. There are at least three constraints; none of them, however, is finally stable.

(1) *The text itself in its original languages.* Texts push and pull us in certain directions and not others. They shape readers; they have an impact on our thinking, speaking, and living. Readers are not in full control of their readings and do not create meanings out of whole cloth. At the same time, as we have noted, texts can be a source of instability.

(2) *Historical background information.* The text has been shaped by the ancient setting in which it was produced, including events, persons, social and political realities, and a limited range of word meaning possibilities. At the same time, this information does not provide the kind of stability one might like, for the data are often ambiguous and historical constructions are often speculative.

(3) *The communities within which texts and readers reside.* Texts are not autonomous but exist only in a web of community beliefs about the Bible and its content. Texts can no longer be read as if for the first time. As for readers, much common ground has been achieved regarding interpretive conventions and meanings of texts, and this narrows reading possibilities.

Recognizing these constraints, the task of biblical interpreters is not to unearth a single authoritative meaning resident in the text but to recognize that various meanings are generated in conversation with the text. If genuine dialogue with the text is another key to interpretation, then readers of the Bible should not be self-effacing, as if the only approach were to receive the text, listen to the text, or get out of the text's way. What we bring to the text will inevitably affect what we see in the text, and so our full engagement is called for, and this will enhance the work of the Holy Spirit in and through us. One key reminder is to have the biblical center in place. Then we can with confidence use our creativity and imagination in exploring the several meanings that a text may have, let them interact with one another, and focus on the meaning that we discern most clearly speaks a word of God to the people in our time and place.

Bible reading is a dynamic process in and through which the Holy Spirit can open us up to new possibilities of meaning that move beyond those with which we may be familiar. The openness in the text itself will foster more new insights, give more room for the play of the imagination, encourage deeper conversation, and provide more avenues in and through which the Word of God can address people in ever more diverse communities. By being freed from the search for a single meaning, the authority of the Bible is enhanced, the various avenues in and through which the Spirit can work are diversified, and the spoken word can reach deeply into a much greater number of life situations. [13]

7

On the Authorities of Scripture

ROBERT W. JENSON

The ecclesial tradition from which I come is Lutheran, specifically the Scandinavian Lutheranism of the Middle West. In my youth this tradition so battered me with talk about Scripture's authority and inspiration that for decades I avoided these notions altogether in my theological writing. Now, alike in mainline Lutheranism and in the ecumenical milieu I have for many years inhabited, any authority is widely regarded as a "legalistic" imposition, and the notion of scriptural inspiration as a relic of unenlightened thinking. Even so, these matters have recently become, much to my surprise, major concerns of my thinking.

Lutheran theology has traditionally discussed the authority of Scripture almost exclusively as its authority for *theology*, broadly construed as explicit knowledge of God.[1] Thus, for instance, Scripture is authoritative for our celebration of the Eucharist because it tells us that God intends us to "Do this in remembrance of me" and tells us what God means by our doing it. The more direct presence of Scripture in the prayers and rubrics of the Eucharist itself was scarcely considered. This narrowness can be explained: Lutheranism was born in a university theological faculty; during Lutheranism's theologically formative time, Scripture's more immediate presence in liturgy and piety and moral guidance could still be taken for granted; and the Lutheran churches developed their doctrine of Scripture during constant theological controversy.

The general scope of Lutheran theology was firmly soteriological: God provides knowledge of himself for no other reason than that thereby we may be brought into union with him; therefore, Scripture as a mediation of that knowledge is also directed strictly to that end. To be sure, by the end of the seventeenth century the doctrine of Scripture's inspiration was thought to exclude error of any sort—however materially unrelated to soteriology—but even so, only because it was thought that any error would compromise confidence in Scripture's inspiration and so eventually in its soteriological authority.

HISTORICAL SKETCH

For Luther himself, it was the *content* of Scripture that was authoritative. What is authoritative in the church is, in his notorious phrase, *was Christum treibet*, "what deals with[2] Christ." Scripture is authoritative because and insofar as it does just that. It should be noted that Luther found in this position no reason to relativize the actual texts.[3] One cannot claim Luther's example for jejune arguments of this sort: "But that was written in another time. We now think otherwise."[4] Nor was Luther's famous "distinction of law from gospel" intended to diminish the authority of the former, for the "law" also deals with Christ in its own ways.

Luther's colleague Philipp Melanchthon, who outlived Luther, supposed that since Luther's description of Scripture's authority was cast in terms of what Scripture *does*, Luther must have had a purely functional understanding of the matter, and he followed him in this supposed method. Thus Melanchthon and his disciples, the "Philippists," did not attempt to analyze the nature of Scripture or the inherent ground of its authority. In their writings, the authority of Scripture is taken up simply within discussion of how to do theology, which requires checking one's teachings against the teachings of Scripture.

Lutheranism in the Seventeenth Century

But then a succession of Lutheran thinkers, through roughly the seventeenth century, developed what is probably the most thorough and conceptually sophisticated doctrine of Scripture ever attempted. These theologians separated from the Philippists by discovering that one could not in fact be faithful to Luther's insights while forswearing all use of philosophical analysis. So they set out to create a version of inherited Aristotelian metaphysics adapted to Reformation theological proposals[5] and worked out also their construal of theology and of Scripture's theological authority in its terms. They looked for the "grounds" (*principia*) of theology and of Scripture's authority over it; they linked the phenomena involved by the four ways by which Aristotelian thought analyzed the connections of things and events, the four kinds of "causes" (*causae*),[6] and they analyzed the nature of theology and so of Scripture by the distinction between "matter" and "form."

Thus God is the "ground of being" (*principium essendi*) of all knowledge of him. That is, if there *is* truth about God, if there is theology to be had, this is solely because God is who God is; we do not in any way project, shape, or posit the truth of God. Scripture, as the Word of this God, is then the "ground of knowing" (*principium cognoscendi*) his truth; we can know it because God tells it to us in Scripture.[7] The old Lutherans posited the differentiated concept "ground of" to tie Scripture as God's Word to God himself—they are together the ground of our knowledge of God—and to articulate the distinction between God and God's Word within that unity. Scripture's authority is, in its specific way, God's own authority.

This theological construction, of course, supposes that Scripture is indeed the Word of God. Usually it was taught that "inspiration" constitutes the identity of Scripture as God's Word: Scripture is the Word of God because God's Spirit is its "efficient cause," the agent who makes it be what it is. For most of the period, however, inspiration was not conceived as a provision of the text but rather as a descent of the Spirit to make prophets and apostles, persons enabled to speak and then write for God.[8]

Perhaps the most distinctively "Lutheran" construal—by the truly great theologian Johann Gerhard—began with an understanding of God's Word as first and fundamentally *proclaimed* word, as a verbal utterance enabled by the inspiration of prophets and apostles. Scripture, then, is the written version of the prophets' and apostles' verbal preaching; the written documents are "materially" (*materialiter*) the same as the inspired proclamation.

This way of identifying Scripture as the Word of God opens up some interesting possibilities. J. F. König, whose work can summarize the period, distinguished between Scripture as materially the Word of God and Scripture as a collection of written documents. In the first identity, Scripture is prior to and independent of the church, since the proclaimed Word of God creates the church. In the second identity, Scripture originated within the church and is one vital means of the church's effort to fulfill its calling. This distinction opens up ecumenical possibilities—of course unnoticed at the time—since it both maintains Scripture's givenness to and authority over the church, on which Protestantism has insisted, and allows for the recognition of the historical facts on which Catholic concern for the broader churchly tradition insists—the recognition that it was, after all, the episcopally governed church, following churchly teaching, that put together the book we call the Bible.

A remarkably original thinker, Johann Musäus, proposed a related distinction between these two modes of Scripture's authority. As proclaimed to the church and read liturgically and devotionally, Scripture possesses the Word's divine power to evoke faith. As documents used by the church in its theological labors, Scripture moreover has the very different authority of a criterion by which to test proposed teachings. More fully recognizing the *first* role could open space to consider all those ways in which Scripture is authoritative in the church insofar as its texts, language, and images are omnipresent in its actual life, thereby remedying the narrowness of Lutheranism's traditional construal.

To complete the old Lutherans' basic analysis, the text as such (e.g., the phrases, propositions, genres, and narratives) constitutes the "material cause" of Scripture—in the Aristotelian sense of that which is potentially the entity in question, as the piece of marble is potentially the statue. The "formal cause"—in the Aristotelian sense of the shaping purpose by virtue of which anything is what it actually is—is God's own knowledge of truth about himself. Thus the texts indeed *are* the Scripture, as the marble is indeed the statue, but they are the *Scripture* only in that they are informed by God's intention for them, as the marble is the statue only as formed by the artist's intention. We should note that in this doctrine the Scriptures are not authoritative by virtue of the propositions and phrases, and such, of which they consist, but by virtue of a divine intention that is beyond these yet gives them their power.

Rounding out our discussion, the "efficient cause" of Scripture's authority—the cause in the modern sense—is God alone, who gives Scripture that characteristic. And the "final cause" of Scripture's authority—the purpose taken for itself—is the saving knowledge of God.

Finally, theologians of the period discussed Scripture's authority directly, as one of Scripture's "predicates," one of the things that can truly be said of it. The ground of Scripture's *possession* of this predicate is again "God," the claim that Scripture is authoritative has no other basis than God's will that it be so. The ground of our *knowledge* that Scripture is authoritative is constituted by others of its predicates, "evidences" that enforce this conviction (*testimonia*). Chief among these is a witness of the Spirit manifest in the texts themselves, as the general impetus the Spirit gives them. We should note that such "evidentiary" characteristics of Scripture, of which they listed many others—perspicuity, efficacy, and so on—do not, as in some Protestant thinking, establish or constitute its authority. They serve only to signal that authority is there.

The Enlightenment

All this fell apart in the Enlightenment of the eighteenth century, as did such constructions in other confessional groups. Through the modern period, Lutheran theologians have, like others, proposed various theories of either biblical authority or why such authority is not needed.[9] If modern Lutheran proposals have had any mitigating unanimity, it has been their continued insistence that Scripture's authority is soteriologically based and intended. As to modernity's chief way of dealing with Scripture, "historical-critical" study, we can only note that some Lutherans have tried to rescue scriptural authority *in spite of* historical-critical methods and their results, while others have tried to rescue it precisely *by* them. At present chaos reigns in Lutheranism as elsewhere.

A PERSONAL PROPOSAL

So what do I propose? Having refreshed my memory of the old Lutheran doctrines, I find—again, rather to my surprise—that their analyses of the grounds and nature of scriptural authority are convincing. I could simply recommend them, thereby imposing on readers a set of concepts now unfamiliar to those outside scholarly circles. Instead, I will propose a reorientation of the context within which to appropriate the old doctrines. Then I will exploit features of the old Lutherans' analyses that they themselves did not develop, in ways of which they would probably not approve. The result of all this will hardly, I think, be specifically Lutheran in character.

Reorientation

The reorientation I propose is a reconsideration of what kind of book the Christian Bible is. As devotees of the Fathers, the old Lutherans knew and approved figurative reading, especially of the Old Testament. That is, they thought that all Christian Scripture told the one story of Christ's coming, and so should be read as any dramatically unified story should be read, namely, by looking for the ways in which earlier events prefigured later ones. But when they came to discuss scriptural authority directly, they nevertheless tended to treat the Bible as a sort of theological textbook. All manner of modern developments demand a firmer adherence to Scripture's narrative character: The Bible is authoritative precisely *as* a single narrative of Christ's coming.

But how can a *narrative* be religiously or theologically authoritative? It can be if it tells God's own story, and that is what the Bible narrates, God's history with us. The Christian Bible—Israel's Scripture with a second volume, the New Testament—tells of God's life with creation from its beginning to its fulfillment.[10]

Thus the character of Scripture's authority is that it tells the true story of the Creator and his creation, within which all other presumptively true stories—from the quantum history of the cosmos to the story of your struggles with faith to the account of organic evolution to the history of the French Revolution to the story of someone's marriage, and so forth—must find their place and so their meaning, or otherwise be unveiled as illusion. Such a claim is indeed hard for us to credit, since it reverses the priorities in which the modern period has indoctrinated us. But just so it must be made; for as the history shows, the modern reversal of these roles, making "secular" truth the determining context of "revealed" truth, ultimately allows the latter no authority at all.

Karl Barth notoriously found his theological and religious way when he was compelled as a preacher to confront a "strange new world" that appeared in the assigned texts of Scripture. The point is: the strange (to us) world that Scripture narrates, the christological world, is the real world, strange to us only because our fallen eyes mistake habitual old illusions for reality. We, for example, inveterately suppose that security rests in the ability to employ overwhelming violence or that it rests in some such empty dream as "eliminating the root causes" of evils. In Scripture we see a world secured only by the Lord.

Opening: Scripture's Exercise of Authority

We turn, within this construal of Scripture, to exploiting those openings we found among the old Lutherans. To begin, we can recognize that Christian Scripture has no authority outside the church, so that we need not look or argue for it there. As the old Lutherans put it, Scripture's authority is to save, and by salvation they meant only the specific fulfillment proclaimed in the church. Indeed, the documents assembled as Scripture belong together as one book only because the one church assembled them to serve its one mission to speak the gospel, whether to people in proclamation or to God in prayer. Apart from this purpose, there is no reason whatsoever for these particular documents of ancient Near Eastern religion to be under one cover. When academic study abstracts from this churchly purpose,[11] the Bible quickly falls to pieces: on the one hand, into "Hebrew Scripture,"[12] and on the other hand, into a miscellaneous pile of evidences for Christian origins that can be added to or subtracted from at the whim of the scholar.

We may next pick up the possibility opened by Musäus, doubtless pushing beyond anything he would have countenanced. Mere observation of the church's life must discover that as Scripture tells the story of God and ourselves, it acquires *many* different roles in the church's life, all of which can come under Musäus's rubric of Scripture's free power to evoke faith. It is especially the Old Testament, with its rich language and stories, that acquires these roles, since it most clearly represents the Word of God's antecedence to the church.

Scripture, thus, exercises authority to create faith when we pray the psalms and other prayers of Scripture or make new prayers on their templates. Scripture exercises authority to create faith when a hard text is laid on the preacher and he or she tries to say what it says, successfully or not. Scripture exercises such authority when we simply read or hear it—regardless of our subjective motivation at the moment. Scripture exercises such authority when our communal rhetoric is formed around its laws and stories—for example, when a mere reference to "Gilead" can call up a whole narrative style and morale. Scripture exercises such authority when the rhythms of its prosody determine the rhythms of churchly music.[13] Scripture exercises such authority when its way of talking about politics or sexuality shapes a believing construal of these central features of humanity. Scripture exercises such authority when the plot of the story it tells shapes the plot of our services. And one could go on with this list. In general, we could say that we are open to Scripture's authority to create faith when we intellectually and spiritually hang out with it, on the corner labeled "church."

In the summer of 1963, I and some other then "younger" theologians were variously occupied in Harvard's libraries, while Cambridge's NAACP was recruiting for what turned out to be the "I have a dream" march in Washington. We dithered. On the Sunday before the march, at the service most of us attended, the lectionary Gospel was the parable about the son who said, "I go" and went not, and the son who said, "I go not" and went. The preacher then mounted the pulpit and simply repeated the address of the sign-up center. That afternoon we marched straight there. This too was scriptural authority in action, to mandate and liberate, or in the Lutheran phrase, to be "law and gospel."

Scripture as Theology's Norm

Lastly, we turn to Scripture as the final norm of theology,[14] of truth and falsity in teaching, whether by word or by practice. Here, too, a firm grasp of Scripture's narrative character enables differentiation.

The "Old Testament," Israel's Scripture, was there before the church and was the *given* text for the birth of the gospel. At least for the first decades, the question was not "Can we accept the Jewish Law and Prophets?" but rather, "How can we justify our new sort of Judaism before the Law and the Prophets?" Thus the Law and the Prophets are *text* for the church, *Scripture* in a sense in which the New Testament is not. The church in fact could and did live for decades without a New Testament, inspired and led by the living apostolic witness. The church came to need something like the New Testament only as an emergency measure when it became apparent that the apostles' personal witness of the gospel would cease before the Lord's return. The New Testament is thus something like an *aide memoire* of what the apostles said.

The faith of the church came into being as interpretation of Jesus' life, death, and resurrection through Israel's Scriptures and as interpretation of those Scriptures through Jesus' life, death, and resurrection. The Old Testament is the constituent antecedent text of the church's message and life. Thus it has, or loses, authority as preaching, moral paraenesis, and sacramental practice take and face up to the Old Testament as text,[15] or do not. The theological authority of the

Old Testament is primal: We have to justify our message and practice by its theology, not the other way around.

The theological authority of the New Testament works in a very different way, as a means provided by God to preserve the apostolic integrity of the church's message and practices, through the time created by God's decision not to make Jesus' resurrection the final fulfillment. We may most conveniently get at this by considering the grammar of the gospel's primal claim: "Jesus is risen." When a gospel speaker makes this claim, he or she must anticipate two questions: Who is this Jesus? and What does "is risen" mean?

An answer to "Who is Jesus?" is vital; "Stalin is risen" would not be good news. But if, when I say, "Mary is sick," you ask, "Who is Mary?" I cannot simply repeat the statement. I have to further identify her and will do this by providing a long or short narrative about her: I will say, "Mary is the one who was valedictorian, moved to New York," and keep going until you have sufficient notion of her identity for purposes of the occasion. Just so with Jesus: Each of the Gospels is a long proposition of the form, "The one who did . . . , said . . . , was crucified on account of . . . , and is risen." The specific theological authority of the Gospels is that they enable us to identify *who* is risen, the friend of publicans and sinners.

But what does "is risen" itself mean? What difference does it make that Jesus or anyone "is risen"? Reflection on this matter became vital at the very outset. The claim of Jesus' resurrection was immediately meaningful within the apocalyptic thought of much contemporary Judaism: If the God of Israel had indeed raised someone from the dead, then the promised fulfillment of God's history with humankind was beginning, and already this specific Jesus had somehow to be Lord. To be sure, disagreement about appropriate practice was possible between the initial Jewish Christians, and this disagreement could be extreme, such as about observance of Jewish law. But when the Paul of Acts spoke in Athens of *anastasis*, the "philosophers" thought this might be the name of a new goddess, which was a different kind of problem altogether (Acts 17:18). The misunderstandings and questions that arose within the congregations of new converts and the apostolic conceptual work to deal with them are the matter of much of the rest of the New Testament.

We are not commanded to reproduce historically the theological moves of the apostolic church. Indeed, we cannot, because however *compatible* the theologies of, say, Paul and John may be, they are nevertheless different. Their authority is that of models, of what the real problems are, and of how to go about dealing with them. We cannot, for instance, simply reproduce Paul's reflections on the place of Torah in Christian faith and practice (even if we could sort them out!), but we can let him lead us to analogous problems among us, and to analogous moves in dealing with them. It remains that the law is holy and good, and yet Gentile Christians are to be brought into the *ecclesia as* Gentiles, that is, without the obligation to obey biblical law in its entirety. It remains that we may learn from Paul something of *how* to think about our analogous problems, not necessarily *what* to think about them.

POSTSCRIPT

I fear this long train of argument and reflection may have more complicated than simplified the question of biblical authority. That may be because some of what I have offered is still undigested, or it may be simply because the matter is complicated.

8

The Bible's Authority for and in the Church

Luke Timothy Johnson

Scholars writing a series of essays for theology students providing their individual views on biblical authority instantly reveal their place in the history of Christianity. That biblical authority can be posed as an issue for discussion or even dispute means that such scholars stand on this side of the Reformation and Enlightenment. Earlier in church history, the subject would not be a matter of explicit debate but an implicit premise so universally assumed as to need no formal attention.

The Reformation made the issue explicit because Scripture was asserted as the measure for all Christian thought and practice over against a tradition that was viewed as overgrown and misrepresentative of simple faith and authentic piety. Note how the Nicene Creed (325 CE) has no statement about Scripture except the single phrase that the Holy Spirit "spoke through the prophets"; and how, in contrast, virtually every profession of faith from the Reformation contained extensive statements on the authority of Scripture over human tradition.

The Enlightenment of the seventeenth and eighteenth centuries demanded explicit attention to the authority of the Bible because it challenged biblical revelation as a whole on the basis of the pluralism of cultures discovered by world exploration; the rise of empirical inquiry, which challenged the veracity of biblical narratives; and a moral revulsion at centuries of internecine Christian strife carried out in the name of biblical authority. If the Reformation principle of *sola scriptura* ("scripture alone") put the authority of the Bible on a pinnacle, the Enlightenment principle of *sola ratio* ("reason alone") put the Bible's authority in peril. The principles have gone to explicit war in the "modernist-fundamentalist" debates within Christianity over the past hundred years, making it necessary even within the church to declare precisely how Scripture speaks with authority.

The fact that I have entitled my essay "The Bible's Authority for and in the Church" also immediately reveals something about where I fit within the spectrum of positions in the modernist-fundamentalist controversy. By speaking of the Bible's authority "for the church," I signal my conviction that the Christian Bible's significance is not absolute, but draws its authority from the decision of the Christian community to canonize these ancient writings as its sacred texts. By speaking of the Bible's authority "in the church," I want to suggest that its authority pertains not to all things everywhere but to the life and practice of the church. Indeed, I think that the issue of authority arises not so much with respect to the individual believer as with respect to the practice of the church as such.

PERSONAL PERSPECTIVE

My perspective on these matters is undoubtedly shaped by my own ecclesial context and experience. Six specific facts, I think, are pertinent. First, I am a sixty-two-year-old Roman Catholic who grew up in a pre–Second Vatican Council church. Second, I was a Benedictine monk from the age of nineteen to age twenty-eight. Third, while I was a monk, the effect of the Second Vatican Council—and its liturgical reforms—created debate and dissension within Catholic communities. Fourth, I went from monastic theological formation to Yale University, to become a New Testament scholar. Fifth, my decision to leave the monastic life and marry a divorced woman with six children eliminated any remaining sense of certainty I once had about righteousness (at least my own). Sixth, my continuing experience as a theologian within the church has required me to reexamine Scripture in light of the great debates, especially those concerning gender and sexuality, which have arisen in our generation.

While these factors have definitely placed me more on the "modernist" than on the "fundamentalist" side of things, I prefer to think of myself as a liberal in the name of the tradition rather than as a liberal opposed to the tradition—as a theologian who tries to combine deep loyalty with genuine criticism. This is not a particularly comfortable place to occupy in present-day Catholicism, where a form of "magisterium fundamentalism," or even "papal fundamentalism," asserts itself as the only legitimate form of loyalty and regards any form of intellectual inquiry as dangerous.

I think that the most positive influence exerted by my Catholic and monastic background has been my appreciation of Scripture as formative of Christian identity through practice and prayer. Long before I began to study the

Bible from the perspective of *scientia* (knowledge), I had experienced it as a form of *sapientia* (wisdom). My first and enduring impression of "the world Scripture imagines" was through the church's liturgy: the Eucharist, certainly, but even more powerfully in the monastic prayer of the *opus Dei* (Divine Office) and in daily *lectio divina* (meditative reading). I understood Scripture to be authoritative above all in its capacity to form and transform humans according to the mind of Christ.

Such influence was (and is) all the more powerful because it is indirect and mediated through a multitude of practices that themselves arise out of an immersion in the symbolic world of Scripture, from prayer and fasting to all the ways "almsgiving"—the sharing of possessions—can be expressed as the symbol of faith and the enactment of love. Nothing is more Catholic in me, perhaps, than a tendency toward a "both/and," rather than an "either/or." I see tradition and Scripture not as opposed but in dialectical relationship. God's Holy Spirit works through both, but God also works outside the church's Scripture and tradition, so that the experience of the living God presses on the church's reading of its sacred texts and its traditional practices, sometimes enlivening them, sometimes calling them into question.

THE FRAMEWORK

Before addressing the question of *how* the Bible is authoritative for and in the church, it is helpful to set the framework for that discussion. My self-characterization as a liberal in the name of tradition is pertinent here. My approach to the Bible's authority can fairly be called liberal in three ways: First, I think of that authority in terms of the Bible's actually being read, in distinction from the sorts of authority that might be called talismanic (taking an oath on it or invoking its power). Second, I regard its authority as relative, never to be separated from other and equally important sources of authority. Third, I think that the reading of Scripture must always be open-ended, responsive to the experience of God in human lives.

My liberal perspective, however, is embedded in an equally strong affirmation of tradition. First, Scripture is not something nebulous but highly concrete, namely, the specific compositions of the Old and New Testaments that the church has declared to be its canon. The concepts church and canon are correlative. Ancient compositions are canonical because the church declares them so, and the church in every age defines itself as church by affirming these compositions and these alone as its measure. For the church to maintain its identity through the ages, moreover, the canon must necessarily be closed, with compositions neither added nor dropped. The affirmation of canon also bears within it recognition of the special character of these compositions. At the church's earliest stage, it sensed that what Paul said to the Corinthians in the past was relevant to others in the present. Canonization is the particular and historical reaching to the universal and the eternal. By reading these and only these writings of the past in the assembly, the church makes its fundamental act of self-identity in each generation. In so doing, the church implies that these compositions are prophetic: They speak God's word to human beings everywhere through human words written and spoken in the past. This is another way of describing the traditional attribute of inspiration, not as a theory of how these compositions were written but as an acknowledgment that in this human language God's word is spoken and God's Holy Spirit is at work for all who read in faith.

Canonicity is not the only way in which the Bible fits within tradition. As a Catholic deeply influenced by Saint Irenaeus of Lyons (*Against All Heresies*), I hold that Scripture must always be read in conversation with the Rule of Faith (the creed), and the teaching magisterium of the church, found above all in the bishops. The creed is a framework for reading Scripture according to the sense of the church. The apostolic succession of teachers provides a continuous commentary on the meaning of Scripture and the creed within the faith of Christians through the centuries. None of these authorities trumps the other, and each is answerable to the other. The authority of the Bible for and in the church, in short, is less a matter of dictation from on high than of conversation in context.

I am not only a Roman Catholic ex-monk but also a professor of New Testament, who after thirty years of teaching in Protestant churches and seminaries embraces an ecumenical sense of church. My years of teaching at Candler School of Theology have made me appreciate particularly the Wesleyan Quadrilateral (Scripture, tradition, reason, experience) as a healthy way of thinking about the authority of the Bible in the church. As a liberal Catholic interloper, to be sure, my understanding of the four elements of the Quadrilateral does not necessarily align with John Wesley or Methodist theologians, but as I understand the terms, they fit well with my sense of a properly Catholic framework.

By placing Scripture in an imaginary "quadrilateral" with three other elements, Wesley, perhaps inadvertently, placed the first element, Scripture, in a dialogical relationship with the other three, and this seems right to me. Here is how I understand the other three elements. I have already said a word about "tradition," as involving creed and teaching authority. But in the broadest sense, tradition encompasses all the authentic realizations of Christian life based in Scripture and all the profound interpretations of Christian life by theologians grounded in the interpretation of Scripture. And, in the most proper sense, tradition ought to include as well all the saints through the ages whose lives have embodied the vision of God found in Scripture. All this life and thought of the church before us is also an "authority" for and in the church.

The element of "reason," I think, has three dimensions, each of which is significant for the conversation with Scripture within the church. The first is the freedom of the mind to think as rigorously and critically as it can; the meaning of Scripture both for the past and for the present is not obvious, and basic skills in logic (above all, analogy) are required of interpreters. The second is the information and insight on specific issues of human life in the world offered by the best of contemporary history, science, and philosophy. On this point a disclaimer is perhaps required: I emphatically do not want to put what is sometimes called "enlightenment thought" or "rationalism" as the measure for the truth of Scripture, especially in forms that exclude the possibility of revelation from the beginning. But it would be utterly irresponsible to interpret Scripture's witness concerning sexuality, for example, without consideration of what we have learned about sexual identity and behavior, or to interpret scriptural passages concerning the household without consideration of what we have learned about gender, or to read Genesis without taking into account the findings of natural science.

All exercise of critical intelligence and all insight offered by contemporary thought, however, must be shaped by the third aspect of "reason," namely, thinking according to "the mind of Christ." The phrase comes from 1 Cor. 2:16, where Paul demands of the community that they think, not according to "the spirit of the world" but according to the "Spirit that is from God" (v. 12). By "the mind of Christ," then, I mean the deeply instinctive sense for what is fitting for Christian thought and practice among the saints, shaped by the Holy Spirit. But this is a real way of thinking that demands its own rigorous reasoning (as Paul's letters demonstrate), not in opposition to Scripture but precisely in accord with the deepest significance and point of Scripture, the transformation of human life.

The final element in the Quadrilateral is "experience." What humans experience in the world makes a difference for the reading of Scripture in the church and must be taken into account. Once more, though, a distinction is important. The experience that the church must consider is not individual or subjective "experience," much less private revelations or idiosyncratic feelings. It is surely not to be equated with the lowest common denominator of what is "normal" in a specific culture, or "what everyone is doing." What the church is called to discern in its reading of Scripture is the experience of God at work in human lives. The "experience of God" is not obvious and, like all experience, is deeply ambiguous, requiring interpretation as well as close and critical examination. This element is essential, however, because the truth that God acts in the world in every age is precisely the message of Scripture, which testifies to a "living God" who always moves ahead of human understanding, opening human beings to a better understanding of the world as God's creation. However difficult the discernment of experience is in practice, without it the interpretation of Scripture would lack its most vital and life-giving impetus.

A final and difficult aspect of the framework for Scripture's authority returns us to the subject of the canon, namely, the relation of the Old and New Testament. In place of a full discussion, a few brief and undeveloped affirmations must suffice. First, the church's decision to canonize the Old Testament means that it has the same overall authority as the New Testament. Indeed, its authority can, in one sense, be regarded as even more fundamental: The Old Testament establishes the vision of the world as created and commanded by the living God that is reaffirmed by the New, and the New Testament is best understood as a reinterpretation of the Old in light of the crucified and raised Messiah, Jesus. Second, the elements of discontinuity between the Testaments cannot be so emphasized as to negate their even stronger continuities; the church has once and for all eschewed explicit Marcionism (the teaching that the Old Testament testifies to an evil creator God responsible for the world's evil)[1] and needs always to be vigilant against the anti-Semitism implicit in a suppression of the Old Testament's voice. Third, it is entirely appropriate, as well as inevitable, that Christians read the Old Testament through the lens of the New Testament, and to give special importance to the ways in which the New Testament makes use of the Old, such as in the prophecies that find fulfillment in Jesus or in the frequent assertion of love of neighbor as the heart of the law. Fourth, the New Testament's appropriation does not exhaust the significance or the authority of the Old Testament: The prophetic protests against unjust wealth and oppression, for example, retain their force as witness to God's vision for the world.

KINDS OF AUTHORITY

To affirm that the Bible has authority for and in the church does not yet answer the question of how it has authority, or the manner in which that authority comes to bear. Before addressing that question directly, I want here to repeat my earlier point that this authority has to do with the Bible's actually being read, and read by the church for the church.

Now, if Scripture spoke uniformly and clearly on every subject, if its commands and directives were entirely consistent, if all its compositions represented precisely the same perspective on identical issues, then the only real hermeneutical problem would be that of translating both its words and the situations it addresses to present circumstances—not a small task, to be sure, but not an impossible one, either. Scripture, however, does not speak in so straightforward a fashion. Besides speaking in ancient languages only partly grasped by contemporary readers and addressing situations mostly obscure to them, Scripture presents an almost bewildering variety of perspectives among its compositions and reveals in its directives inconsistencies and even contradictions on a significant number of issues. Finally, Scripture simply does not speak either clearly or directly to any number of issues that are important to its present-day readers.

Interpreters must deal with this complexity. Avoiding or denying it is simply a form of intellectual dishonesty. Many interpreters solve the problem of diversity by choosing one set of biblical witnesses as more authoritative than others, thereby holding a "canon within the canon." The most radical form of such selection was Marcion's rejection of the Old Testament in favor of the New Testament, and many Christian interpreters have practiced, whether deliberately or not, some form of mitigated Marcionism. I have already stated that such a decision is inconsistent with the canonical status of the Old Testament and its continuing role as shaper of the world in which Christians choose to live. In any case, there is equally great diversity in the New Testament compositions to which interpreters have also applied a "canon within the canon," making Romans or James or Revelation the text by which all others are to be measured.

Others have employed history to establish degrees of relative authority. In this approach, the "historical Jesus" is considered more authoritative than the letters of Paul, or even than the Gospels. The earlier ("authentic") letters of Paul are considered more authoritative than the later ("disputed") letters attributed to him. In general, the historical approach privileges the earlier over the later, the great exception being that the authority of the New Testament is greater than that of the Old. Some interpreters have deemed a single principle (e.g., love, liberation) as the lens through which all compositions are evaluated, while others have deemed certain literary genres as more authoritative than others (prophecy over law, narrative over wisdom).

While I respect these various efforts—they must all be applauded for recognizing and trying to deal with very real problems—and while I acknowledge that some element of these various approaches is almost inevitably going to affect individual interpreters as they seek to make sense out of the confusions in Scripture, I also consider each of them, when raised to the level of an explicit principle, to be inadequate. In my own work, I think of the authority of Scripture in terms of three distinct functions. I will first describe them, state how I see them work together, and then close this chapter with an example that also puts the framework I described earlier into play.

1. Scripture "authors" a certain identity. This is the most fundamental and important of the functions, located in all the practices of the church's common life. Scripture read liturgically and in the practices of the church shapes readers (or often, hearers) in a powerful fashion. Here is where Scripture is most powerfully transformative. It reveals a world that is created, sustained, saved, and sanctified by the living God, and invites humans to enter "the world that Scripture imagines" and make it real in the empirical world through the way they live. When the Bible's world is presented within the faith and practices of a community that already acts as if that world was true, the word of Scripture is plausible and powerful. For this identity process to happen, Scripture must be read as a whole and regularly; it must enter not only the minds but also the hearts and even the bones, of its readers. Here it is a matter of *sapientia* ("wisdom") more than *scientia* ("knowledge"), a matter of living in a certain way rather than solving problems. Here is also where Scripture as a whole speaks with the greatest degree of consistency, concerning the nature of faith and the demands of love. Here is where the Gospels and Epistles are most consistent in their portrayal of Jesus: not in the diverse incidents of what he said and did but in the pattern of his death and resurrection and in the character of his humanity (radically obedient to God and selfless in love toward humans) that the pattern reveals. Scripture read for wisdom in the church has the function of transforming Christians into this "mind of Christ," into the same character of faith and love shown by Jesus.

2. Scripture "authorizes" its own reinterpretation. This aspect of authority plays off the nuance of the Greek term *exousia*, which points toward "freedom." To take Scripture seriously means taking the task of reinterpreting it seriously, and Scripture itself provides us with the best model of the process, above all in the way in which the compositions of the New Testament reinterpreted Torah in light of the crucified and raised Messiah, Jesus, and of the work of the Holy Spirit among the first generations of believers. We sometimes insufficiently appreciate the magnitude and decisiveness of this reinterpretation, as when "the Holy Spirit" is defined as the fulfillment of the promise to Abraham (Acts 2:32–39) or when Jesus is declared to be "the end/goal (*telos*) of the law" (Rom. 10:4). The important thing here is not simply *that* the New Testament reinterpreted Scripture, but *how*. It provides a paradigm for how later Christians, also guided by the Holy Scripture, might engage the sacred texts.

3. Scripture provides "authorities" for Christian discernment and decision. This is the aspect of the Bible's authority on which most discussions focus, but it is actually the most superficial and least powerful. Scripture provides a wide range of "authorities," analogous to those used in law as legal precedents or "cases." It is at this level that Scripture is most diverse and most constrained by its historical circumstances and literary forms and theological perspectives. Here is where we meet the most difficulty if we ask the question, "What does God's Word have to say about *x* or *y*?" The answer is, all too frequently, "What passage of Scripture have you last read?" Nevertheless, responsible interpretation must take all these voices, all these perspectives and "authorities" into account when trying to discern God's will in the present and seeking to decide in a manner that is obedient to God.

I see these authority functions working together in this way: When faced with the need to discern and decide in the face of pressing circumstances, the church is true to its identity when it seeks wisdom and guidance in Scripture. If it is to take the authority of Scripture seriously, it must first listen to *all* of Scripture: it cannot eliminate from consideration any of the "authorities" offered by the Bible. Second, the church must also assume the responsibility to interpret "authorized" by Scripture itself, which means that in the face of sharp diversity in the texts some words of Scripture are going to be taken as more normative—that is, as more obligatory—than others.

Reading all the texts of Scripture—and engaging them with integrity—constitutes a recognition of their authority, but authority does not immediately translate to normativity. Which texts are to prove normative in any instance derives from the church's freedom (and responsibility) to interpret and reinterpret what Scripture itself authorizes. How, then, is a decision between texts to be made? Here is where the "authoring" function of Scripture enters: All discernment and decisions must be measured ultimately by their conformity to "the mind of Christ" that Scripture in its formative function instills in the church. How is this decision consonant with faith, understood as radical obedience to the living God? How is this decision an expression of the selfless love and service revealed by Jesus? If the church makes a decision that happens to agree with some text of Scripture yet offends the deepest and truest message of Scripture, then the church betrays its own identity and cannot be said to live "according to the Scripture."

EXAMPLE: HOMOSEXUALITY IN THE CHURCH

I choose this example precisely because it is one of the hardest cases facing the church's discernment and appears directly to challenge the authority of Scripture. Should the church welcome homosexuals into communion? Most say "yes," but some say only on the basis of a celibate lifestyle. Other communions are split on the question of ordaining sexually active homosexuals or recognizing same-sex unions as marriages. Due to the constraints of space, my discussion will be purely formal and suggestive rather than substantive. I want to illustrate how my views of scriptural authority would affect the way the process of discernment would proceed.

First, I assume that the entire process of debate and discernment takes place within the symbolic world of Scripture, that is, within a community whose members are all committed to living in obedience to God and are sincerely committed to discovering the truth of God's will more than a position that will support their own desires. Part of this commitment, as I understand it, is the willingness also to acknowledge the framework of creed and teaching authority within the church, however those are expressed. In short, deciding "hard cases" demands not less but more integrity of life and witness within the church.

Second, all the "authorities" of Scripture need to be considered. In this case, everyone knows that Scripture appears to speak with one voice against homosexuality. But taking all the "authorities" into account would also involve paying attention to the amount of attention given to sexual sins compared to other moral instructions, how direct or indirect such statements are, and how they fit within the extraordinarily complex set of statements in Scripture concerning sexuality, including such apparently dissonant passages as the story of David and Jonathan (1 Sam. 18:1–5). Responsible interpretation, in other words, cannot cherry-pick texts but must place them responsibly within the discourse of Scripture as a whole.

The same applies to the second element in the Quadrilateral. A superficial look at "tradition" easily concludes that the church's teaching on same-sex relations has been completely consistent. But, once more, invoking tradition means placing those statements in the context of a complex history of attitudes toward sexuality in general, as well as those minority witnesses that suggest approval, or at least benign neglect, toward same-sex activity.

The two remaining elements of the Quadrilateral impel reconsideration of this issue. The first is the use of reason. History provides insights into sexuality in antiquity. Biology instructs us in the physical aspects of gender and sex. Anthropology reveals a wide range of human behavior with respect to same-sex relations. And so on. None of these is probative, but they must be allowed to enter the discussion and help to shape it. Reason in its other dimensions, the use of good argument, and thinking with the mind of Christ can also have the effect of casting the bald prohibitions of Scripture in a different light.

It is undoubtedly the human experience of perhaps 10 percent of those in the church who claim that they are homosexual not by choice but by creation that most presses the church to reexamine Scripture and tradition concerning this issue. The real difficulty here is discerning the character of experience. Does it serve as a cloak for vice? Or does it reveal how God might be at work, in a manner as surprising as the inclusion of the Gentiles in the first generation (Acts 10–15)? While the church cannot say "yes" in principle to what

Scripture calls *porneia*, the question is whether homosexual relations, especially those that are covenantal and give rise to greater life, fall into that category. In this case, the church needs to exercise the greatest possible discipline in discerning claims to experience: Are they from humans alone or are they also from God?

Neither individual Christians nor the church as such can ever be certain that they have made a *right* decision in such difficult matters of moral discernment. Humans do not have access to such knowledge. But they can have confidence that they have made decisions *righteously* if they work together within the symbolic world of Scripture, taking all the texts seriously, taking their responsibility to interpret seriously, but above all taking seriously what it means to live according to the mind of Christ.

9

Inhabiting Scripture, Dreaming Bible

SERENE JONES

"What is your view on scriptural authority?" Every time I hear that question, my first thought is, "Oh, no, if I tell the truth, they're going to nail me." "They," of course, refers to a whole host of folks who seem utterly self-assured when asked about Scripture, absolutely certain they have figured it out, in contrast to me—someone who after twenty years of teaching theology is still fumbling around, looking for something halfway intelligible to say.

Such know-it-alls, real and imagined, come in various shapes and sizes and show up in church, the news, politics, and, not surprisingly, seminary. At times, I feel as if they've also taken up full-time residence in my own head. There's the fundamentalist who knows exactly what every passage in the Bible means and how to apply it, the historical scholar who is certain the Bible's meaning lies buried in the past and knows exactly how to dig it up, the modernist philosopher who has identified its metaphorical solutions to the deep existential questions of life and knows exactly how to describe them, and the postmodernist who is confident that it means nothing at all but enjoys reading the Bible anyway.

Admittedly, there's a bit of truth in each of these positions. But what frustrates me is that they offer such clear, sharply formed answers. And yet when I try to describe how Scripture actually functions in my life—and what kind of authority it wields—the answers I come up with hardly amount to a grand "theory of interpretation" or a "conception of canonical normativity." It is much murkier, more confused, and just plain messy.

If asked how I read Scripture when I sit down at my desk and open the Bible to write a sermon, I would give a formal answer that my colleagues in biblical studies would no doubt appreciate: I start with word study, move on to history,

73

do a little redaction criticism, and then end with application. Similarly, if asked how I would lecture on scriptural authority, I would give my spiel about the canon-within-the-canon, and so forth, a good systematics response. But if someone really wants to know how Scripture plays itself out in my life on a daily basis, my answer is guaranteed to be more fuzzy than either of these pat responses. When I stop to consider, for example, what Scripture might have to tell me about recycling or how much television to let my daughter watch or what my pledge should be this year at church, I come up with insights, make decisions, and then do things that I know are scripturally informed but whose precise logic escapes me. It is even more complicated when I consider those times when I am not even thinking about the Bible at all—when I am grocery shopping or out jogging in the neighborhood or even when I am dreaming away about one thing or another in the middle of the night—times when I know that, even though it seems absent, Scripture is exerting formative pressure on my experience anyway.

Given how difficult it is to describe how Scripture works at these times, it often seems to me easier to avoid thinking about it at all, to just let the process of scriptural formation happen in its own mysterious way. I realize, however, if we want to get to the heart of the matter about the authoritative influence of the Christian Scriptures in the lives of the faithful, it is worth pausing to reflect on the messy, murky ways the Bible shapes us at these times—not just when we're consciously asking, "What would Jesus do?" or, "What would Paul tell us?" but also when we are going about the regular business of trying to live responsible Christian lives, doing much of what we do in a "shoot from the hip" fashion more than in a carefully formulated exegetical manner. Describing this amorphous form of scriptural authority is tough, because it is more associative and ad hoc than it is orderly and logical, more primitive and reactive than considered and volitional. For these reasons, it proves as inaccessible as it is ever present. It happens where life happens, in the chaotic coursings of the everyday, that place where God is alive in the mysterious fullness of each moment's unfolding.

SCRIPTURE AND I

In my own life, Scripture started having this kind of authority in my early childhood, before I could even talk or make conscious sense of things around me. My parents were very active church folks, my father a professor and minister, my mother a regular Sunday school teacher. Every Sunday, week after week, I spent the day in rooms where Bible stories were being shared, sometimes read, sometimes told by heart, sometimes sung about, sometimes repeated in the chorus lines of prayers, sometimes enacted around a Communion table. These stories—their characters, plot lines, poetic rhythms, and, at times, awkward wordings—were announced and enacted everywhere with great and serious enthusiasm. In this way, the world of Scripture and the world of church occupied often indistinguishable spaces in my imagination. Moreover, it was a world full not just of spoken words, but of sights, smells, and tastes as well. Jesus felt like bread and grape juice on my tongue, Moses looked like an African American slave singing spirituals on the road to freedom, and the fierce God of the Old Testament smelled like incense, glowed like a candle, and made my heart beat fast with both awe and fear. In the midst of associations like these, I was given a Bible that we all—friends, family, rich, poor, young, old—inhabited together in embodied ways. Its world is our own.

It is hard to say exactly how that ongoing church-Scripture experience impacted my life or, even more importantly, my developing imagination. I often think of the biblical stories (and all that went with them) as being lodged somewhere way down in my brain stem, stuffed into that special area where foggy but powerful memories get stored and used. They are packed in right next to the feel of my mother's rocking arms and the sound of my father's strong voice. In this deep place, they are no doubt intermingled with other worlds of meaning that formed me during those years—and continue to—like the words of the Pledge of Allegiance, the silly sound of that tune "I Wish I Were an Oscar Mayer Wiener," and the crazy antics of the TV's Three Stooges. What is different about the world of Scripture, however—something that made all the difference in the world with respect to where Scripture lodged (and still lodges) in my forming imagination—is that when I stepped into the landscape of the Bible, I was told repeatedly that I was stepping onto the terrain of "Truth" itself. Of all the stories that were to shape me, I was assured from day one that none would take precedence over Scripture. Even my mother's smile and father's voice came under its pronounced authority to define and organize life at its bedrock best. In my emerging Christian imagination, it was the story that anchored all others.

The "Pull" of Scripture

As to how this anchoring process works, I can't precisely say. It would be a gross exaggeration to claim that my conscious and unconscious thoughts were so efficiently trained by my early church experiences that my mind has always given priority to biblical stories over everything else. I am sure it rarely happens that way. What seems more likely is that Scripture's authority takes the form of a pervading feeling, on my part, that there is no place I can go—physically or psychically—that the Bible is not big enough to embrace and define, and that no matter what kind of person I become and what events I live through, the God who comes to us in those stories is a God who will never stop coming to me with steadfast, gentle assurance. Its authority is also embedded in the "stuff" that my mind and body use to make sense of this all-pervading, ever-alive, graced presence. God tastes like wine, sounds like the crackle of a burning bush, feels like wind, and hangs out with tax collectors and prostitutes. These biblical associations, and countless more like them, are so deeply imprinted on my imagination that it is impossible for me to think about God and about the world without them.

Over the years, the shape of this churchly, scriptural world has no doubt changed and grown as my experiences have shifted. Not only has my interpretive agility increased; the other worlds of meaning that intermingle with it have become more complex and thick. When I was baptized at age thirteen, I started associating "responsibility" with Scripture—it was the place I went to learn from Jesus about being an adult and caring for others. In my twenties, I was taken with the Prophets, and the world of Scripture became for me a place of rebellion and social critique as I marched against apartheid and wrestled my way into feminism. When my daughter was born, the psalms for the first time sounded to me like lullabies. And when I grappled with cancer several years ago, the hemorrhaging woman and the tale of the great flood came alive for me in ways hitherto unimaginable. As I look back over it all, it strikes me that at each step along the way, the stories pulled me into their realm of imagination in radically different ways. What has remained constant, however, is this dynamic of the stories pulling me in, sometimes kicking and screaming, at other times without a struggle, and at still other times without my knowing it has happened.

Even now, I am not sure how to describe this *pulling-in* authority that Scripture holds for me, because it is so unlike what we usually think of as authority. For example, I don't believe that everything written in the Bible is true, if "true" means that each story gives us the absolute, factual lowdown on who God is and what God does. I do not think that God kills people for being bold enough to build tall towers, or that God washes civilizations away with floods when he gets mad—I even do not think of God as being a "he." I do not believe that there is a hell waiting for the evil ones at the end of time or that a golden heaven flitters somewhere above us all, waiting to welcome the righteous. In cases like these, I reject Scripture's picture of God quite forthrightly. What is odd, however, is that even in the face of this rejection, my imagination still continues to enact what I think of as a biblical drift. Often, much to my surprise, I find my thoughts floating onto the landscape of these tales I supposedly do not believe in, and I discover that they are forming my experience anyway. So, for instance, at night I sometimes dream of fiery hells and of buildings falling and floods raging and of a God who is there in the middle of it all, an awful specter, terrifying me more in my sleep than he would if I thought of those scenes as true events. The feeling of these stories in my body is real, emotionally dense, and visceral. Similarly, when a close friend died last year, I found it easy to let my heart and mind wander off into comforting visions of golden gates and glorious throngs of angels rushing forth to receive her; in those moments I knew that what Scripture says about heaven is not true, and yet is.

How does one define this odd kind of scriptural authority? If I were a Freudian analyst, I would sketch out an account of the unconscious that would help explain it.[1] If I were a cultural anthropologist or social linguist, I might turn to Claude Levi-Strauss, Mary Douglas, or Clifford Geertz for assistance.[2] If philosophy were my field, I would perhaps pull Ludwig Wittgenstein off the shelf and let him figure it out for me.[3] What all these thinkers point to, in different ways, is the role played by those deep-structure stories that make it possible for us to perceive and order reality in meaningful ways, special stories that take priority over others, stories that cannot be lined up next to other, more casual stories and analyzed in the usual manner because these special ones are the normative stories that provide us with the logic of analysis itself. They mark the space of what it is. This does not mean we cannot examine them, make judgments about them, and even change them at times. It does mean, however, that unlike most of the stories we tell, we cannot leap outside of these deep, ordering tales or structures or languages (or whatever a particular theorist happens to call them) and expect to continue making sense— because these are the tales that circumscribe the realm of sense itself.

In my own tradition, John Calvin's view of scriptural authority comes close to making the same point. In the *Institutes of the Christian Religion*, he refers to the Holy Bible as the "lens of faith."[4] For him, Scripture is not just an encyclopedia stocked full of true propositions about reality or a history book full of interesting facts about God. Instead, he suggests that it is like a pair of glasses: you put the Bible on and then look through it to see the world—not just a few things in the world, but everything in the world. Like the carefully crafted curves of spectacles glass, the Bible not only brings focus and clarity to all aspects of our lives, it lets us see what we otherwise would not. And once we have put these glasses on our face, there is nothing, absolutely nothing, that escapes their vision-framing power. It is hard to imagine a more robust, comprehensive account of authority than this!

I have also been helped to understand the "pulling-in" authority and the "eyeglass" power of Scripture through the work of my teacher, Hans Frei. Following a line of thought that he traced back to Karl Barth and then farther behind him to Reformation figures like Calvin, Frei taught his students to think of the scriptural text *not* as a set of stories that Christians were called to read, figure out, and then apply, as if the job of the biblical interpreter were to decipher texts written in secret code or a language in need of constant translation so that they could hook up correctly with real life.[5] No, Frei suggested that quite the opposite is true. When read as an authoritative witness to the real-life truth of God in our midst, the Bible is the place where *we* are deciphered, translated, figured out, interpreted, and lexically ordered into real-life meaning, and not vice versa. It is a book that reveals not just how we see God but, more importantly, how God sees us, how God narrates reality, how God in Jesus Christ engages our worldly existence. As such, the Bible functions authoritatively when it reads us as we read it. It inhabits us as we step onto its terrain, inhabiting it. It pulls us into its world at the very moment our lived reality meets its living truth.

This may sound quite abstract. When I step back, I even find it a bit hard to grasp this notion of Scripture's authoritatively "pulling us into" its world, and doing so in ways so profound that it shapes not only our waking thoughts but our sleeping ones as well, even those dreamlike associations that we have seemingly no conscious control over. To help make it a little clearer—and again, I am not sure it is possible for us ever to get a completely clear picture of it because so much of it escapes our conscious knowing—let me describe just a few of the many ways in which my imagination has been inhabited by Scripture, my dreams infused with the world of the Bible. Bear in mind, however, that these descriptions point to the dynamic ways in which Scripture authoritatively shapes things such as my intellectual impulses, my bedrock desires, my ever-ambiguous attitudes, my wily and often confused emotions, and the wide range of things I consider imaginatively possible, and not just the more obvious content-specific surface claims of what I know to be true.

Habits of Imagination

The first of these impulses or habits of imagination is one I mentioned above. Shaped in the world of churchly, scriptural speech, it is impossible for me to imagine a world without God because, in the biblical world that has long deciphered me, God is always there, as the grounding reason for the story. Whatever happens to be happening, there at the edge of the page, at the end point of the horizon, hovering over the roof of the house or at the far edge of the parking lot, is God. Call it an overwhelming, all-encompassing trust in divine presence, a constant sense of divine thereness. God is here, and the story of life transpires in God. In this way, the world of Scripture has nurtured in me a profound and abiding feeling that existence is not only contingent on God's will but is unfolding in space that exists only and forever in God. The scriptural story—my story—discursively unfurls as a witness to the God who constantly witnesses it into being. This means that God reigns over everything not only as its ongoing creator, but also as the judge of its truth, its law, its order. In this regard, the habit of reading Scripture as God's Word has become a habit of mind that, even when Scripture is not being invoked, thinks of the world and of history as God's own.

In the ongoing play of my imagination, there is also a strong tendency for me to impose on everything I experience some sort of story about sin and redemption. It becomes instinctual, this habit of mental organization. Wearing the eyeglasses of faith, I experience events in my life as constantly following a narrative arc, wherein a problem is identified (something is wrong) and its solution is promised and sometimes delivered (salvation happens). My mind has been structured to follow the storied logic of falling and being liberated and delivered: sin and grace. I see it everywhere, both in its grandest form as the dialectical story of human history and in its more miniscule form as the chronicled pattern of my everyday comings and goings. In the midst of all life, Jesus is constantly being born, living, confronting sin, being nailed to the cross, and resurrected into life eternal with God.

There are other ways that Scripture inhabits me as well. For instance, I cannot look at any person without seeing Jesus loving him or her. This is true even in those moments when all I can honestly feel for someone else is hate, jealousy, or fear. It is impossible for me to frame humanity in any other way than as Jesus-loved—this is my gut response to people. All human beings are God's beloved children, my imagination insists, even when we are messing up and refusing to live justly and failing to love each other as God intends. We are all constantly walking with Jesus, friend or foe. He walks beside us, healing, teaching, challenging, provoking, and comforting. And he is there laying his life down at every moment and just as persistently rising up before us as the promise that makes us all the more human in him. This strong conviction about the profound, enduring, ever-resilient truth of the blessedness and equality of all people in Christ is something I cannot escape. It is, in short, the most authoritative truth about who we are, and it lives in my bones.

When I think about the deep habits of mind shaped in me by the scriptural story, I realize that I have learned to glance continually at the border of any story to make sure nothing is being excluded from it, and, if it is, to try to pull it into the main frame. I constantly see Jesus looking up at Zacchaeus in the tree or toward the lepers living in caves outside the city walls. I see, deep in my mind, his cross too, standing hauntingly beyond the gates of the civilized world. Call it a penchant for the marginal, a habit of mind that moves toward the edge of what we normally see in search of what we do not. It is an impulse that drove me toward feminism, toward liberation theology, toward a deep commitment to racial justice, and, interestingly, toward the eccentrically destabilizing claims of deconstruction and postmodern aesthetics. I hope it has also pushed me to be suspicious of the exclusions and repressions that religion itself is constantly enacting, such as our present cultural inability to think honestly about sexuality, violence, or the deeply conflicted passions that mark our collective humanity, and, perhaps most importantly, the captivity of our minds and desires to the consumptive pull of market capitalism, a story that more than any other competes for the prized place of being the "grounding story" of contemporary Western culture.

There is much more to be said about the habits inculcated in me by the biblical story. There is the sense I have, constantly, that God might burst into our reality, rupturing and undoing everything we love and treasure—an apocalyptic play of mind. There is the fact that in the face of the excessive claims of no-nonsense science or the stultifying rules of my ordinary days, I often drift off into a world where lepers are magically healed, where seas are calmed by the hands of a prophet, where I meet again and again a Messiah who one day hangs dead on a tree and the next walks through a door toward the disbelieving Thomas and me.

Each time I return to the holy text, I am surprised by what I find there, by the miraculous play of possibilities it insists on opening up before me and before the church community that lives in its divinely enchanted world with me. Each time I open its pages, I embark on a journey to a land far away and yet closer to me than the words on this page, a place where the sun is always rising over Golgotha, where one wrestles with demons that constantly take flight into the flesh of wild pigs, a place where unmerited grace is not just a doctrine, it is a patch of ground, a smell, a feeling that comes when you walk next to Jesus and find the world always new and so strangely alive.

10

Authority and Narrative

Sarah Heaner Lancaster

My father was a Methodist minister, and my mother had been a Methodist missionary before she married, so I grew up in the church, knowing that a vocation to church service was highly valued. It never crossed my mind, though, nor the minds of my parents, to think that I might have a vocation to ordained ministry. It was not until I graduated from college and spent a few years as an adult member in a United Methodist church in a different region of the country that I began to consider a call to ministry. And even then it was not my own idea. The pastor of the church I was attending had to call to my attention that something might be going on in my life that I had not recognized myself. That began my long journey first to ordination, then to working on a PhD, and finally to teaching at a United Methodist seminary.

Why would my imagination have been so limited? I did not hear sermons from my father as I grew up that were against women in ministry, or even against women in general. I had been successful in school, and my parents expected me to continue to be successful. I enjoyed being active in church. But it never occurred to any of us that I could use my gifts as the pastor of a congregation. I was not aware of anything negative preventing me from doing such a thing; I was just not positively supported to recognize and follow my vocation.

My story points more to the subtle ways that Scripture and its interpretation in the church works on women, rather than to the more overt and quite serious problems that are both real and devastating for many women. Even when Scripture is not used consciously and pointedly against women, it can contribute to assumptions and expectations that limit women's imaginations about how God is working in our lives. It never occurred to me to connect those call stories of men in the Bible to a vocation to ordained ministry for

myself. While I felt quite free to question overt attempts to make me subordinate to men, I did not notice the effect of having so few women's stories in
sacred writ. Nor did I notice the way that so many stories in the Bible that
stressed humility, passivity, and obedience reinforced conventional understandings of what it meant to be a woman and thus discouraged active engagement of imagination about things like vocation.

Only when I began to study feminist theology did I become aware of the
effect that the Bible and its interpretation that I had grown up with had had
on my self-understanding and on my ability to imagine certain possibilities for
my life. I learned to recognize things I had not seen before, and I started to
"talk back" to Scripture in a way I had never done before. The Bible had supported me through many hard times, and it had helped me know God, but it
had also fallen short of offering me the "fullness of life" that the Bible itself
promised. I wanted to find a way to understand this book that had brought me
life in so many ways, so that it would not also work against me in other ways.
The question of Scripture's authority, especially as I increasingly claimed my
own authority to raise questions and speak from my own experience, became
a persistent concern that has shaped my work as a scholar.

As a United Methodist, I do my work as a scholar in a denomination that
considers the Bible to be primary for theological reflection, but that also recognizes the importance of tradition, reason, and experience in this task. What
is often known as the "Wesleyan Quadrilateral" was not in fact developed by
John Wesley, the founder of Methodism, but it does reflect much of his practice. He called himself a "man of one book," but he read widely. (He recorded
reading more than fourteen hundred different authors.) He sought wisdom in
theologians of the past, particularly from the "primitive church." Trained in
logic, he employed careful distinctions as he worked through the meaning of a
biblical text. He tested interpretations of Scripture against the effect they had
in the lives of real people. In addition to these four concerns, he believed that
individual texts had to be interpreted in light of the "whole tenor" of Scripture.
Thus, wherever the surface meaning of a text seemed to contradict what he
believed the Bible said about God's nature and work on behalf of our salvation,
he looked for a deeper meaning that was consonant with this larger message.[1]
In the position I outline below, I am drawing from this heritage of how to read
Scripture for thinking about the concern I have as a woman reading the Bible.

THE CONCEPT OF AUTHORITY

The word "authority" is problematic for women because of our long history
of being told that we are "subject to" someone else's authority. It is language

that evokes control, and as subjects of authority, women have had little opportunity (or have had to fight for the opportunity) to speak for ourselves, make our own decisions, or be considered valuable contributors to communities. The Bible has supported this understanding of authority by those passages that explicitly tell women to submit to their husbands, as well as in countless stories that place women on the lower side of a power relationship. "Authority" understandably brings out a strong negative reaction among women who have recognized the ways it has been used against them.

On the other hand, part of the feminist breakthrough has been to allow women to recognize and embrace our own authority. Learning to speak for ourselves, to make our own decisions, and to develop and share our talents with others have all been major gains for women. Many feminist theologians have recognized that authority is not something we can or should avoid talking about. What we need to do is redefine it so that it does not lead to unfavorable power relationships that threaten the full humanity of women.

Feminists are not the only ones who have recognized that the very concept of authority can be problematic. Several philosophers have examined the notion of authority in order to distinguish it from authoritarianism (a misguided use of and distortion of authority) and to develop a genuine understanding that will foster a healthy society in which all participants are able to make distinctive and valuable contributions. The work of Richard De George has been particularly helpful in this regard.[2] From observation of how authority actually functions in society, he is able to make several points that I have found useful for thinking about the Bible's authority.

First, authority is at its heart a relational concept. It can only function when more than one party is involved; it describes a particular way in which these parties relate to each other. One has or exercises authority, and the other is "subject to" authority. The one who "bears" authority is usually a person, but it can be an object that stands in for a person or persons. The one who is "subject to" authority is always a person. While there is an unevenness between "bearing" and being "subject to" authority, the legitimate engagement of this relationship does not place the one "subject to" authority at a disadvantage.

In fact, and this is the second point, the authority relation exists for the benefit of the one who is "subject to" it. The one who has or exercises authority is in that position because of something that this party can offer to another, whether that may be knowledge or experience, or that the role itself is necessary for carrying out some valuable function. The relationship actually exists because the person who is "subject to" authority should benefit in some way from the relationship. The phrase "subject to" is clearly problematic, but notice how the picture changes if we talk about the authority relation in terms of benefit instead. The student benefits from the knowledge and experience of the teacher. The citizen benefits from the order that comes from those who make and enforce law in society. Authority should function in this way; it exists so that some members of a community gain from the talent and expertise of others. When the relationship is used in such a way that the party on the "having and exercising authority" side of the relationship benefits and the other party does not, then the relationship has slipped from genuine use of authority to authoritarianism. The sad truth is that this slippage happens all too often, and for that reason many fail to distinguish between genuine authority and the misuse of authority. It is important to do so, though, because social relationships cannot function without authority. We need to have a clear idea about what authority is supposed to be so we can recognize when it has turned into something else.

Third, authority in human life is never authority in general. In other words, one party is never the sole authority over everyone and for everything. If one party attempts to become the sole authority, then again we have an instance of authoritarianism. Genuine authority is held and exercised in a specific domain: for instance, math teachers are certified as authorities in math but not political science, and police officers are empowered in their positions to write traffic tickets but not business contracts. They have been authorized in a particular domain to play a certain role, usually because they have met standards deemed necessary for that position. Recognizing the appropriate domain for the exercise of one's authority is an important step for ensuring its proper use.

Fourth, as the examples above begin to indicate, there are different types of authority. There is authority in a field of knowledge (math), authority to perform certain actions (writing traffic tickets), authority in an area of skill, authority to make decisions for an organization, and more. It is important to remember the variety of ways in which people serve as authorities because the dominant image is often authority to command. Imperative authority does have its place in certain areas of life, but it is not the only or even supreme example of what authority is. Because it lends itself so easily to dominance and submission, imperative authority captures attention, both by those who want power and by those who have been mistreated by the abuse of power. Careful examination of when and where command and obedience are appropriate is important precisely because their misuse can be so damaging. Command and obedience are not all that authority is about.

Finally, if authority is relationally based and thereby exists to benefit the members of a community because some have expertise or play roles that others do not, then there will necessarily be multiple authorities in a community as different people provide what others lack in specific domains. Those who know math may need to consult others who know medicine; those who run companies may need legal advice; a worker skilled in automobile repair may need the help of a worker with different skills to build a house (and vice versa). Each has something to offer; each requires what another has to offer. The fact that we need each other in different ways is the basis for the authority relation in society. Recognizing this situation can help explain how a woman may both exercise her own authority and benefit from authority held and exercised by others.

READING THE BIBLE AS NARRATIVE

Human beings are storytellers. We pass on knowledge from generation to generation through the telling of history, anecdote, fable, and more. "Story" is often associated with artistic creation, but even our most precise, technical language is embedded in narrative, that is, in a larger context of telling about the world in a certain way. Even in mathematics and science, some overarching, descriptive framework allows ideas to be connected and "followed" the way one "follows" a plot. Narrative, then, has a deeper meaning than simply telling stories. It is, in fact, defining of the way humans think, organize experiences, find relevance, and make meaning. This deeper meaning of "narrative" is what I have in mind when I talk about the Bible as narrative. It does not refer to genres of literature within the Bible, nor does it claim that the Bible is like a novel. It does indicate that the discrete texts find their place in a framework so that they cohere or "hang together" in an understandable way.

Over the long period of time in which the discrete texts were written, collected, and edited in a community that read them as having religious significance, the narrative structure for understanding the Bible as Christian Scripture came into being. The texts chosen by the community for reading and the way they were read mutually reinforced certain commitments that shaped both canon and the identity of the people who used this canon. For Christians, those commitments include the following: there is one, true God (so literature that fragmented the deity was rejected), who created the world and called it good (so literature that indicated a distaste for the material world was rejected), made covenant with Israel (so the Hebrew Scripture was accepted), and then was disclosed in Jesus Christ for our salvation (so new Scripture was added). The Bible that is used in Christian churches thus provides a perspective on the world by providing a narrative framework in which these commitments make sense. As we enter the narrative world of the Bible to understand it and find our place in it, we come to share this perspective and these commitments.

The narrative world that is produced by reading the Bible in this way not only makes sense of the discrete texts within it, but it also helps readers make

sense of their lives in light of God's involvement in history and self-disclosure
in Jesus Christ to bring them wholeness. By reading these texts in a community that assumes their relevance for guiding one's life, members of the community are encouraged to approach them, listening for what God may have to
say through them. Thus, while the texts are based in ancient situations, written
by human authors shaped by their own contexts, readers presume that these
words have some relevance for their own lives. Nevertheless, because of the vast
difference in time and place between the text and the reader, listening for God's
guidance necessarily involves some kind of creative appropriation. God
"speaks" through the text when some aspect of my life is illumined by the reading of it in such a way that my relationship with God is brought to bear on my
daily experience. Knowing the text well, for instance its literary context, the historical situation that produced it, the meanings of its words, and so on, greatly
assists making appropriate connections in a new context. But knowing those
things does not strictly determine the way the text may be relevant. One's own
context also matters, much the same way a musician has to take into account
the acoustics of the hall in which a piece of music will be played. Adjustments
have to be made from one performance to another so that the music may be
brought to life adequately in each case.

Putting these ideas about the Bible together with the understanding of
authority that I have described allows an approach to the authority of Scripture that can be very helpful to women. Starting with the Bible as the bearer
of authority, we can say that women may benefit from what the Bible has to
share. The narrative structure of the Bible offers to women and men a perspective that allows us to see God's involvement in the world to offer us salvation, that is, fullness of life, through Jesus Christ. This perspective is the
domain of its authority, so, as theologians have long recognized, it may be said
to have authority in matters pertaining to salvation.[3] While specifying a single domain may seem restrictive, the very nature of this domain is expansive.
If "salvation" involves the whole person, then to benefit from the Bible's
authority one must bring one's whole life into the perspective that Scripture
offers to us. That is, every aspect of our lives should be seen in light of God's
involvement in our own real histories. We benefit from the Bible's authority
when we attend to God as we make decisions, live out relationships, react to
events around us, and much more. It is when we do so that we actually experience the wholeness that God offers us through Jesus Christ.

In order to do its work in this domain, the Bible has to do much more than
command. It provides knowledge of God; it gives examples of what life with
God is like; it bears varied witness to the power of God in human life. In many
ways, the Bible functions as a teacher, guiding us into understanding through

its diverse materials. Women accept the authority of Scripture when we allow ourselves to be taught by it in order to gain this perspective on the world and on our lives.

Women know all too well, though, that those diverse materials do not always promote our well-being. Instead of experiencing wholeness, we experience limitation and sometimes pain. To deal with this problem, it is helpful to remember that the Bible bears authority as an object does, that is, standing in for the one or ones who authored it. A theological understanding of the Bible recognizes that it is authored by both humans and God. Even the most highly developed dictation theory, which sees the Bible as the direct words of God, acknowledges through a theory of accommodation that the human authors have some effect on the way the text is written. Recognizing this distinction allows women to have a twofold response to the Bible. To the extent that the "author" is God as God "speaks" to us through these human words in the way I have described above, the appropriate response is to open oneself to the illuminating and edifying relationship that is being offered. To the extent that the "author" is the human who recorded the words, the way is open to engage in honest conversation about the effect that those words have on one's life. Many think that questioning the human words is questioning God, but that is not the case when one distinguishes between the words themselves and how God may use the words for God's own purpose. If the purpose of the Bible's authority is to bring us fullness of life, then we have the authority in the domain of our own personal experience to say whether the words help or hinder that fullness. We know the effects and our changed context in a way that the human authors never could, and it is essential in the task of appropriating the text for a new situation to take that knowledge into account. Far from defying or replacing the Bible's proper authority, this exercise of our own authority is crucial for the Bible to do its work. Without such an honest exchange, the Bible will not be able to draw us into the perspective that it wants to share and thus come alive for us.

HERMENEUTICAL IMPLICATIONS

To see how this approach to the Bible might help women interpret texts, I want to look at Hebrews 5:5–10. This passage appears in Year B of the lectionary for the fifth Sunday in Lent, a season when great emphasis is placed on self-denial and a Sunday on which the Gospel lesson shows Jesus speaking openly about his impending death. In this context, it is easy to read the Hebrews text as a lesson in submission to God's will, especially when one phrase in v. 7 is rendered in English in the NRSV as "he was heard because of his reverent submission."

Read in this way, the text reinforces all the problems that women face in yield-ing their own wills to others in authority, even to the point of self-destruc-tion—and it does so without ever mentioning women. Being attuned to this sort of problem, though, can lead one to ask whether this kind of submission actually brings wholeness to women. The personal experience of many women authorizes a searching exploration of this text in light of the potential harm it holds, while still expecting that God may find a way to speak through the text for our wholeness when such criticism is engaged. In this way both the author-ity of women as interpreters and the authority of the Bible as means to salva-tion are held together.

When questions about submission are at the forefront of interpretation, the text itself read in light of the larger biblical narrative provides material for a construal that does not support passive submission to the point of self-destruction. First, the larger context of the epistle shows that "Son" is the reflection of God's own glory and the imprint of God's own being. The refer-ence in v. 5 to Psalm 2 specifically calls to mind the larger context of the canon and thereby underscores the royal position of the Son. Whatever the rela-tionship between Jesus and God that this epistle intends, it is clearly not a rela-tionship based on vast inequality, such as master and slave, in which obedience is simply expected because of disparity in status. Second, a look at the original Greek shows that the word "submission" has been inserted in the English translation. The Greek instead indicates reverence in the sense of godly fear, the kind of awe that trembles when confronted with ultimacy. Third, the word translated as "learn" indicates a kind of learning through experience. There are some things that one can learn only by doing them: One learns to dance by dancing, to write by writing. That kind of learning is not usually easy. One has to put oneself out there and try something for which one cannot com-pletely prepare in advance. This kind of learning is anything but passive, espe-cially when the learning comes by confronting a difficult and costly task. It requires commitment and involvement. Finally, the word translated as "per-fect" is important because it is also used at the beginning of the next chapter, where readers are urged to become "perfect." This word involves the idea of fulfillment, or even maturity. There is a connection between what has hap-pened to Jesus and what we should aspire to.

So if this text is not really about submission in the sense of bowing to some-one in an unequal power relationship, if the key to facing a task with a tremen-dous cost is reverence, if obedient learning is not passive learning, and if the result is some kind of fulfillment or maturity, then what can we learn from this text that might promote women's well-being rather than diminish it?

If we think about Jesus as the Son, the heir, the reflection of God's glory, the imprint of God's own being devoting himself to the difficult and costly task of our salvation (our wholeness), learning and maturing into the role of Savior through facing death with the kind of trembling understanding of what was at stake, then we have a very different picture from a passive obedience that submits to a death sentence imposed from outside. Following this Jesus takes more than passive submission. To see this Jesus as our teacher, to learn from him what he learned so that we ourselves can become mature requires active commitment and involvement. There is a "giving of oneself" to a task, but it is freely undertaken because of the value of what is to be gained, not because of the disvalue of the person submitting. Anything that is worth learning takes that kind of commitment, and learning to be a follower of Jesus Christ takes no less. Women who follow this Jesus will not be passive but be courageous participants in their faith.

The authority of Scripture and the authority of women do not have to be thought of in opposition to each other. In fact, when women's questions are given voice, they can lead to opportunities for Scripture to speak in a new and vital way. In the dialogue that results, women may be empowered to imagine the fullness of life that God intends.

11

Alternative Worlds

Reading the Bible as Scripture

JACQUELINE E. LAPSLEY

INTERPRETATION AS JOY

I began really thinking about the authority of Scripture about fifteen years ago when I entered seminary. While the other first-year students and I shared a number of characteristics, namely, lots of free-floating anxiety, a still-amorphous desire to engage in ministry, and faith enough to have brought us this far, we differed, sometimes dramatically, in how we read the Bible. Most everyone thought the Bible was authoritative, but how we construed scriptural authority varied considerably around the room.

My Presbyterian upbringing had emphasized the life of the mind as an important site of God's activity. God has given human beings the ability to think deeply; therefore, Christian life means wrestling with the Bible, asking questions about the world and about God. It is "faith seeking understanding." This passion for the intellectual life as both divine gift and mandate was tempered by another Reformed conviction: our striving after truth sometimes, indeed often, leads us astray because of sin. But to neglect the life of the mind—to think that the Bible requires no interpretation, for example, or to reject scientific inquiry—is to fling a gift of incomparable beauty and value back in the face of the Creator. All truth is God's truth, but it is not easy to put our hands on it—we must think together toward it.

I had also gone to seminary with an undergraduate and graduate degree in the interpretation of literature. Great works of literature reveal so much about the world and about the human heart that I found (and still find) sustained joy in reading and interpreting literary texts. When I came to seminary, I wanted to read the Bible in the same way, for it seemed that if great works of literature reveal the beauty of the world, along with its complexities and sorrows, would not the Bible do so even more and with more profound results? The joy of interpreting George Eliot's novel *Middlemarch* (which for me is considerable) would be surpassed only by reading and interpreting Scripture, the unique and authoritative witness[1] to the ways in which God was historically in relationship to God's people Israel and then to the church in the coming of Jesus Christ into the world. For the most part, my hope that interpreting the Bible for the life of faith would offer joys similar to, but even more profound than, the reading and interpreting of insightful works of literature has been fulfilled whenever I engage deeply with a passage from Scripture.

ENTERING INTO ALTERNATIVE WORLDS

When first asked to reflect on "my view of biblical authority," I found it difficult to order my thoughts (despite years of opportunity!). It took some time before it dawned on me that the Bible functions authoritatively not in one single way, but in many different, complementary ways. For example, the Decalogue is widely held to be authoritative for the way our communities are formed and the way we treat one another within them (although that authority is often misconstrued). But the kind of authority I lay out in this chapter is rather different from that kind of authority. It is concerned less with what we do, or how the Bible shapes our behavior, and more with who we are and how we perceive—how the Bible can change the way we see God, ourselves, and the rest of the world. Or, more accurately, how the *Spirit*, through our reading and interpretation of Scripture, can change the way we see God, ourselves, and the rest of the world.

One day my two children were disputing possession of a toy. The toy itself had lain neglected and unvalued for countless months, but as my daughter picked it up, its social value suddenly skyrocketed. Her attention to, and now physical grasp of, this object implicitly conveyed to my son that (a) the toy must be more valuable than he had previously realized, and (b) his sister was making an exclusive claim to its possession that would counter any claim he might make. No words were required, of course, for any of this to take place. My son reached out to grab the object, and my daughter naturally resisted this show of aggression. The two were engaged in a classic tug-of-war with the toy between them, each calling out in increasing frustration and anger, "MINE!" As I watched them, it dawned on me that I had seen this play out somewhere else recently, in a more pleasant context, and so I said, "You remind me of the seagulls in *Finding Nemo*."

In the Pixar animated film *Finding Nemo*, the seagulls represent mindless orientation to self. When they see potential food (a hapless crab in one case),

they immediately begin to intone the only word they know: "MINE . . . MINE
. . . MINE." The seagulls cannot be understood to offer a chorus of "MINE,"
because "chorus" implies cooperation, whereas competition for the crab is the
order of the day. Each cry of "MINE" is answered by another seagull's coun-
terclaim of "MINE." The word in their mouths sounds like the noise that
seagulls actually make when they screech and squawk, which makes the scene
quite funny. The scene is funny also because each person in the audience
simultaneously judges the mindless fixation of the seagulls and recognizes the
anthropomorphizing: This is how human beings behave, even perhaps *I* behave
sometimes.

When I mentioned the seagulls in *Nemo* to my children, they suddenly
stopped pulling on the toy and turned to look at me. A longish pause ensued.
The abrupt change from cacophony to silence enhanced my impression that I
could *hear* them thinking. Then, suddenly, they both began to laugh. I cannot
remember who ended up with the toy because the conflict was at an end.

What had happened? In that moment *Finding Nemo* performed a scriptural
function: it abruptly changed the way my children saw themselves at that instant
and brought them to a new understanding, ultimately effecting positive change.
Their laughter was a form of repentance. In one sense this is not a very profound example of a text's functioning scripturally; after all, it would not take
long to plumb the movie's spiritual depths, and my children continue to bicker
over stuff. But what *Finding Nemo* did in a very limited way in that argument
between my children is precisely what Scripture is capable of doing in a much
more profound way. In our cocky self-assurance we think we see clearly, but the
clarity of our vision is akin to the clarity of a peephole in a wall—we see some
things with relative acuity, but we cannot see the whole picture, how everything
behind the wall is connected. Scripture brings us to the point of realizing our
own blindness and of seeing God, ourselves, and our world anew.

I need to clarify two points here. First, I am not equating the Bible with
other texts that might occasionally function in a way similar to Scripture. Only
the Bible, or more precisely, the spirit of God at work in the reading and interpreting of the Bible, creates the possibility for its readers to see *all things* new
in a unique and authoritative way and to be changed in the process. The
authority of the Bible is entirely different from that of any other literary work,
but the *ways* we read them should perhaps not be all that different, at least for
many biblical texts.

Secondly, my *Finding Nemo* example might suggest that I think that the primary function of Scripture is to modify behavior. This is a secondary scriptural function, and as such not an unimportant one, but it is far from the most
significant role of Scripture for Christians. First and foremost, Scripture
reveals to us *who God is* and *who we are.* Out of these central questions of iden-

tity flow possibilities for the kinds of relationships (with God, each other, the rest of creation) that will foster flourishing for humanity and world. New understanding of who God is and who we are makes possible profound change in how we relate to others and to the world.

In an article on the importance of music education for children, Alex Ross cites Maxine Greene's conviction that arts education is crucial to democracy, not simply a privilege of it. Tapping into children's imagination by means of the peculiar perspective offered by the arts leads to profound differences in the way children learn to perceive the world. The arts empower them to break with what appears to be given and unchangeable about the world and to see new possibilities.

> Children learn to notice surprising details that undermine a popular stereotype; they grow tolerant of difference, attuned to idiosyncrasy. They can also experience a shock of perception that shows them alternative possibilities within their own lives, whether or not those possibilities or those lives have an obvious surface relationship with the art work in question.[2]

In its capacity to open our imaginations to potential realities other than the one we wake up to every day, Scripture functions something like the arts. I am not suggesting that their respective functions are identical, only similar in some interesting ways. Christians hold that the Bible is God's word to human beings and for human beings, that is, for their flourishing in every generation. What the arts may do for democracy, Scripture may do for the fundamental questions of existence, of who God is and who we are in relation to the God-given world we inhabit, a world that God loves. Scripture opens alternative worlds that we could not perceive otherwise, possibilities that God would have us see, explore, embrace, and become.

In her novel *Middlemarch*, George Eliot plumbs the ambivalences and complexities of the human condition in a profound and illuminating way. As I was listening to National Public Radio recently, I heard the writer Francine Prose express similar admiration for *Middlemarch*, but it was the metaphor she used to describe the experience of reading the novel that brought me up short: "It's like getting a stronger eyeglass prescription and a new pair of lenses through which to see more deeply into the hearts and lives of 'grown-up people.'"[3]

I was brought up short because this is the same metaphor John Calvin employs in describing Scripture. Scripture for Calvin is a pair of "spectacles" through which we as believers may, indeed must, peer in order to see God more clearly. Calvin puts it this way: "So Scripture, gathering up the otherwise confused knowledge of God in our minds, having dispersed our dullness, clearly shows us the true God."[4] He makes the process of seeing the "true

God" somewhat easier than it actually is, I think, but his central claim seems justified: Scripture provides us with lenses through which God (and I would add humanity and the rest of creation) appears with clarity. George Herbert expresses something similar in his poem "The Holy Scriptures I":

> Thou art all health, health thriving till it make
> A full eternity: thou art a mass
> Of strange delights, where we may wish and take.
> Ladies, look here; this is the thankful glass,
> That mends the looker's eyes: this is the well
> That washes what it shows.[5]

It is a fundamental irony of the Christian life that we must get involved in the messy act of interpreting Scripture in order to achieve some of the clarity to which Calvin and Herbert, more indirectly, allude. Interpreting Scripture is not an easy enterprise. For one thing, how tedious the life of faith would be if it were! As Brian Blount memorably says: "It's supposed to be hard!" Why? Because "every word is a *living* word for people living where they are in their present and future, not in somebody else's past."[6]

How can Scripture exert this shaping influence, this power to make us see God, ourselves, and the world differently? A fundamental problem in ecclesial life in the United States is that those who spend a lot of time reading the Bible reduce it to moralism, while those who do not spend much time reading the Bible are disdainful of its power, largely because they too think of it as a rule book. These two groups share a belief in the fundamentally moralistic character of the Bible, the difference being that one group accepts the rules while the other rejects them.

The Bible has some rules in it, of course, but they are given by God as a gift to human beings so that their communities may thrive. They are not given to punish people or to demand obedience for no reason. The perception of the Bible as principally a rule book is based on this misunderstanding of Scripture, and its consequences for ecclesial, social, and political life are distressingly pervasive. The church needs to take Scripture seriously, and also to realize that its genuine power lies in freeing us to live in joy with God, with other human beings, and with the whole of creation.

Yet I still have not answered the question of how Scripture makes it possible for us to see God, ourselves, and our world from a completely different angle (perhaps with the result that we stop clenching the toy long enough to see ourselves from the outside for a moment and, as a result, repent). If this is a crucial function of Scripture, how does it achieve this effect? First, we must read it, often and slowly, paying considerable attention to the details and how they work together to create a world of meaning. Yet paying careful attention to the Bible does not mean treating it as an answer key, as though life were a really Big Exam, and God the great Test Giver. Reading Scripture means entering into the worlds it evokes, and abiding there for a time until you are changed. It is more about encountering God and ourselves in the text than about explaining away textual difficulties or justifying our opinions and prejudices. Of course, I do not mean that we should pretend we live in ancient Palestine and adopt the customs and culture of that time. That is neither possible nor desirable. Rather, Scripture conjures *theological* worlds different from the one(s) we live in, and these require our urgent attention. I draw from Ezekiel to illustrate what I mean.

READING EZEKIEL 1

In the first verse of the first chapter of the book that bears his name, Ezekiel sees "visions of God." This turns out to be not simply visions with a divine source but actual sightings of God! Very early on, the rabbis understood the profundity and gravity of the claim, which has no equal anywhere else in Scripture, and allowed only select individuals to interpret Ezekiel's vision. Yet Ezekiel is very careful in his description of what he sees. After his description of the "creatures," who are like human beings yet also like and unlike other creatures (Ezek. 1:5–12), the prophet describes a kind of fire that accompanied them.

> And the appearance of the creatures! With them was *something that looked like* burning coals of fire. This fire, *suggestive of* torches, kept moving about among the creatures; the fire had a radiance, and lightning issued from the fire. Dashing to and fro [among] the creatures was *something that looked like* flares (1:13–14).[7]

The most striking linguistic feature about Ezekiel 1 is the number of similes (such as those I have emphasized here), the number of ways and times that Ezekiel tries to avoid saying exactly what this God looks like, all the while describing what God looks like. Most translations try to clarify too much; the Hebrew is difficult, hard to understand, and more diffuse and opaque than any translation can convey. The prophet glimpses God, and yet that glimpse also points away from God. The substance and solidity of the language evoking the creatures, their wings, their faces, and the like, alternate with the destabilizing language of simile: likeness, appearance, and so on.

The dynamic between articulacy and inarticulacy, so palpable in the vision, announces, *paradoxically through language itself*, one of Ezekiel's major claims: the gods whose reality *appears* more palpable (i.e., the gods of the nations) are in fact impotent and unreal; the God who *appears* to be absent is actually the only God who is powerfully at work in the world.[8] This paradox at the heart of the vision—the simultaneous absence yet powerful presence of God—is also the central paradox and theological claim of the book of Ezekiel itself. On the one hand, Ezekiel must persuade his audience that God is actively present in both Babylon and Jerusalem, not destroyed with the Jerusalem Temple, but on the other hand the aniconic tradition, so powerful in the Old Testament witness, prohibits physical representations of God.

Ezekiel's description is a step removed from the reality of God. The early church fathers emphasized this dimension in their interpretations of the passage; it was an effective argument against the gnostics in the second century CE and later against the neo-Arians in the fourth century, who claimed that God could be completely known.[9] It is not that Ezekiel is not saying something important about who God is in his visions. On the contrary, he is making serious claims: God is not limited in time or space, for example, and God's power and sovereignty are evoked through the immensity of the creatures and the radiance of the fire and flame. Yet language about God can never define who God is completely—and this is true even of biblical language, as Ezekiel's vision attests.

In what way might Ezekiel's vision be considered authoritative? It calls us to see ourselves from outside ourselves for a moment, to examine the ways in which we attempt to domesticate God for our own purposes, whether they be political, religious, social, or economic. In general we act as though God were manageable; we believe we understand what God is doing in the world and what God wants Christians to do and how they should act and who is a faithful Christian and who is not.

Ezekiel, however, opens an alternative world in which a more appropriate posture embodies humility before the One who eludes our constant attempts to make God conform to our own visions. And so, like my children with their fists clenched around the toy, it may be a moment to stop yanking, to reflect, and repent. It is actually liberating to realize that God cannot be stuffed into the box we have personally outfitted for our purposes.

Ezekiel's book is so weird in part because of its purpose to disorient us, to disengage us from the safe, reliable God we think we know and can direct to our own ends, and to reorient us to an alternative view of reality. That alternative world most thoroughly unfolds in the last part of the book, a world in which human beings come to a more humble, realistic, and life-giving understanding of a God who is unmanageable yet acts for our ultimate well-being in unpredictable ways. The result is not to feel constrained or punished, but to feel released into the joy that comes from the realization that the God who reigns over the cosmos is not of our own making: Scripture points toward One who is more mysterious and sublime than the little, safe god we have constructed to suit ourselves. The unmanageability of God may produce anxiety at first, but ultimately it must come as something of a relief.

Again, I make no claim that my articulation of Scripture's authority somehow trumps others (although some I find to be manifestly better than others). On the contrary, if we are to take Scripture more seriously, we would do well to attend to the *multiple ways* that Scripture can function authoritatively, but always with the core conviction that God wants Scripture to benefit us,[10] to bring us into better, more life-giving relationships with God, with each other, and with all the world God has made.

Biblical Authority and the Scandal of the Incarnation

Frank J. Matera

The claim that the church makes for the Bible is analogous to the claim that it makes for Jesus Christ. For just as the church proclaims that Jesus Christ is the incarnate Word of God, so it proclaims that the Bible is the Word of God in human words.[1] Each claim is scandalous in the biblical sense of being a "stumbling block." After all, how can the eternal Word of God be enfleshed in a human being? And how can the Word of God be present in a book written by human beings? But if students, pastors, and exegetes are to understand what it means to say that the Bible is the Word of God, authoritative and normative for the life of the church, they will do well to pay attention to this analogy between the scandal of the incarnation and the scandal of God's Word that expresses itself in human words.

A PERSONAL WORD

My own engagement with the issue of biblical authority began in the 1960s, when I was a seminarian at the Catholic University of Louvain in Belgium. To that point in my life, my knowledge of the Bible had been mediated through the liturgical life of the church. It was not necessary for me to ask if the sacred text was normative. I knew that it was because I heard it repeatedly proclaimed in the church's liturgy. But in the lecture halls of Louvain, where I was introduced to source, form, and redaction criticism, I began to realize how the Word of God had been communicated in and through the words of human beings. And for the first time, I understood the need for some kind of historical-critical exegesis.

After seminary, the first ten years of my ministry were spent in parish work. In accordance with the directives of the Second Vatican Council, the Roman Catholic Church was introducing its revised Lectionary for Mass (1969) and its revised Liturgy of the Hours (1971). These texts made the riches of the Bible more available to Catholics, and they required pastors to be more intimately familiar with the Bible and its interpretation. Immersed in the liturgical life of the church, in which the sacred Scriptures played such a central role, I had little doubt that the Bible was normative for the Christian life. But it now became more challenging to explain this normative character, given my new appreciation for the way in which God's Word was communicated in and through human words.

Aware of my need for further study, in 1978 I undertook doctoral studies at Union Theological Seminary in Richmond, the first Catholic to do so. I had chosen Union because of its rich tradition of biblical theology, and I was not disappointed. While deeply invested in the academic guild, Union's faculty understood that the ultimate goal of exegesis is the proclamation of God's Word. And because it appreciated how the Word of God is communicated in human words, it applied all the methods of historical-critical exegesis to the text.

As a professor at the Catholic University of America, I have followed in the steps of my teachers. I apply the methods of historical, literary, and narrative criticism to the text because I believe that the Word of God is communicated in human words that need to be explained and interpreted for every generation. Although this approach to the text has been enriching for me, I am keenly aware that the historical-critical method is threatening and disturbing to some. For if God's Word is communicated in human words and interpreted by this method, then how can these writings be authoritative for the life of the church?

THE AUTHORITY OF BIBLE: A PROPOSAL

My proposal for understanding the authority of the Bible revolves around three concepts: revelation, inspiration, and canonicity. After explaining the significance of each for the authority of the Bible, I will return to the analogy between the incarnation of the Word in Jesus Christ and the communication of the Word of God in the human words of the Bible in order to explain how the Bible is normative and authoritative for the life of the church.

Revelation

The Bible is authoritative because of the unique witness it bears to God's self-revelation.[2] This divine self-revelation was prior to the written text of the Bible, inasmuch as it occurred in God's mighty deeds to which the Bible bears witness. For example, God revealed himself to Israel through the powerful deeds performed at the time of the exodus, long before there was an Old Testament. And God revealed himself in the life, ministry, death, and resurrection of Jesus Christ before there was a New Testament. Accordingly, there is an intimate relationship between God's mighty deeds and the words of the Bible, which the Second Vatican Council expressed in this way: "This economy of revelation is realized in deeds and words, which are interconnected in such a way that the works accomplished by God in the history of salvation show forth and confirm the teaching and realities signified by the words, and the words, in turn, proclaim the works and illumine the mystery contained in them."[3]

Although God's self-revelation is broader in scope than the word of Scripture, the written word is a privileged witness to God's self-revelation. For in and through the biblical stories of Israel and Jesus, God reveals himself to the world. The Bible, then, is authoritative not because it is a book about God but because it is a book of divine self-revelation. Although some may think of this revelation as a series of propositional truths about God, the narrative and poetic nature of the biblical writings suggests that God's revelation is more personal. It is a self-revelation of God to the world that comes to its climax in Jesus Christ, whom the Father sent into the world to reveal the Father to the world. In the language of the Johannine Gospel, whoever has seen Jesus has seen the Father (John 14:9).

Inspiration

Because the Bible witnesses to God's self-revelation, it is appropriate to speak of God as its author and of the sacred text as inspired by God's Spirit. Thus, in addition to revelation, we must also speak of inspiration if we are to understand biblical authority.[4] The concept of inspiration, however, which is so closely related to revelation, is fraught with historical and theological problems.[5]

On the one hand, as we become aware of the ways in which specific biblical writings originated, it is more difficult to speak about inspiration solely in relation to a particular author. For example, we may call the final editor of the Fourth Gospel the author of the Gospel, but contemporary scholarship has taught us that this editor was the beneficiary of earlier traditions and editions of the Gospel. This history of the Gospel's growth and development suggests that God's Spirit was active in the process that brought about the Gospel, as well as in the person who brought this process to its completion.

On the other hand, as we take into account the human dimension in the Bible's composition, it becomes apparent that, while inspiration assures the believing community of the truth of God's self-revelation, it does not necessarily endow the sacred writings with historical and scientific knowledge that transcends the understanding of those who composed them. As the Second Vatican Council noted, the authors whom God chose "made full use of their faculties and powers, so that, with God himself acting in them and through them, they as true authors committed to writing everything and only those things that he wanted written."[6] Inspiration guarantees the truth of God's revelation rather than the historical and scientific accuracy of every statement the Bible makes. To talk of inspiration and even inerrancy, then, is to speak about the Bible's authority in matters of God's self-revelation for the sake of the world's salvation.

Inspiration, then, is best viewed as the attendant of revelation, for it empowers the human authors of the text to express God's self-revelation in human words. Apart from the Spirit's inspiration, there would be no possibility of expressing God's Word in human language. But through the Spirit's inspiration, human words express God's self-disclosing Word for the salvation of the world.[7]

Canonicity

Whereas revelation and inspiration assure the church of the Bible's authoritative character as the Word of God, the canon is the church's authoritative list that identifies which writings constitute the church's Scripture, normative for its life.[8]

How the church determined its authoritative list of writings is a complicated and fascinating story. Although some would argue that the establishment of the canon was a "power play," whereby the bishops of the fourth century imposed their will on the church in order to define Christianity in their own way, the reality of the canonical process was more subtle. For even though the final shape of the New Testament canon was not settled until the fourth century, its central core was already in place by the end of the second century.[9]

Rather than view the canon as something "imposed" from without, then, it is more helpful to understand its development as a slow and intricate process whereby the church identified and recognized certain writings as authoritative for its life and others as not. The writings of the New Testament, then, did not become inspired because they were accepted into the canon. They were accepted into the canon because the church recognized and identified them as God's self-revelatory word.

To understand how the church was able to decide which writings were authoritative and which were not, it is important to recall that the church existed before the New Testament. It was the church that gave birth to the New Testament, and inasmuch as the New Testament grew out of the bosom of the church, it should not be surprising that the church recognized what was its own. To be sure, other writings were helpful and beneficial to the life of the church, but the church eventually judged that they were not the inspired bearers of God's self-revelation.

To summarize, the Bible is the authoritative Word of God, normative for the life of the church, for at least three reasons: (1) it witnesses to God's self-revelation; (2) it enjoys the inspiration of God's Spirit; (3) the church identified these writings as those in which God revealed himself to humanity for its salvation.

GOD'S WORD IN HUMAN WORDS

Understanding the Bible as the Word of God in human words is analogous to understanding Jesus as the incarnation of the preexistent Word of God. Consider for a moment the challenge of the Fourth Gospel. Jesus comes into the world claiming to have been sent by the Father to teach the world what he has seen and heard in the presence of his Father. Not surprisingly, the world rejects what it considers to be a scandalous claim: that the human one, Jesus, comes from God to reveal the Father to the world. Although Jesus is the Word made flesh, the world refuses to see the glory of the only-begotten Son because it is scandalized by his humanity. In contrast to the world, Jesus' disciples believe that he comes from the Father to reveal what he has seen and heard in the Father's presence. The disciples see the glory of God in and through the flesh of the incarnate Word. Jesus' humanity is not a stumbling block for them but the means by which they see the glory of God. This challenge of interpreting the Bible as the Word of God is analogous to the challenge that the incarnation presents in the Fourth Gospel. Just as one must hear and see the Father in the words and deeds of Jesus, so one must hear the Word of God's self-revelation in the human words of Scripture.

Luis Alonso Schökel once noted that misunderstandings concerning the Bible as the Word of God are analogous to the great christological heresies of the first four centuries, which tended to veer from one extreme to the other. He writes, "There can be a sort of Docetism or Monophysitism which denies or diminishes the human quality of the inspirited word; there can be a Nestorianism which denies its divine character."[10] For example, biblical fundamentalism rightly affirms the importance of the Bible as the Word of God, but in "refusing to take into account the historical character of biblical revelation, it makes itself incapable of accepting the full truth of the Incarnation itself."[11] In other words, just as Docetism and Monophysitism did not fully appreciate the humanity of Christ, so biblical fundamentalism does not fully grasp the paradoxical way in which God's self-communication occurs in the human words of

Scripture. Conversely, the proponents of the historical-critical method rightly seek "to shed light upon the historical process that gave rise to the biblical texts."[12] But when the historical-critical method becomes an ideology or an end in itself, it fails to hear the Word of God in the human words of the text. In effect, just as Nestorius "refused to attribute to the Word of God the events of Jesus' human life,"[13] so an ideological use of the historical-critical method denies the presence of God's Word in the words of the Bible.

THE AUTHORITY OF THE BIBLE IN PRACTICE

Paul's teaching on the Parousia—the return of Christ at the end of the ages—provides a test case for understanding of the authority of the Bible. The Parousia was central to Paul's theology, as it is to the church's creed ("He will come again in glory to judge the living and the dead"). But history has shown that Paul was mistaken insofar as he thought that the Parousia would occur in his lifetime, or soon after. Indeed, a good part of early Christianity was mistaken in this regard, so much so that it became necessary for the author of Second Peter to provide the Christians of his day with an *apologia* for the delay of the Parousia (2 Pet. 3:1–13). So what are we to say about the authority of the Pauline letters if Paul was so mistaken about the imminent return of the Lord? To answer this question, I turn to Paul's discussion of the Parousia in 1 Thessalonians.

The immediate occasion for 1 Thessalonians is the positive report that Paul has just received from Timothy about the faith and love of the community and its longing to see him again (1 Thess. 3:6). Overjoyed that the community has been faithful to the gospel and is desirous to see him, Paul writes 1 Thessalonians to encourage and strengthen the Thessalonians in their faith, hope, and love. Toward the end of the letter, however, he also discusses the question of the Parousia, presumably because he has learned that the Thessalonians are fearful that the deceased members of their community will not share in the victory of Christ's Parousia. In face of this crisis, Paul must explain that those who have died as Christians will not be excluded from the victory of Christ's Parousia because there is an intimate relationship between the resurrection of Christ and the resurrection of those who believe in him. Consequently, those who have died in Christ will not be forgotten when the Parousia occurs. Paul then describes what will happen. At the archangel's call and the sound of God's trumpet, Christ will descend from heaven, and those who have died as believers in Christ will rise. Then those who are still alive at the Lord's return will be "caught up in the clouds" with those who have been raised from the dead to meet the Lord in the air (the so-called rapture). Thus all, the living and the deceased, will be with the Lord (1 Thess. 4:13–18).

This is the oldest description of the Parousia in the New Testament, and on face value it would appear that Paul expected to be alive at the Parousia ("Then we who are alive," 1 Thess. 4:17). Although brief, this description of what will occur is quite specific: the archangel's cry, the sound of a trumpet, the raising of the dead, the descent of Christ from heaven, the gathering of the elect with the Lord in the air. But what kind of authority does this text hold for us today? After all, the Parousia has not come as Paul thought it would, and while Paul's cosmological description of the Parousia may have cohered with his understanding of the cosmos, it no longer coheres with our knowledge of an infinitely expanding universe.

If we approach the text as biblical rationalists who try to explain everything historically and reasonably, there is little hope of finding a divine word of self-disclosure in this text. The biblical rationalist will assert that Paul was wrong about the arrival of the Parousia, and so it is illusory for Christians to continue believing that Christ will come again. Furthermore, since Paul employed the Hellenistic imagery of the imperial visitation to describe the Parousia, biblical rationalists may be tempted to assert that his description does not correspond to any transcendent reality. Consequently, Paul's teaching about the Parousia is no longer authoritative for contemporary believers, who are better advised to conceive of the future in another way.

If we approach the text as biblical fundamentalists who do not distinguish between the Word of God and the human words that communicate it, we will be inclined to say that Paul provides us with an authoritative description of what will actually happen at the Parousia, a kind of preview of the future. Christ will descend from heaven just as Paul describes, and when he does, the rapture will occur. The elect will be taken up with Christ into heaven, and unbelievers will be "left" behind. Many faithful Christians firmly believe in this scenario and prepare for it daily. But despite the comfort and assurance it brings, it is difficult to reconcile this scenario with the world in which we live. So where is the biblical authority of 1 Thessalonians? Has it completely vanished because Paul was so utterly mistaken about the timing of the Lord's return? Or is it found in a literal interpretation of his words?

It is at this point that we need to return to our analogy of the incarnation and affirm yet again that the Word of God is revealed in and through human words. If we are willing to affirm this with the same faith that we confess the incarnation, then we will understand that Paul's rich description of the Parousia in 1 Thessalonians, or any other letter, is not the essence of God's Word. What the New Testament affirms in proclaiming the Parousia is that God will be victorious. In God's own time, in God's own way, in a manner that will utterly astound us yet again, God will be victorious over the powers of sin and death. Paul knew this because he had encountered the risen Lord, who is already victorious over sin and death. As a former Pharisee, Paul realized that the general resurrection of the dead had already begun in God's Messiah. And because the general resurrection of the dead had already begun in God's Messiah, Paul understood that the return of Christ is always imminent, no matter when it occurs. *Paul was mistaken* in thinking that the Parousia would occur in his lifetime, *but Paul was not wrong*. In light of Christ's resurrection, Paul understood that the general resurrection of the dead had already begun in one man, God's Messiah. Aware that the general resurrection of the dead had begun in Christ, Paul understood that Christians are living in the final age. Consequently, the Parousia will always be imminent for them, no matter when it occurs. Paul was *mistaken* about the timing of the Parousia, but he was *not wrong* about God's final victory.

The New Testament describes the Parousia in a variety of ways: the return of the Son of Man at the end of the ages (the Synoptic Gospels), the conflict between Christ and the "lawless one" (2 Thessalonians), the conflagration of the universe (2 Peter). The reason for these multiple descriptions is that the Parousia belongs to the mystery of Christ's resurrection and the general resurrection of the dead. And just as we cannot adequately describe the mystery of the resurrection, so we cannot adequately describe the Parousia. The authority of these texts, then, is found not in their descriptions of the Parousia but in their witness to God's Word that God will be victorious and Christ will be the agent of God's victory.

To summarize, the authority of the Bible is not found in the words themselves but in the reality to which they point and witness—the Word of God. In and through the human words of Scripture, we encounter the authoritative Word of God. It is *this* Word to which the Bible testifies. It is *this* Word that endows the Bible with authority.

13

The Charter of Christian Faith and Practice

S. Dean McBride Jr.

The Scriptures of the two Testaments are uniquely authoritative in matters of Christian faith and practice because they reveal to us whose we are and how we should respond to this knowledge.[1] They disclose the cosmos to be the intentional, uncontested creation of a beneficent Deity and construe our human vocation within it to be one of honoring the Creator's enduring sovereignty and gracious providence, exemplified especially by Israel's formative history, as comprehended under the aegis of the covenants and epitomized in the singular personhood and redemptive work of Jesus the Christ.

In their disclosures of divine character and purpose, both Testaments are theologically and ethically imperative, or prescriptive, as well as indicative. They urge us to celebrate life as at once a gift to be treasured and enjoyed and a sacral calling to service of the Holy One in whom we, together with the rest of creation, subsist. Accordingly they command us to love the Lord God—the sole Creator, who still claims us in spite of our many failings—and also our neighbors as ourselves. They commission us to do so through praiseful and repentant worship that eschews idolatry, vigorous and effective stewardship of the resources that sustain life throughout the created order, and diligent proclamation and pursuit of compassionate justice in temporal affairs. The Scriptures are thus the theopolitical charter that forms and reforms communities of God's people and directs their ministries of reconciliation, nurture, and renewal in the world.

I understand this definition to be in substantive agreement with the confessional tradition to which I—an elder in the Presbyterian Church (U.S.A.)—willingly subscribe.[2] As a Christian of Reformed persuasion, I affirm that the testimony of the Scriptures to the sovereign identity, providential work, and salvatory purposes of God is preeminent and indispensable for true knowledge of the world and ourselves. As both a Calvinist and a child of the Enlightenment, however, I also acknowledge that this testimony, firmly rooted in antiquity, is neither self-explanatory nor altogether perspicuous in its applicability to the complex challenges of modernity. The crucial question of scriptural authority, then, is not whether we revere the Testaments as peerless anthologies of eternal divine decrees—the pristine, immutable "Word of God"—but how we responsibly receive, interpret, and implement the particular theological visions and ethical guidelines they invite us to share with those who first apprehended and recorded them and with their heirs who ardently conserved them and, in turn, bequeathed them to us.

Here are five, interrelated considerations that I find to be especially important in thinking about how these ancient Scriptures still function authoritatively in matters of contemporary faith and practice.[3]

"The Wisdom of God in Its Rich Variety" (Eph. 3:10)

First, far from advocating either an insular or a monopolistic view of efficacious knowledge, the Scriptures themselves attest that wisdom whose source is the Creator permeates the interfacing realms of heaven and earth, and is both desirable and ordinarily accessible through observation, reason, and examined experience.[4] To be sure, many texts also remind us that human beings have the capacity to overlook, obfuscate, and misuse knowledge whose significance should be sensible to us.[5] Whether because of innate cognitive limitations, a rebellious and fallen state, divine judgment, or lapses of common sense, we often lack "hearts [prepared] to understand" the true import of what we observe and experience.[6]

The overarching problem that the Scriptures indicate in such cases is human failure to discern that phenomena of the natural order are not themselves divine or self-referential but point instead to the independent will of their sovereign Creator.[7] Similarly, the human penchant for egoism, sometimes involving a pretense of radical moral independence as well as a compulsion toward personal aggrandizement, can obscure the effects of divine agency in our own lives and those of others or, worse, distort these effects into idolatries of self, nation, privileged group, cherished cause, or elite status.[8] In glorifying the sole God, the Scriptures unmask idolatry. They reveal its many forms to be pernicious distortions of knowledge about the world and ourselves. The Testaments function authoritatively, not because they negate or replace such knowledge, as cultivated especially by the physical and social sciences and the humanities, but when they expose defective habits of mind, ancient and modern alike, and provide the theological language and perspectives that allow us to perceive reality with greater humility, depth of understanding, sense of wonder, and openness to transcendence.[9]

This I take to be the import of Calvin's assessment that "God has provided the assistance of the Word for the sake of all those to whom he has been pleased to give useful instruction, because he foresaw that his likeness imprinted upon the most beautiful form of the universe would be insufficiently effective."[10] The scriptural manifestation of divine "Word" is the Creator's complementary, restorative instruction. It is the sufficiently effective catalyst that facilitates our evaluation, integration, and faithful application of genuine wisdom whose proximate sources and forms are manifold.

"The Word of God Is Living and Active" (Heb. 4:12)

Second, Calvin's use of the familiar appellation "Word" of God underscores the point that the two Testaments have been transmitted to us primarily by communities of faith who curated them not as cultural artifacts or compendiums of traditional learning but rather as extraordinary textual media through which divine communicative intention may still be discerned.[11] Already in antiquity Jewish Scriptures are variously described as foundational, inspired, oracular, and hallowed.[12] They, and eventually their New Testament extension, are deemed revelatory and sacrosanct in ways that differentiate them categorically from other literatures, even those widely acknowledged to be theologically edifying or otherwise invaluable spiritual and ethical resources.

Such claims can easily, but not necessarily, encase the privileged texts in shells of hermeneutical and doctrinal certitude and conceal them behind defensive bulwarks of hardened apologetic tradition. Thus there is need to be on guard against making idols of the Scriptures themselves. For this reason Calvin objected strongly to the argument that the Scriptures are the creation of the church, which consequently retains definitive authority to decree what they do and do not mean. In effect, this reduces them to a fossilized replacement for the living God and permits ecclesial interests to exercise "unbridled tyranny" over their interpretation.[13]

The problem is an old one (e.g., Jer. 8:8; Matt. 15:6). An important corrective involves recognition that the terminology of inspirational divine "Word" essentially reflects prophetic idioms that express God's discrete commissioning of and communication through human instruments.[14] The principal overtones of such language are intrusion, empowerment, momentum, effectivity, immediacy—much more so than stasis, or the conservation and constraint of permanently fixed pronouncements that are supposed to articulate inviolable divine truths. As literary vehicle for the "living and active" Word of God, the Scriptures are fraught with the power to critique intellectual inertia as well as stagnant political and religious institutions; they carry the potential to produce change, to generate new fruits of insight and reform in human affairs.[15] But the hermeneutical implications are even more elemental. The prophetic associations of the language of "word" assist us in acknowledging that the "voice" of the transcendent God may be heard through biblical texts only because and to the extent that they address us "in the language of human beings."[16] This recognizes that the Scriptures, as well as the cumulative interpretative traditions that should extend and renew their testimony from one age to the next, are culturally and historically conditioned. These "many and various" witnesses and traditions have been shaped by human minds, in specific contexts and for particular purposes, and they are formulated in conventional, sometimes flawed patterns of human thought and language. An understanding of them requires careful as well as faithful listening, with our critical faculties fully intact.

Karl Barth summarized the basic point this way: "In the Bible we meet with human words written in human speech, and in these words, and therefore by means of them, we hear of the lordship of the triune God." [17] Authoritative use of the Scriptures must give cogent attention to the mundane words and the specific cultural-historical situations in which the divine Word is ineluctably humanized and particularized.

"These and These Are Words of the Living God"[18]

Third, the embedded and engaged, or "situational," character of the scriptural witnesses pertains directly to the question of their coherence or, conversely, their conspicuous and sometimes disconcerting multifariousness. How should we attend cogently to dissonance and dissent between the Testaments and within each of them?

Important differences of dispensational emphasis notwithstanding, both individually and in conjunction with one another the two Testaments have a unifying theocentric focus: they exalt the God who creates, governs, and invites humankind into covenantal relationship and reconciliation.[19] Israel and the church alike, together with their shared and distinctive scriptural corpora, are called into existence by the "living and active" Word of God, which was instrumental in the creation, became audible as a voice at Mount Horeb on "the day of the assembly," empowered the prophets, and "tabernacled among us" in the person of the historical Jesus.[20] But neither Testament makes consistency a ruling criterion for what is and is not included as authentic testimony about the ways in which divine sovereignty and providence are experienced, articulated, and put into practice. To be sure, while rejecting bland uniformity and featuring a lively array of distinctive, sometimes argumentative human voices, neither Testament encourages theological diversity or contentiousness per se.[21] Each Testament amplifies certain witnesses as pre-eminently trustworthy or normative, but without silencing all others.

The Jewish Scriptures clearly privilege Moses as the singular, incomparable figure who acted and spoke most decisively to Israel on the LORD's behalf and whose promulgation of Torah reverberates authoritatively through the Prophets and Writings and well beyond into the scholarly deliberations, debates, and decisions of rabbinical Judaism.[22] Yet Jewish tradition not only respects the considerably more restrained witnesses of Esther and Qohelet to divine involvement in temporal affairs, but also attributes to Moses the audacity to argue with God, on Israel's behalf as well as his own; and, consistent with this, he is even named as the author of the book of Job, with its sharply provocative questioning of divine justice.[23]

New Testament writings indicate that controversy regarding crucial matters of belief and practice was rife within the early Christian fellowship as well as between it and major Jewish parties of the time.[24] While the design of the New Testament features the collection of Paul's epistles—thereby underscoring the centrality of Paul's personal testimony and mission to the Gentiles—his ambivalence toward Moses' legacy of Torah and his version of the gospel of the crucified and risen Christ are complemented and corrected by the varied witnesses of four evangelists and other apostles whose voices are at least occasionally oppositional to his.[25]

Long before the advent of historical criticism it was recognized that there are many important biblical texts—such as the two accounts of creation juxtaposed in Genesis 1–2, the variant versions of the classic Decalogue (Exod. 20; Deut. 5), and discrepant reports of Jesus' life and teachings in the Gospels—that resist harmonization. Rather than leveling these and many other ostensible irregularities of the received textual landscape, canonization preserved them, thus allowing them to provoke our own reflections on the presence and absence of God in our lives and challenging us to hear—even through contrapuntal choruses of testimony, "these and these" alike—what God expects of us in faithful, situational response to our individual and communal callings.

"He Opened Their Minds to Understand the Scriptures" (Luke 24:45)

Fourth, each of the points sketched above indicates that authority does not adhere to the Scriptures in metaphysical fashion, but is a function of why, for whom, and how they are interpreted. Though they certainly can be and are studied profitably in other contexts as well, when the Scriptures are in view specifically as the charter of Christian faith and practice, the chief purpose of interpretation is to discern the Word of God conveyed through human words as it addresses especially, but not exclusively, the church as God's covenanted people who seek forgiveness, illumination, comfort, and guidance. The methodological "how" of such interpretation is a crux that has received—and requires—perennial attention.

Augustine's classic handbook on Christian education, completed in the early fifth century, introduces the work of biblical interpretation with a trenchant hermeneutical distinction: "There are two things which all treatment of the scriptures is aiming at: a way to discover what needs to be understood, and a way to put across to others what has been understood."[26] As Augustine develops it, this formulation locates the interpreter not on the detached, objective outside of the interpretative process but in its very midst, as a mediator who must competently engage both the scriptural texts in their literal, contextual particularity and the interpreter's own contemporary community of faith with whom the Scriptures want to converse. The engaged mediator is thus doubly accountable, both for cogent discernment of the sense and significance of the inspired witnesses and for effective communication that enables the meanings discovered in the words of the text to be understood by those in the church who need their guidance.[27]

These tasks are conjoined and, at least in considerable measure, reciprocal. The first, which we are accustomed to label "exegesis," involves disciplined listening to the biblical sources in their original languages, giving immediate attention to matters of text, grammar, semantics, rhetoric, poetic idiom, context, and literary genre. Augustine sets out a coherent method for dealing with such matters, closely informed by his knowledge of classical scholarship. While emphasizing that the literal-grammatical sense of a passage does not always yield its correct or fuller "spiritual" meaning, which often entails interpreting any given scriptural witness in the light of others, Augustine insists that a responsible exegete must "make every effort to arrive at the intention of the author through whom the Holy Spirit produced that [particular] portion of scripture."[28] The interpreter's second task is to assist the faithful in understanding what specific texts are saying and not saying to them, which is performed through expository teaching and preaching. In Augustine's view, the principal goal of exposition, and the measure of its effectiveness, is increase in the "twin love of God and neighbor" through which Christian faith is rightly practiced.[29]

Augustine's model of linguistically rigorous, theologically astute, and communally engaged interpretation exerted significant influence on subsequent Christian interpreters, including Erasmus, Luther, and Calvin. It is worth observing, too, that the model has important Jewish counterparts, notably in the hermeneutical work and commentaries of Abraham ibn Ezra (ca. 1150).[30] In my judgment, the Enlightenment should not be blamed for undermining the integrity of these models, even though it clearly did produce shifts in methodological emphasis and stimulate new insights into the human dimensions of the composition and transmission of Jewish and Christian Scriptures.[31] But to the extent that the Enlightenment honed reason as an exegetical instrument, which was used to critique anachronistic interpretative constructs and allegorical flights of fancy, it contributed positively to the effectiveness of the hermeneutical agendas already developed by Augustine and Abraham ibn Ezra and utilized by Calvin, among others.[32]

If there is to be a genuine dialogue between the Word of God and the church, mediated through faithful, engaged interpretation of the Scriptures, they must be allowed to speak in their own voices and distinctive theological accents, especially since what they may have to say to us is not always what we want or expect to hear.

"How Then Can We Live?" (Ezek. 33:10)

Finally, in order to function authoritatively, scriptural witnesses must not only be rightly understood through informed interpretation but become affective and "effectual" in matters of faith and practice.[33] In both Testaments, the divine "word" is usually experienced as a commanding or commissioning presence that should reorient and renew human lives, individually and communally, in accord with divine priorities.[34] In the psalmist's apt metaphor the divine "word" is authoritative when it serves as a "lamp," guiding our walk of faith with one another and in testimony to God's ways in the world (Ps. 119:105; cf. 1 John 1:1). The Scriptures are a charter because the theology and ethical principles they attest are constitutive of knowledge seeking faithful and effective responses.

What counts as a faithful and effective response to the knowledge that our creaturely existence is wholly dependent on the providence and grace of God? There are familiar guidelines offered in the Scriptures themselves, probably none more useful than the double commandment identified and exposited by Augustine as "the rule of love."[35] But other summaries are compelling as well.[36] They emphasize that the theologies developed in scriptural contexts are essentially practical and situational. They encourage us to understand the gift of faith as a discipline through which we honor God by ministering on God's behalf to the particular needs and specific circumstances of those with whom we share life in God's world.

14

The Bible's Wounded Authority

PETER OCHS

INTRODUCTION AND SETTING

To make a claim about the authority of the Bible is also to situate oneself some-where in the world, within some society that shapes one's relation to the Bible. Of course, in this modern world of fractured communities and plural mem-berships, one may not truly know what inherited presupposition guides his or her receptivity to the Bible. But, as Deuteronomy puts it, "It is not in the heav-ens, that you should say 'Who among us can go up to the heavens and get it for us, that we may observe it?' . . . No, the thing is very close to you, in your mouth and in your heart, to observe it" (Deut. 30:12, 14 NJPS). So, without striving to peer beyond what I know, let me tell you this much of my orienta-tion to the Bible. I write to you as a scholar of Jewish philosophy, which means someone who engages the technologies of Western philosophy and logic as helpful tools for more clearly hearing the implications of the biblical word. "Jewish" refers, however, not simply to a biblical tradition, but to one shaped in particular by the interpretations of rabbinic sages: the cultural leaders of the people Israel in the days of the destruction of the Second Temple and then for about five or six hundred years thereafter.

Among the various practices of Jewish scholarship, I work within a commu-nity of philosophers and rabbinic text scholars that calls itself The Society for Tex-tual Reasoning.[1] This group was formed in 1991 out of some dissatisfaction with factionalism in the Jewish academy and in Jewish religious life, a factionalism that at times pits rabbinic historians and philosophers against one another as if their differences displayed not a division of labor, but a division of commitments to the

truth. This is a factionalism that pits one denomination of Jewish religious observance against another, as if "both this and that" were not comparably "words of
the living God," but competing words, one true and one false.

"Textual reasoners" seek to represent the whole spectrum of Jewish practice
and of Jewish academic disciplines. Their shared commitment is to a love of the
texts of Bible and rabbinic literature, of fellowship with one another, and of the
activity of *limud torah l'shma*, "the study of Torah for its own sake." The central
activity of textual reasoning is to gather together in groups ranging from ten to
thirty participants, to read, interpret, debate, celebrate, challenge, and be challenged by sample texts of both Bible and rabbinic commentary. Members of the
group prefer to study together for hours at a time, or if possible over a couple
of days, so that there is time for the group to assimilate itself to the words, gram-
mars, and semantic range of some small collection of verses. If they do this, they
find that after several hours or a day of sustained study and conversation, something initially unexpected and delightful may take place: a time of increased
insight into the texts and into one another. This insight stimulates patterns of
reasoning together that are possessed by no one person in particular. The patterns belong to the group, then and there. As for their style and content, these
patterns are at once "of the text," in the sense that they are about the specific
words and rhythms of specific biblical and rabbinic texts, but they are also "of
reason," in the sense that they display practices of reflection and analysis that
cannot be traced to any one set of verses. This is "textual reasoning," however,
not just "reasoning," since the group finds these reasonings are not simply
brought in from outside the world of the text—not simple applications of, say,
"postmodern philosophy" or "modern ethics." Individual thinkers in the group
tend to speak out of such singular disciplines and also out of particular denominational devotions. Each individual is, however, also committed to intense
engagement with each other and with the specific texts on the table. As a result,
shared study generates patterns of reasoning that are not dominated by any one
discipline or devotion but belong to the whole group and to that moment. In
this chapter, I speak not only in my own voice, but also out of the habits of trust
and commitment that are generated by textual reasoning.

BIBLICAL AUTHORITY:
A TEXTUAL REASONER'S VIEW

Authority Revealed: The Written Torah

> God spoke all these words, saying, "I am the LORD your God, who
> brought you out of the land of Egypt, the house of bondage: You shall
> have no other gods besides me." (Exod 20:2)

A textual reasoner's relation to biblical authority is, first, one of inheritance: "Moses commanded the Torah to us as an inheritance of the Congregation of Jacob" (Deut. 33:4). From Israelite ancestors through rabbinic sages and medieval and modern teachers, textual reasoners receive the text of the Tanakh (Torah, Prophets, and Writings) as part of a covenantal tradition. This text delivers the literal words, black on white, of God's revealed covenant with Israel.

Authority Received: The Oral Torah

> Ezra opened the scroll in the sight of all the people, for he was above all the people; as he opened it, all the people stood up. Ezra blessed the LORD, the great God, and all the people answered, "Amen, Amen," with hands upraised. Then they bowed their heads. . . . Jeshua, Bani . . . and the Levites explained the Teaching to the people, while the people stood in their places. They read from the scroll of the Teaching of God, translating it and giving the sense; so they understood the reading. (Neh. 8:5–8)

The Talmudist David Weiss Halivni argues that, for a significant stream of Talmudic thinking, Ezra acquires a status near, or in ways equal to, that of Moses.[2] There is a tradition, for example, that the Torah texts transmitted by the priestly scribes to Ezra were imperfect, that Ezra instituted a process of restoring those texts, and that the dots that appear over ten verses in the Torah (*eser nekudot*) mark places where Ezra did not yet carry out the revision.[3] According to this tradition, Ezra's corrections were transmitted as oral Torah: "for Ezra had dedicated himself to seek [interpret, *l'drosh*] the Torah of the LORD so as to observe it, and to teach laws and rules to Israel" (Ezra 7:10).

> Moses received the Torah on Mt. Sinai and transmitted it to Joshua, Joshua to the Elders, the Elders to the Prophets, the Prophets to the members of the Great Assembly. (*Mishnah Pirke Avot* 1.1)

According to the rabbinic sages of the century after the destruction of the Second Temple (70 CE), this "oral" (or enacted) tradition of the repaired texts of Torah was transmitted alongside the written text: from Moses, Joshua, and the Prophets, by way of Ezra, to the scribal priests, then to the Pharisees, then to the rabbinic sages whose Mishnah (codified in the second century) and Talmuds (codified in the third and sixth centuries) guided the people Israel (Jewish people) into the medieval period and beyond. But is the "oral" Torah a preset rule for reading God's word, or an evolving practice for interpreting its meaning?

Authority Interpreted: Studying and Performing Torah

The Bible scholar Michael Fishbane devoted his lengthiest book to studying how the Bible interprets itself: for example, how Deut. 4:15–17 ("be most careful . . . not to act wickedly and make for yourselves a sculptured image . . . : the form of a man or a woman, the form of any beast on earth") reapplies the creation imagery of Gen. 1:14–27. Fishbane suggests that we can imagine how one such passage interprets another one. In this case, "the Deuteronomist . . . establishes a distinct rhetorical nexus between the themes of creation and idolatry . . . , [reinforcing] the . . . [theological claim] that idolatry is a sin against the creator and his transcendence."[4] Fishbane suggests that almost every passage of written Torah can be reread as interpreting another.[5] In this way, the teachings of Torah appear first as interpretive judgments about other teachings rather than as judgments about the world itself beyond the text. In light of Fishbane's study, the rabbis' oral Torah appears to continue rather than intrude on the Bible's own tendency to display meaning by way of reinterpretation. For Halivni, this means that Torah is received only through Israel's interpretive practices of God's Word, as they are exemplified in the interpretive practices of the rabbinic sages and completed only when we enact them, as well, within our own communities of interpretation and practice. God's teaching thus appears to us in the relationship that binds written Torah and oral practice. But what warrants our interpretations and guarantees their truth?

Wounded Reading

In traditional Jewish schools, or yeshivas, when children begin studying Bible they do not read it alone, nakedly, but with the accompaniment of rabbinic commentaries collected by the medieval scholar Rashi (Rabbi Shlomo Yitzchaki, also known as Rabbi Solomon ben Isaac of Troyes, 1040–1105). This means that, right from the beginning, the scriptural text is read alongside its rereadings. And how are text and Rashi related? The teacher asks: "Given what Rashi says, what problem did he find in the text? What were his questions? It is the questions that matter." Study thus proceeds not from text to answers, but from question to question. That is the tradition: a line of reading questions to questions. But what prompts the questions? This is a question more for adults than children. Rashi suggests an answer in his reading of the psalmist:

> Like a hind crying for water,
>   my soul cries for You, O God. . . .
> O my God, my soul is downcast;
>   therefore I think of You
>   in this land of Jordan and Hermon,
>   in Mount Mizar,

where deep calls to deep
in the roar of Your cataracts,
all Your breakers and billows have swept over me.
(Ps. 42:2, 7–8)

Rashi reads "deep calls to deep" as "trouble calls to its fellow": the psalmist's troubles multiply like the surging waters, as if each trouble calls its fellow to join it. I take this to mean that wound speaks to wound, that, in words of Halivni, the holiness of Scripture inheres in its maculations, its points of error or woundedness. As I understand them, Rashi and Halivni teach that when I bring my suffering to the text of Scripture I notice *its* wounds first. I am drawn to tend to them, and only after being engaged in the work of "mending" them do I realize that my own wounds correspond to the text's and that the more deeply I care for the text's wounds, the more deeply are my own wounds healed.

But what does a wounded text look like and how is it "mended"? As Halivni notes, one kind of wound concerns grammatical and syntactical incongruity:

> The incongruities of the Pentateuch, and its disparities with observed law, are not the new discoveries of modern textual science. . . . Traditional sources dating back to the time of canonization itself seem already to have struggled with the insufficiency of the Pentateuch's literal surface, searching the text for hidden meaning and mining the traditions for corrective oral law. . . . We must therefore begin with the premise that the literal source of the canonical Pentateuch is marred by contradictions, lacunae, and various other maculations whose provenance appears more human than divine.[6]

Another kind of wound concerns the ways that a scriptural text's meaning appears to contradict historical reality or religious experience. One classic case is Isaiah 60:21: "Your people shall all be righteous, they shall possess the land forever; they are a shoot of My planting, the work of My hands in whom I shall be glorified." When read by the rabbinic sages who observed the ruins of the Second Temple after 70 CE or the exile after 136 CE, this text must have appeared counterfactual indeed. What possession? What glory?

For textual reasoners, to "mend" the text is to answer such questions by way of a *derashah*, a "searching out" or interpretation of the text that settles its syntactical or semantic incongruity at the same time that it both uncovers and heals complementary incongruities or wounds in the reader's own heart. *Mishnah Sanhedrin* 10:1 appears to read Isaiah 60:21 in just such a way. Its profound midrash (the product of *derashah*) is displayed in a single phrase: "All Israel have a portion in the world-to-come, as it is written, 'Your people shall all. . . .'" The Mishnah reads Isaiah, in other words, as referring not to *this world* of tribulation and exile but to the future, messianic world to come. It is traditional to recite this midrash just before ritual readings of *Pirke Avot* for Sabbath afternoons between Pesach (commemorating Israel's exodus and freedom) and Shavuoth (commemorating Israel's receiving the Torah). In that setting, the midrash appears to display another level of meaning: the words of the sages' oral Torah not only anticipate but also belong to the world to come, for in the study and performance of those words ancient Israel receives its enduring life.

Performed this way, the midrash serves as a prototype for readings that mend both text and reader at once. *The mending does not rewrite the written Torah nor replace its authority as the unchanging source text for all rabbinic study.* It is not, in other words, a mending of some object out there—the text by itself— for all time and for any reading. *Instead, it mends a time-specific relationship between the written text and some community of readers: a meaning of this given text as intimately joined to this given community of readers.* This relationship cannot be characterized as "subjective," as opposed to "objective." It belongs to the real life of Torah in the world, which means that this life is always relational, displaying to us analysts no less than three constituent elements: (1) the black-on-white letters of the written text and (2) the text's midrashic or performative meaning (3) *for* a particular community of readers. The Bible's authority, in other words, is displayed generically but realized and performed only in historically particular ways.

Today's Wounds: Modernity and Shoah

And today? How is the Tanakh received by the community of textual reasoners? At this point in the history of this community, I cannot speak of any single drama of woundedness-and-mending, but only of a family of related dramas. There are dramas, for example, conditioned by the incongruities of Scripture when read in light of modern rationality; dramas conditioned by modern text–historical science in particular; dramas conditioned by the "postmodern" collapse of faith in reason; dramas conditioned by the Shoah or Holocaust; and dramas conditioned by the Jewish people's divided sociality— in part, landed in a troubled holy land; in part, in exile among the nations; in part, at home among the nations. The Bible's authority is received only by way of such dramas. By way of illustration, I will close by observing some consequences of the drama of life after the Shoah.

Most readers will be familiar with the question that haunts Elie Wiesel's *Night*: "Where is God?" For Halivni, a fellow survivor from Wiesel's town of Sighet, the challenge is not to locate God but rather to face the current reality of God's speaking a word that is "maculate"—not immaculate. "As religious Jews," Halivni writes, "we have to know that without God there is no humanity. . . . 'Walk humbly with the Lord thy God' (Mic. 6:8)—like a child holding hands. You must hold hands, and walk. But this does not mean that you always have to say, particularly in remembrance of the Holocaust, 'What you did was right.' It was terribly wrong."[7] This clash of obligations—to honor one's relation to God and one's experience of what went terribly wrong—provides the setting for Halivni's understanding of the maculate, or wounded, text. For Halivni, there is no life without relation to God; there is no such relation except by way of God's spoken word in Scripture; there is no receiving that word after Shoah except as wounded; and there is no way to read and thus observe that wound without seeking to mend it. By way of such mending, one participates in the life that mends Israel's broken heart (and body). And that life is the only access one has to God's authority and the authority of God's Word.

This leads Halivni to conclude that, just as the kabbalists taught that our prayers and our deeds of loving-kindness are the primary means through which God mends the world (*tikkun olam*), so we learn after the Shoah that our reparative study of Torah (written and oral) mends not only our world but also the Torah (*tikkun Torah*) and thus the divine Word and thus the world that God creates through his Word. But "our reparative study" means nothing other than the way we meet God in and through the drama of reparative reading. Since our "meeting God" is precisely where the wound lies after Shoah, how is such reparative study possible? Halivni's Holocaust memoir ends with the drama of a religious Jew walking hand in hand with the God "who was terribly wrong."[8] Halivni's general book of hermeneutics after the Shoah ends with a yearning for "continuous revelation," the still unfolding display of God's word in our wounded lives and God's wounded text.[9]

EPILOGUE: HOW, THEN, TO READ TANAKH AND RECEIVE ITS AUTHORITY TODAY?

And what of those of us who are neither Holocaust survivors nor Talmudic scholars? What lessons can be drawn about how to address the Bible at a time of wounded relations? I close with one set of lessons learned so far from the work of textual reasoning. The lessons are presented as if they were responses to the question: "But, with all these wounds, how shall I read the Bible today?"

(1) *Don't worry so much.* Set out assuming that you can read the text of Scripture in ways that respect its authority while also respecting the demands of critical rationality. For, if you begin with anxiety, do not expect that the anxiety will be magically removed; it may simply propel you back and forth between competing certainties and doubts.

(2) *But how, then, to remove anxiety?* You need to rely first on the traditions of practice that lie behind your own orientation to reading, not just officially "scriptural" traditions, but whatever traditions of wisdom you have already

affirmed. Perhaps this has to do with exercise, or family life, or disciplines of prayer. Come to these resources first before you read and, thereby, increase the chances that you can begin reading *as if* you were at peace. If Scripture is itself your source for this, then seek out the prayer of Psalm 23: "The Lord is my shepherd. I shall not want; he makes me lie in repose along still waters; he restores my soul." Regard that kind of repose as a way of opening your powers of attention and reasoning, not of closing them.

(3) *If you can, begin reading in the company of others who share at least some of your reading interests.* Read Scripture as a context for deep conversation among fellow readers. Begin with a conversation about the letters, words, and verses of the texts you read, but also allow the conversation to be transformed by the reading so that Scripture may itself turn the conversation toward issues of belief, responsibility, and action in the world.

(4) *Whether or not you read in community, also learn to read alone.* In the words of Steven Kepnes, student of Martin Buber, engage the "text as thou," "thou" in the sense of the intimate other rather than of some austere, distant one. Bring your deepest concerns to the text and thereby hear the deepest concerns of the text at this time of your reading.[10]

(5) *Read, ideally, both alone and in community.* When reading in community, converse with others from out of your intimate relationship with the text as "thou." But such deep reading must never replace reading in the plain sense. Then seek to bring the fruits of such interpersonal conversation with you when you return to your solitary encounters with the text.

(6) *Respect the authority of the text in its graphemic, or black-on-white, body.* That is, respect the body of the text the way you would respect the body of any member of your community of readers. Do not identify words of the Bible with any of your own statements of what one should believe and do.

(7) *But recognize the text's incapacity to speak without your help.* In order to find out (*l'drosh*, "inquire after") what Scripture demands of you, you must walk together with Scripture for quite a while. The rest of our lessons have to do with this walking together.

(8) *Acknowledge the place of tradition and the past.* The less you know consciously of the personal and communal past you bring to the text, the more it may cloud your reading—for example, by uncovering wounds in the text that are *not* your wounds but those of a prior community whose habits of reading you retain. The more you know of this past, the more it may lighten your reading—for example, by exhibiting your inherited familiarity with many ways of receiving the text and thereby refining the way you read it today.

(9) *Discern the place of wounds now and the potential dangers of authority.* In a time of peace—which also means a time when your communal and religious life appears untroubled and biblical texts appear unburdened—you may not

need to worry about "authority." You will probably receive the biblical words simply as enrichments to your present life. But authority matters in times of crisis. Scripture speaks as authority when the reader is wounded, and reading is a means of urgently searching out God's help. Then the reader lends the divine word authority to repair the wound. *This is, ironically, also when such authority is most dangerous.* The greater the wound, the greater desire there is for its repair, the less concern there is for errant reading, and the more willingness to submit to authority carelessly. Halivni's reading is most pertinent in this setting. At a time of unfathomable woundedness, God's word is also most unfathomable. In such a setting, hasty readings and hasty cures tend to be signs of serious error. That is why faith—with its complements of patience, trust, and diligent work—is most crucial in times of greatest loss. The greatest loss and the greatest need mark the time of greatest peril for those who seek God's presence. Is this not, in the words of Exodus 3, the time when God is most present? "I will be with you" (*ehyeh 'imach*). . . . Tell them *ehyeh* ('I will be') sent me" (3:12a, 14b). And does the psalmist not read Exodus 3 to say, "*ehyeh 'imach b'tsarah* ('I will be with you in suffering')"? Yes, but the midrash in *Exodus Rabbah* 30:24 also rereads Ps. 91:15 to say, "I will be with you in suffering. When you [Israel] suffer, I suffer."[11] And, for Halivni, God's suffering is a mark of wounds in the very text to which we turn in need.

15

Authority and the Practice
of Reading Scripture

ALLEN VERHEY

GROWING UP DUTCH REFORMED

The best—at least the funniest—guide to the Dutch Calvinism in which I was reared was Peter DeVries. The opening scene of *The Blood of the Lamb*[1] lampooned the sort of pious and provincial Dutch Calvinist household in which DeVries and I, as well as Don Wanderhope, the tragicomic hero of the story, were raised. There was a family crisis at the kitchen table. Don's father, Ben, was questioning the infallibility of Scripture. He was lost, Don reports, "in seas identifiable among the . . . Dutch Reformed with whom he sought his portion as those of Doubt" (p. 4). While Don's uncle Hans, a "dominee," did his best to administer "theological first aid" (p. 5), the conversation moved quickly from infallibility to evolution to the virgin birth to election to total depravity, "a tenet for some reason always especially dear to our folk" (p. 18). The conversation and the crisis, however, always circled back around to Scripture. Don's older brother, Louie, who had lost his faith at the university, took up his father's case, ridiculing the notion of infallibility but conceding that the Bible was, nevertheless, "great literature." What Louie thought a generous concession excited "a special murmur of dismay" around the table. Uncle Hans in his distress turned directly to God. "Next he'll call Thy word poetry," he said. "He's going to call it gracefully written. Forgive him, O Lord, I ask it in advance" (p. 7). Such worldliness!

In this contest between the obscurantist piety of Uncle Hans and the worldly sophistication of Louie, it is hard to have much sympathy with Uncle Hans. DeVries, however, also lampooned pretentious sophistication, including the pretentious sophistication of biblical criticism. In *The Mackeral Plaza*, for example, the Reverend Andrew Mackeral—affectionately known as "Holy

122

Mackeral"—had made a "reverse pilgrimage"[2] from the Calvinism of his youth to theological liberalism. He built People's Liberal Church, where the area for worship was the smallest room in the complex and where the pulpit was constructed of four different kinds of wood to signify the disagreement of the Gospels. An associate said to him one day, "Your anti-Calvinism is the most Calvinistic thing I've ever seen."[3] DeVries did not nurture much sympathy for either obscurantist piety or worldly sophistication.[4]

The family crisis in Don Wanderhope's kitchen was repeated countless times in the kitchens of Dutch Reformed homes, with slightly different characters and considerably fewer theatrics. I watched my older brothers play the roles of Ben or Louie more than once, and I played those roles myself a time or two. My pious and patient father, with his high school education and his considerable wisdom, was usually cast in the role of providing "theological first aid." He did better, I think, than Uncle Hans.

My father had several balms in his theological first-aid kit. The most healing was surely his own piety. The evening meal was not over, or the children excused from the table, until Scripture had been read and prayers offered. Scripture formed those prayers, and we had the sense that it should form our lives as well. On Sundays he would sometimes read the passage that had been the text for the sermon that morning, and he would ask his sons, "So, what did you think of the sermon this morning?" After my brothers and I responded in unison that it was too long, he would say, "Besides that, I mean." He was patient with our criticisms then, as long as we criticized the sermon in the light of the text, and we had the sense that Scripture should form—and reform—the life of the church.

There were arguments, of course, in which his sophisticated sons would criticize Scripture. There were arguments about Genesis and the age of the earth, about whether Moses wrote the first five books of the Bible, about whether Isaiah was one book or three, about "the Synoptic problem," and about assorted other questions of biblical criticism. At the end of those arguments (which in my view he usually lost), he would usually say something like, "Well, I don't know about that, but I do know that the Bible is God's Word and that we better listen—and live—carefully."

That simple and pious remark was important for its suggestion that the authority of Scripture is not the conclusion of an argument that starts with an objective, scientific examination of these writings. It is rather the confession of the believing community and of the members of that community that their submission to God and to the cause of God will be guided and tested by attention to these writings. And, if the authority of Scripture is not established by a "scientific" examination of these writings, neither is the authority of Scripture threatened by the critics' best worldly and sophisticated judgment about the historical origins and contexts of these documents. The authority of Scripture is threatened, rather, by the "objectivity" that regards these writings simply and merely as human words, simply and merely as a miscellaneous collection of ancient Near Eastern religious writings.[5] For my father—and for the church—these writings are Scripture, the rule, or "canon," by which we may measure our thoughts and lives. Indeed, "church" and "Scripture" are correlative terms. One of the things we mean when we say "church" is that this community reads Scripture together as somehow normative for its common life. And to say "Scripture" is not simply to name a little collection of ancient Near Eastern religious texts; it is to name the writings that Christian churches receive as "canon," as somehow authoritative for their life.[6] Ignoring Scripture is not an option for the church, not, at least, if it is to continue to be the church.

There were other occasions on which my brothers or I, like Ben and Louie, would question the infallibility of Scripture. It seemed clear to us that the Bible not only contradicted itself on certain narrative details but also was inconsistent about the relation of sin and sickness, about the legitimacy of divorce, and about much else. On such occasions my father sometimes replied, "If you ask the wrong question, you will get the wrong answer, and don't go blaming Scripture when you get the wrong answer." The obvious retort was, "So, what's the right question?" And to that my father's response was sometimes, "I'm not sure exactly, but I'm pretty sure you are asking the wrong ones if Scripture contradicts itself," and sometimes, "I'm not sure exactly, but perhaps we would do better by letting Scripture question us." There was wisdom there, although it was not clear then to his "sophisticated" sons.[7]

My father had one more balm in his "theological first-aid kit." He delighted in jokes that displayed the abuse of Scripture by those who held it in high regard. There is a story told in more than one pious Dutch Calvinist household of Great-great-grandpa in the Netherlands. He was famous for his piety and especially for his ability to recite a Scripture verse appropriate to any occasion. People would come to consult with him about a verse to use at a particular funeral or wedding or baptism. He was, however, infamous as a horse trader. None of the villagers who so admired his ability to quote Scripture would deal with him when they needed a horse. One day a stranger's horse went lame, and Great-great-grandpa sold the stranger an old nag for about four times its value. Great-great-grandma complained about this behavior, giving Great-great-grandpa a little nag of her own. Great-great-grandpa retorted quickly, "But Great-great-grandma, I did it by the command of the Lord: I saw a stranger, and I took him in."

It was a cautionary tale, of course, warning against the abuse of Scripture by those who call Scripture an "infallible rule" and treat it as an oracle. It is not just the worldly sophistication of the "critic" that threatens the authority of Scripture, but also (and more fundamentally) the dead orthodoxy of those who say the "right words" about Scripture but are not guided or tested by it and by the cause of God made known in it.

Such was the landscape in which I sought to negotiate a path between obscurantist piety and worldly sophistication. I knew from my parents' lives that the Bible was important, indeed somehow authoritative for the common life of the church and for the individual lives of its members. I also knew, however, from my brothers' questions, that there are some problems here.

One problem is the silence of Scripture. Scripture is silent, for example, about stem cell research. That, however, is not the biggest problem here. There is also the strangeness of Scripture. When Scripture does speak, its words are sometimes, well, quaint. It is a strange world of sex and gender in the Bible, a strange world of economics and politics, a strange world of sickness and healing. When the Chronicler chides King Asa for consulting physicians about a gangrenous leg, for example, we are forced to admit that the words of Scripture are human words, words we may not simply treat as a timeless moral code dropped from heaven. A third problem is the diversity in Scripture. The authors of Scripture do not all speak in the same voice or even always in harmony. Job, for example, gives an account of evil different from the conventional wisdom of Proverbs. And we may add, finally, the problem of the difficulty of Scripture. It is sometimes difficult to determine just what Scripture means.

But if there are these problems with Scripture, there are greater problems with us as readers of Scripture. There is, first, a widespread lack of familiarity with Scripture. That is easily enough remedied. The problems with us as readers, however, go deeper than our ignorance. Call it pride, or interpretative arrogance, but we too frequently "use" Scripture to judge others as "sinners" and to defend ourselves as the "righteous." We use Scripture like a weapon against others and in defense of our own interests and opinions. A bad joke or two may provide cautionary tales here, but we need not resort to bad jokes to be reminded of the possibilities for abusing Scripture. We need only remember our history.

Scripture has been used to silence women, to license abuse, to defend slavery and apartheid. It must simply be admitted that appeals to Scripture have sometimes done a great deal of harm. When Genesis 3:16, "in pain you shall bring forth children," was quoted to oppose pain relief for women in labor, a great deal of harm was done. When some people pointed to the Bible to claim that AIDS was God's punishment for homosexual behavior, a great deal of harm was done. It may be said, and rightly said, that these uses of Scripture are all abuses of Scripture, but people have nevertheless sometimes been harmed by appeals to Scripture, notably women and children and those on the margins, seldom "righteous" adult males. Such abuses of Scripture may make us a little suspicious of the authority of Scripture.

But if, as we have said, "Scripture" and "church" are correlative concepts, then the authority of Scripture is given in the very notion of "church." Without the church, the writings we call "Scripture" are simply a little library of ancient Near Eastern religious texts. And without the Scripture, the church loses its identity and way. For the church, it cannot be a question of whether the Bible has authority, but how. Somehow—but how? That is the question.[8]

AUTHORITY AND THE PRACTICE OF READING SCRIPTURE IN CHRISTIAN COMMUNITY[9]

If we learn that Scripture has authority in the very notion of church, perhaps we can learn something about how it functions appropriately as an authority if we consider the church's practice of reading Scripture together in Christian community.

A "practice" may be defined, following Alasdair MacIntyre, as a

> socially established cooperative human activity through which goods internal to that form of activity are realized in the course of trying to achieve those standards of excellence which are appropriate to, and partially definitive of, that form of activity with the result that human powers to achieve excellence and human conceptions of the ends and goods involved are systematically extended.[10]

Christians learn to read Scripture (and to read Scripture as authoritative) by being initiated into the practice of reading Scripture in Christian community, not by being informed that a creed calls Scripture an "infallible rule," nor by being taught by a biblical scholar that the Bible is a little library of ancient Near Eastern literature. The creed and the scholar may both be right, and Christian communities should affirm their creeds and be hospitable to scholars, but this practice of reading Scripture is a "cooperative human activity" that is "socially established."

In learning to read Scripture as a practice of Christian community, Christians learn as well the good that belongs to reading Scripture, the "goods internal to that form of activity." They learn, that is, *to remember*.[11] To remember, however, is not just an intellectual exercise, not just the mental process of recollection, not just the disinterested recall of some historical facts. To remember is to own a past as our own past in the continuing church, and to own it as constitutive of identity and determinative for discernment.

Neither we nor our communities live in simple transcendence over time. Against Kant and Kierkegaard, we do not discover ourselves as "noumenal" selves in moments of radical freedom cut off from past and future. On the contrary, we find ourselves by remembering. Without remembering, there is no identity. In amnesia, one loses one's self. In memory, one finds an identity. And without common remembering, there is no community. It is little wonder that the church sustains this practice of reading Scripture and is itself sustained by it.

Through this remembering we are freed from being "fated" by our past, for remembering sustains the possibility of repentance as we learn to tell a different story of our lives. By this remembering we interpret the present and make sense of it. And by this remembering we sustain certain possibilities and nurture certain expectations. By remembering, we learn to hope. Without memory, there is no hope.

There are temptations to forgetfulness in public life, when Enlightenment assumptions demand generic principles and "scientific" knowledge, pushing "God" to the margins. There are temptations to forgetfulness in personal life, when the private realm is construed as a space for the self-centered quest to satisfy desire. And there are temptations to forgetfulness, ironically, in the sort of historical reading of Scripture that treats these writings simply as the (more or less reliable) record of a figure of the past whose life ended with his death. Then the memory of Jesus is "merely a memory,"[12] an intellectual process of recollection, a disinterested reconstruction of some historical facts, *not* the memory that is constitutive of identity and community and determinative for discernment. In Christian community, Scripture is read on the Lord's Day, in celebration of resurrection, and in the confidence that the remembered Jesus lives. Forgetfulness threatens a loss of identity, but the remedy for forgetfulness is remembrance, and remembrance is served by reading Scripture.

Moreover, in learning to read Scripture and to remember, Christians learn as well certain "standards of excellence," certain virtues for reading Scripture that are "appropriate to" and "partially definitive" of this practice. Consider three pairs of such virtues: holiness and sanctification, fidelity and creativity, discipline and discernment.

Holiness is the standard of excellence for reading Scripture in Christian community that sets these writings apart from others, sets them apart as authoritative, as "canon," and also sets apart a time and a place to read them and to remember.[13] *Sanctification* is the virtue for reading Scripture that is ready to set the remembered story alongside all the stories of our lives—stories of sexual desire, stories of sickness and healing, stories of wealth and poverty, stories of our politics—until our conduct and character and communities are judged and made new by the power of God, until they are formed in remembrance and hope and themselves render the story rendered by Scripture.[14]

Remembrance provides identity, and *fidelity* is simply the standard of excellence in reading and performing Scripture that is ready to live with integrity, ready to live faithfully in the memory that the church has owned as its own and in the hope that memory endures. Fidelity, however, requires a process of continual change, of *creativity*, for the past is past and we do not live in it, even if we remember it. We do not live in David's Jerusalem or in Pontius Pilate's Judea, and an effort to "preserve" the past is doomed to the failure of anachronistic eccentricity. Moreover, God's good future is not yet, still sadly not yet. We do not live in John's "new" Jerusalem either, and an effort to read Scripture that neglects the continuing power of sin is condemned to the failure of utopian idealism. Creativity is the standard of excellence (nurtured in and limited by particular communities and traditions) that is ready to find words and deeds fitting both to Scripture and to our own time and place, in order to live in the present with memory and hope and fidelity, to perform Scripture with fidelity and creativity.

To treat Scripture as a revealed science text or as a timeless moral code is, then, a corruption of the practice of reading Scripture. It allows the tradition to petrify, to fossilize. It confuses fidelity with an anachronistic—and sometimes less than amiable—eccentricity. And to treat Scripture as simply dated and as irrelevant to contemporary moral practice is also a corruption of the practice. It turns remembrance into an archivist's recollection and runs the risk of alienating Christian community from its own moral tradition and its own moral identity. It invites amnesia.

The narrow path between anachronism and amnesia requires both discipline and discernment. *Discipline* is the standard of excellence for reading Scripture that marks one as ready to be a disciple, ready to follow the one of whom the story is told, ready to order one's life and the common life to fit the story. Discipline, of course, requires a community of disciples, people who are together ready to submit to and to contribute to the mutual admonition and encouragement of Christian community, to its interpretative and moral discourse. Discipline is the humility not to insist that Scripture be read "for ourselves," either by insisting on a "right to private judgment" in interpretation or by demanding that any interpretation serve our interests. It is the humility to read Scripture "over-against"[15] ourselves and our communities, "over-against" our lives, in judgment upon them and not just in self-serving defense of them, "over-against" even our conventional reading of biblical texts, subverting our own efforts to use Scripture to boast about our own righteousness or to protect our own status and power. It is the humility of submission to the authority of Scripture. A costly discipleship tests character and conduct and community by the truth of the story we love to tell.

Yet the shape of that story and of lives formed to it requires *discernment*. Discernment is the standard of excellence that is able to recognize "fittingness."[16] In reading Scripture, discernment is the ability to recognize the plot of the story, to see the wholeness of Scripture, and to order the interpretation of any part toward that whole. It is to recognize how a statute, a proverb, or a story "fits" the whole story. And in reading Scripture as authoritative for the moral life, as "useful . . . for training in righteousness" (2 Tim. 3:16), discernment is the ability to recognize whether an action or a practice "fits" the story of Scripture. It is the ability to plot our own lives in ways that "fit" the whole of Scripture, the skill to order our lives toward that whole, until our conduct and character are "fitting" to Scripture, "worthy of the gospel."[17]

Discernment is learned and exercised in the community gathered around Scripture, and it involves the diversity of gifts present in the congregation. Some are gifted with the scholarly tools of historical, literary, and social investigation; others with moral imagination or with a passion for justice or with sweet reasonableness. But all are gifted with their own experience, and each is gifted with the Spirit that brings remembrance (John 14:26). Discernment requires a dialogue with the whole church gathered around the whole of Scripture; it requires reading Scripture with those whose experience is different from our own and whose experience of the authority of Scripture is different from our own. It requires a dialogue in which people listen both to Scripture and to one another, muting neither Scripture nor one another. In that dialogue and discernment, the authority of Scripture is "nonviolent."[18] The moment of recognition of Scripture's wholeness and truthfulness comes before the moment of submission to any part of it and prepares the way for it. Discernment enables us to see in the dialogue with Scripture and with saints and strangers that our readings of Scripture do not yet "fit" Scripture itself, and that our lives and our communities do not yet "fit" the story we love to tell and long to live. Then discernment is joined to discipline again, and the recognition of a more fitting way to tell the story and to live it prepares the way for humble submission and discipleship.

THE AUTHORITY OF SCRIPTURE AND DIVORCE

To illustrate briefly the practice of moral discernment in the context of such an account of Scripture's authority, consider divorce. We confront a diversity of texts. In Mark's story (10:2–9), Jesus sets aside the Torah, Moses' dispensation for divorce in Deut. 24:1–3, as written "because of your hardness of heart." Instead, he reminds them of the story of the way it was in the beginning. The story, he says, is that "God made them male and female" (Gen. 1:26–28; Mark 10:6), and "For this reason a man shall leave his father and mother and be joined to his wife, and the two shall become one flesh" (Mark 10:7–8; see Gen. 2:24). In "the beginning" there was no divorce. Human sexuality was there, and marriage was there, as the gift of God, but there was—and there was to be—no divorce. Divorce was not what God intended. It is a mark of the fall, a concession to "the hardness of our hearts." And now that God's future is "at hand," now that it is making its power felt in the works and words of Jesus, the statute of Torah is no longer the finally decisive thing. To those who would follow him, to the disciples, Jesus says, "Therefore what God has joined together, let no one separate" (Mark 10:9).

Jesus announces the good future of God and the ways it already makes its power felt, not only in singleness and celibacy but in sexual relationships of equality and mutuality, where husband and wife are "one flesh," joined to each other in an embodied and enduring relationship. The point of Jesus' words was not to provide a new Torah, not to establish a new and extremely rigorous statute. The point was to summon people to welcome God's rule in marriage and sexuality as in all other matters. The power of God makes itself felt when husband and wife are "one flesh." Sin makes its power felt in the patriarchal hegemony of husband over wife and in divorce. God's purpose from the beginning has been revisited and restored.

If those who would remember Jesus and follow him are to renounce divorce, then Christians may ask—and must ask—whether they may ever choose divorce. Matthew and Paul handle that question differently.

Matthew tells the story itself somewhat differently (Matt. 19:3–12). He artfully changes the order of Jesus' reply. Jesus first takes up the Genesis texts and gives the Markan conclusion, "Therefore what God has joined together, let no one separate." When the Pharisees cite Deut. 24:1, Jesus responds by saying that it is a concession to the hardness of their hearts, but he does not for that reason brush aside either the law or the necessity of interpretation. Instead, he interprets the law in the light of God's intentions. He gives a legal (or *halakic*) interpretation for his community, an interpretation similar to the interpretation of Rabbi Shammai (*Gittin* IX.10): "Whoever divorces his wife, except for unchastity, and marries another commits adultery" (Matt. 19:9; cf. also 5:32).[19]

This passage *is* a legal ruling. Should we then revise our renouncing of divorce to make allowance for men to divorce their wives "for unchastity" (*porneia*)? But what of Paul in 1 Cor. 7:10–16? Paul cites the "command" of the Lord "that the wife should not separate from her husband . . . and that the husband should not divorce his wife" (vv. 10–11), but he does not treat it as a moral rule. Faced with the concrete problem, he exercises discernment, offering the church his own judgment ("I say," he says, "I and not the Lord") that certain marriages to unbelievers may be dissolved.

Mark, Matthew, and Paul all remember Jesus, and they all remember him faithfully and creatively. They receive and modify the tradition so that Jesus may be remembered—and so that the memory of Jesus may be performed—in their own communities. None of them, nor all of them combined into some elusive harmony, should be read as a timeless rule (or set of rules) to settle directly and immediately a contemporary Christian community's question about a particular choice to end a marriage. But all of them are a part of the whole Scripture that the churches read and struggle to perform.

Christians read the texts, and by reading they remember. They remember the story of Jesus as part of a larger story that begins "in the beginning" with creation, whose plot thickens with the story of human sin and the curse that came in its wake, and whose end is God's good future and "all things made new." They read them in ways fashioned by these standards of excellence.

They set Scripture aside as *holy*, and they set the stories of their sexual lives and of their marriages alongside the story to be judged, challenged, formed, reformed, and sanctified. *Fidelity* to this text and to its story does not require (or permit) us to read Mark (or any other particular text) like a timeless moral code. We do not live in Mark's community (or in Matthew's or Paul's), but we live in memory of Jesus and test our lives—and our readings—for fidelity. Fidelity requires *creativity*, and creativity licenses the formation of rules and judgments concerning divorce that need not be identical to Matthew's concession or to Paul's, but which respect both the vows of marriage and the partners of a marriage, which protect both the vulnerability of sexuality and the vulnerable, which honor God's creative and redemptive intentions in a world still marked and marred by sin. Although divorce is never to be celebrated as a good in itself or as a way God's good future makes its power felt, a Christian community may acknowledge that, in a world where God's good future is not yet realized, divorce may be necessary in order to protect either marriage itself or one of the marriage partners. As killing is sometimes allowed with fear and trembling, as in a just war, a Christian community may permit divorce "between the times" with mourning and repentance. For example, it might (given the promise of God to protect the weak and to defend the humiliated) permit divorce in cases of abuse. Or, taking a cue from the just war tradition, the Christian community might insist that divorce be "a last resort."

The authority of Scripture and fidelity to its story surely require a disposition not to divorce, even when the law (or a self-interested and patriarchal reading of the law) would permit it. It chastens any effort to read the text of Deuteronomy or the texts of Matthew and Paul as if they provided easily accessible justifications for divorce. The longing to be faithful to Scripture will permit neither treating the text as a manipulable oracle nor treating divorce as if it were a purely private matter. It requires that the community's reading of Scripture *discipline* our dispositions and decisions about divorce. Personal responsibility is not disowned, but it is put in the context of the community that remembers Jesus and is ready to follow him, to be disciples and pilgrims on the way toward God's good future. The longing to be faithful to Scripture will require the community's *discernment*, both that we may see how parts of Scripture fit the whole and that we may learn how our lives and our common life can be made coherent with remembering Jesus.

16

The Word of Creative Love, Peace, and Justice

SEUNG AI YANG

MY COMMUNITIES

I grew up in a multireligious culture in which Confucian and Buddhist teachings were the air that people breathed. Despite their patriarchal elements, Confucian philosophy and ethics (e.g., respect for elders) and Buddhist teachings (e.g., sympathy, respect for life) have positively guided my life. My family was multidenominational and multireligious. Among six of us, four, including myself, were Catholic, one was Baptist, and one was Presbyterian. My precollege education took place at a Methodist school. I have fond memories of my family singing together from different hymnbooks. Denominational diversity had never been an issue among us until much later. We were also multireligious. We all celebrated ancestor rituals several times a year, in accordance with Confucian teaching. When we climbed a mountain, we made sure to visit a Buddhist temple and paid homage to Buddha. Often I brought back a sense of tranquillity from the visit, which I long cherished. I knew, however, that my family was exceptional.

Most Korean Christians, both in the homeland and in the United States, are fundamentalists. This is, in a sense, a postcolonial phenomenon. European and U.S. colonial expansion brought Western missionaries to the East, who began to work actively in Korea during the nineteenth century. Missionaries were catalysts for the change of Korean society in both positive and negative ways. Positively, they raised a new consciousness for sociopolitical reform toward a just society, especially related to the advancement of women's status. Negatively, the Euro-American–centered ethos and binary-oppositional perspective, which missionaries unconsciously or consciously instilled in

132

Korea, still remain as deep (post)colonial wounds. For Christians, they are particularly related to their fundamentalist viewpoint.

Fundamentalist Christians, who have done much harm in Korean society, often justified their attitude with appeals to biblical authority. They crushed many of the Buddhist statues that had dotted the mountainsides for centuries. A loud voice would often cry out on a busy street: "Buddhists for hell; Christians for heaven!" Christians felt ashamed of their non-Christian family members, whom they perceived as stubbornly clinging to evil paganism. Many Christians shunned the traditional family gatherings on the national feast days in order to eschew the ancestral rituals, which they believed to be idol worship. They began to regard non-Christian family members, neighbors, and friends as "the other," or even as the enemy to be conquered. The impact has reached my own family. My sister-in-law and my nephews and nieces stopped coming to family reunions that involved ancestral rituals. A sister of my husband prays daily that God will save us from the "satanic" Catholic Church, which acknowledges truth in other religions. This was the very reason why I wanted to study the Bible. I had to know what the Bible teaches and in what way the Bible is authoritative for Christians.

I came to the United States for graduate studies and have now been teaching in a U.S. Roman Catholic seminary for thirteen years. I am often the only woman or the only Asian in the classroom. As external voices have changed my identity from Korean to Asian, international, minority, or resident "alien," they have ironically helped me to expand my perspective. I increasingly realize that our society is divided by many binary modalities, all of which separate people into superior and inferior groups. My personal experience as a Korean female biblical scholar has led me to be especially attentive to the misuse of biblical texts to oppress people whom the dominating power considers to be inferior on the basis of skin color or gender. The Roman Catholic Church explicitly condemns the use of the Bible to justify racism and sexism and emphasizes that biblical interpretation and its use should be practiced in accordance with evangelical justice and love.[1]

THE TRANSFORMATIVE AUTHORITY OF THE BIBLE

One's understanding of biblical authority is fundamentally based on how one understands the nature of the Bible, and thus on what one thinks of proper methods for reading and interpreting the Bible. The Roman Catholic Church has constantly addressed this issue in response to societal changes. Among various church documents, the "Dogmatic Constitution of Divine Revelation [*Dei Verbum*]" of the Second Vatican Council and "The Interpretation of the Bible in the Church" of the Pontifical Biblical Commission (PBC) are most important in understanding the church's contemporary teachings on the Bible.[2]

According to Catholic teachings, the Bible is God's Word in human language. The languages with which human authors convey the divine truth reflect their contexts, including their historical, social, geographical, cultural, political, and religious limitations. The relationship of the two different realities, divine truth and human limitedness, yields a complex tension. While they are vastly disparate, they are intimately close. Most of my students, with varying degrees of fundamentalist assumptions, struggle greatly with this tension.

A famous Buddhist tradition seems to illuminate well this complex tension. One day Buddha took his disciples to the top of a mountain. Pointing to the moon with his finger, Buddha said to his disciples, "Look at what my finger points to." As the disciples carefully followed his finger, Buddha continued: "What are you aiming to see? Is it my finger or the moon? My teachings are like the finger, and the truth I intend to reveal with my teachings is like the moon. You must aim to see the truth that my words are pointing to. My words are not the truth itself but the guide by which you get to the truth." My students in general immediately apply this analogy to the biblical traditions: The human languages of the Bible are like a finger pointing to God. The human authors of the Bible intended to reveal God in their own limited languages, but those languages are not the precise words of the ineffable God.

Another famous story in the Buddhist tradition illuminates well the relationship among the different, sometimes conflicting, voices in the Bible. Two disciples of a master were arguing. Not being able to reach an agreement, they brought the issue to their master. Disciple A told the master, "I have been arguing with disciple B, and it was so and so. I really think that I am right. What do you think, Master?" The master said, "You are right." Then disciple B told the master, "Master, I argued so and so. I really think that I am right. What do you think, Master?" The master said, "You are right." Disciple C, who was watching this, asked the master, "Master, you said to disciple A that he was right and then to disciple B that he was right. How can both be right? I think either A or B is right. Am I not right?" The master told disciple C, "You are right too." The point of this story is that each disciple's argument has something to do with the truth, but the real truth is beyond each partial argument and exceeds each partial understanding. Because human beings are constrained by space and time, and because of the limited nature of human language used by limited human beings, each voice in the biblical tradition is able to reveal God only from its limited perspective. Different voices complement the limited truth of each voice in revealing God.[3]

Understanding the Bible as God's Word in human language has led the church to interpret the Bible in a way that is essentially congruent with current biblical scholarship. In general, the church recommends that one should rely on all critical scholarship, although one should be careful not to accept its ideologies blindly. The PBC document, however, pays special attention to two methods. It commends the historical-critical method, while rejecting the fundamentalist method.

The historical-critical method is not only helpful but indispensable, for the human authors wrote from their concretely historical and cultural contexts. Their languages are subject to the constraints and limitations of authorial bias and historical contexts. For example, certain accounts present God as a misogynist or as a violent God who commands massacre. The historical-critical method is vital in shedding light on the historical and cultural context of those expressions. In contrast, fundamentalist interpretation naively identifies the constrained languages of human authors with God's exact words and therefore does not account for the Bible's diverse historical origins. As a result, the noncritical reading of the Bible sometimes reinforces social prejudices such as racism and sexism, which are contrary to evangelical justice and love. Not only is fundamentalist interpretation wrong, it can be harmful to society.

Neither *Dei Verbum* nor the PBC document explicitly defines or clearly delineates the concept of biblical authority. Instead, the PBC document provides a rather concrete guideline about how the Catholic interpretation should work in the life of the church. The guideline emphasizes that biblical interpretation, with its message of God's salvation, should nourish faith communities in their diverse contemporary contexts. The church documents not only leave room for diverse contextualizations of the biblical messages, they also underscore the necessity of continual recontextualization. The documents implicitly suggest how one should understand biblical authority: Their authority lies in the ever-renewing nourishment of communities that actualize the biblical message of God's salvation in their own contexts. I understand this authority as transformative, because I believe that this nourishment and actualization transform the individual, community, and society.[4]

My understanding of biblical authority as transformative is reflective of my Confucian heritage. The Great Learning, one of the Confucian canonical scriptures, maintains that the ultimate purpose of learning is to bring peace to the world. The sage explains how each step of learning works to serve its ultimate purpose. One's thoughts become sincere through study and the acquisition of knowledge. Out of sincere thoughts, the heart and mind are rectified so that the person as a whole may be cultivated. Once the whole person is cultivated, the household runs properly. Then the society, and ultimately the entire world, will be at peace.

I find this Confucian wisdom to describe analogically how biblical authority rests in the text's capacity to transform. Believers encounter the revelatory text through their threefold dialogues, attending the three different worlds of the Bible: the world behind the text (i.e., the communities that shaped and passed down the biblical traditions), the world within the text (i.e., the text itself in its literary and canonical setting), and the world in front of the text (i.e., the readers with their communities).[5] This threefold encounter with the text opens the heart of the reader and rectifies her mind. The encounter enlightens her so that she may be able to see who God is and how people are related to each other and to God. The reader sees God as one who continually creates life and saves people from oppression, sees that all are one family of God, and hears God's invitation to participate in God's creating and saving work. This enlightenment transforms the reader, enabling her to participate in God's creative love and thus helping to actualize God's reign of love, peace, and justice.

The understanding of biblical authority as transformative suggests at the same time how it should not be understood or used. The authority of the Bible should not function as a coercive or compelling power that oppresses the reader and undermines the reader's dignity. One should not understand biblical authority to consist of unilateral or legalistic commands that threaten violent sanction or punishment. Nor is the Bible's authority to be grounded in logical necessity, as in a mathematical formula. These approaches present submission to the authority of the text as a function of self-preservation.[6]

In his first encyclical letter, *Deus Caritas Est* (God Is Love), Pope Benedict XVI implicitly addresses the function of biblical authority as transformative. Emphasizing that God is the true source of any kind of love and that love of God and love of neighbor are inseparable, the letter raises an objection to the idea that love can be commanded. This objection alone is cause enough to reject a view of biblical authority that is essentially grounded on coercion. The reader participates in God's creative love, not in obedience to coercive authority but by being transformed by the love of God and enabled to see the relationship between God and humanity. Our love is a participation in the love of God. "Since God has first loved us," love is not a command. Rather, it is a reflection of God's love for us (*Deus*, §1). God is love and is continually creative, for the love of God continually creates love and life in others. One is able to respond to the love of God by virtue of the image of God, which is shared both between humanity and God and within humanity itself (*Deus*, §39).[7]

The inextricable relationship between love of God and love of others is a consistent theme that is expressed in diverse biblical traditions. Certain traditions explicitly address this close relationship, such as those found in the prophetic literature (e.g., Amos 5:21–24) and Gospel traditions (e.g., Matt. 25:31–46). Elsewhere, the language is less direct, as in the Ten Commandments, where the first half concerns the relationship between God and God's creatures and the other half concerns the interrelationships among all creatures of God. In sum, the authority of the Bible rests on how it constantly reminds us of who we are, opens our eyes to see the image of God in others, and moves us to create life in the world by loving others.

THE TRANSFORMATIVE AUTHORITY
OF THE CREATION NARRATIVES

Now I turn to the creation narratives to illustrate how a specific biblical text can enlighten and transform the reader through a threefold dialogical encounter. The two creation narratives (the priestly account in Gen. 1:1–2:4a and the Yahwist account in Gen. 2:4b–25) differ in many ways: the order of creation, the designation of God, the image of God, the method of creation, and so on. Like the disagreeing disciples of the Buddhist story, however, both are truth tellers. Due to limited space, I will focus on the texts describing the creation of human beings. Each story uniquely reveals various aspects about the truth of relationships between God and human beings and among human beings.

The priestly account briefly presents the creation of human beings in two verses (Gen. 1:26–27). God proposes the plan at the divine council: "Let us make 'adam in our image, after our likeness. They shall rule over the fish . . ." (1:26).[8] What is peculiar in God's speech is that God describes 'adam, a masculine singular noun denoting humankind, as a being more than one in number. God explains what the newly created 'adam will do by using a *plural* verb for 'adam: "they shall rule." More interestingly, in the subsequent summary report of the creation of 'adam, the narrator juxtaposes different "numbers" in describing 'adam: "God created 'adam in his image. In the image of God, he created *him. Male and female* he created *them*" (1:27, emphasis added). For the narrator, 'adam is "him," "them," and "male and female" all at once. Such awkward syntax intentionally presents the identity of 'adam as ambiguous and multifaceted. The ambiguity reveals both the distinctiveness and the interconnectedness of human beings: A human being, whether male or female, is individually unique, but all individuals share in "one" humanity; each constitutes a part of the one family of God.

The first creation story, furthermore, grounds the creation of humankind in God's image. Within two verses (vv. 26–27), the variations of "the image of God" appear four times. The awkward syntax noted above and the emphasis on "God's image" work together to manifest a powerful message: every person is related to God and to each other. Later, in presenting the genealogy of Adam, the priestly tradition makes this meaning clearer by applying the same expressions to Adam and his son. After repeating the first creation account about the creation of 'adam, male and female, in God's image (Gen. 5:1–2), the priestly genealogy states that Adam became the father of a son "in his likeness" and "after his image" (5:3). Though the patrilineal genealogy is reflective of patriarchal society, it is clearly inclusive. As God created 'adam, both male and female, in God's image (5:1–2), the descendants of Adam, both male and female, carry the image of Adam, who carries God's image.

The Yahwist creation account is more elaborate (2:4b–25). Except for the beginning two and a half verses, the account essentially focuses on the creation of human beings (2:7–25). After creating 'adam, God judges that "it is not good" for 'adam to be alone. This statement reminds the reader of the first creation story, in which God judges everything God created to be good (1:4, 10, 12, 18, 21, 25, 31). God decides to make a fitting companion for 'adam. God makes all kinds of animals and brings them to 'adam, who names each animal but finds no suitable companion among them. God creates woman from the side of 'adam and brings her to him. 'Adam exclaims: "This one, at last, is bone of my bones and flesh of my flesh!" 'Adam names her wo-man ('ishshah), because she is from the man ('ish). And for that reason, the narrator adds, the man leaves his parents and clings to his wo-man, and they become one flesh (2:24).

The Hebrew text of the Yahwist version consistently uses a singular form in reference to 'adam. Nevertheless, the identity of 'adam is not straightforward. Throughout the story, the Hebrew text almost always refers to the first human as 'adam. The term 'adam appears sixteen times, whereas 'ish appears only twice in the context of the relationship between man and woman. The text explains why 'adam names a new created being as woman: Wo-man came from man (2:23). It is obvious, then, that the second creation account also uses the term 'adam to denote not just "man" but "humankind." Unfortunately, most English Bibles have flattened out the distinction by rendering both 'adam and 'ish as "man" throughout the second creation narrative.

With its consistent use of the term 'adam, the second account reveals significant aspects about the nature of human beings. First, human beings participate in God's work. 'Adam names all the animals. It is also 'adam who names the newly created "wo-man." God embraces 'adam's judgment that none of the animals is a suitable companion. 'Adam should be more directly involved in creating the suitable companion. God had to make the new creature out of 'adam. In short, God creates new life with human beings. The Yahwist tradition repeats this same message when it describes Eve's remark at bearing her first child: "I created [qnh] a man ['ish] with [the help of] YHWH" (4:1).[9] As Adam represents all human beings, so also does Eve (hawwah), as the explanation of her name "mother of all living" suggests (3:20). In short, human beings participate in God's work, God's creation of life.

Second, human beings are to live together in community as most suitable companions to one another. The text reveals this message in multiple ways.

God's judgment will change from "not good" to "good" only when human beings find each other to be suitable companions. Hence, the story concludes with this remark: "Therefore a man leaves his father and his mother and clings to his woman, and they become one flesh" (Gen. 2:25). On one level, the story tells about a marriage between man and woman. Once a man outgrows his parents, he loves his suitable companion and begins a family with her. On another level, it speaks of the relationship shared by all human beings. In the Hebrew Bible, the term "flesh" is communal, with a wide range of meaning, from family (e.g., Gen. 29:14), to clan (e.g., Judg. 9:1–2), to township (e.g., Judg. 9:2), to nation or people (e.g., 2 Sam. 5:1). The Hebrew Bible uses the verb "to cling" to describe a passionate love. It refers to romantic love (e.g., Gen. 34:3) as well as to religious or unconditional love (e.g., Ps. 63:8). This same verb also describes an exclusive attitude of people who are "clinging together" just among their "in-group" members (Sir. 13:16). In light of this, I would paraphrase the concluding remark in Genesis 2:25 as follows: "Therefore people stop clinging to their own kind, find others to be their most suitable companions, and build a loving community together."

Third, the process of the creation of 'adam's suitable companion out of 'adam's side reveals that human beings are interrelated. Adam becomes a part of Eve (hawwah). Eve becomes a part of Adam. Both hawwah and 'adam represent humankind, as the etiological explanations of the Yahwist tradition suggests ('adam as the one who came from the earth, hawwah as the mother of all living in 3:19–20). Hence, the text intends to say that everyone is a part of everyone else. In a sense, everyone is a part of one interconnected body. This is precisely what is conveyed in the man's jubilant cry of kinship with the woman in 2:23a.

The two creation narratives, expressed through the limited constraints of context and language, are like a finger pointing to the biblical truth regarding the relationship between God and human beings. The authority of the creation accounts does not lie in their literary wordings or in any form of coercive commands. Rather, the authority lies in the text's power to transform the reader through revelatory encounter. The threefold dialogue with the creation accounts enlightens the reader to see God's image in everyone. The reader now sees that everyone is interrelated, and all belong to one family of God. The enlightenment transforms the reader to find in the Other the most suitable companion and to build a community of love and justice together.

Such transformation enables the reader to overcome the barriers that divide people. One will not see people with a different religion, race, ethnicity, gender, sexual orientation, or class as the feared or despised Other. For example, one will not perceive an Asian as perpetual foreigner or as yellow peril. One will not regard a woman as an object of man or inferior to man. Instead, the reader will recognize God's image in them and find in them a most suitable companion. The accounts' emphasis on the gift of companionship transforms and expands the reader's heart to embrace the differences among people as God's gift. For example, one will appreciate the Hindu tradition as a helpful tool that may lead one to a richer understanding of God and people. The Bible's emphasis on the interconnectedness of people enlightens the reader with the insight that any action toward others is in fact directed toward the self. This realization can transform people of violence and bigotry to people of justice and peace, since harm to the other causes harm to one's self. To care for the other is actually caring for one's self. One can be transformed to love others, bringing peace and justice to personal relationships, to society, and to the world.

A STORY OF CREATIVE LOVE, PEACE, AND JUSTICE

This vision of the Bible's transformative power is no abstract hope. I have had the pleasure of seeing people transformed by it. A few years ago, I led a workshop with Korean teenagers in a Catholic church in Los Angeles. The workshop addressed the same topic as this chapter, but was designed for the teenage audience. The three-evening workshop concluded with the participants' group presentations on their learning. One presentation was especially powerful in revealing how "biblical authority" is indeed transformative. The group came up with a skit about a young Korean American man and his African American girlfriend. They were confronted by severe opposition from the man's Korean parents about their decision to marry. The opposition in the skit revealed the deeply wounded relationship between Korean Americans and African Americans, as well as the painful reality of racism, sexism, classism, elitism, and ethnocentrism that this young generation had observed in their communities. Overcoming the obstacles, the couple marries and gives birth to a son who becomes the first "nonwhite" U.S. president. These kids, I hope, will continue reflecting on the transformative nature of the Bible and contribute to creating a better world for all God's creatures.

Notes

Introduction

1. See p. 147n5.
2. To resist the temptation to group the chapters according to various contextual criteria, they are simply presented in alphabetical order according to the author's last name.
3. *Webster's New Universal Unabridged Dictionary*, 2nd ed. (New York: Simon & Schuster, 1983).
4. *Webster's Seventh New Collegiate Dictionary* (Springfield, MA: G. & C. Merriam, 1969).

Chapter 1

1. I would like to thank Alan Lenzi, Jeff Leonard, Jon Levenson, Hindy Najman, Jeff Stackert, and Donald Kraus for their very helpful comments on earlier drafts of this essay.
2. In contrast, see the recent article by Benjamin D. Sommer, "The Source Critic and the Religious Interpreter," *Interpretation* 60 (2006): 9–20.
3. See M. H. Goshen-Gottstein, "Tanakh Theology: The Religion of the Old Testament and the Place of Jewish Biblical Theology," in *Ancient Israelite Religion: Essays in Honor of Frank Moore Cross*, ed. Patrick D. Miller et al. (Philadelphia: Fortress, 1987), 617–44; and Goshen-Gottstein, "Scriptural Authority (Judaism)," *ABD* 5.1017–21.
4. *Encyclopaedia Biblica*, 9 vols. (Jerusalem: Bialik Institute), 1950–88.
5. His essay "Why Jews Are Not Interested in Biblical Theology" is most accessible in Jon D. Levenson, *The Hebrew Bible, the Old Testament, and Historical Criticism* (Louisville, KY: Westminster/John Knox, 1993), 33–61. The reluctance of Jewish biblical scholars to write on theology is slowly changing. Among the Jewish scholars who have published in this area (in addition to myself) are Michael Fishbane, Stephen Geller, Tikva Frymer-Kensky, Isaac Kalimi, Joel Kaminsky, Israel Knohl, Jon D. Levenson, Yohanan Muffs, Benjamin Sommer, and Marvin Sweeney.
6. See my "Biblical History and Jewish Biblical Theology," *Journal of Religion* 77 (1997): 563–83; and "The Many Faces of God in Exodus 19," in *Jewish and Christian Biblical Theology*, ed. Joel Kaminsky and Alice O. Bellis (Atlanta: Scholars Press, 2000), 353–67.
7. Throughout this chapter, I will be using the term Bible to refer to the Hebrew Bible or Tanakh, since I am writing this explicitly from the perspective of my faith community.
8. *The Jewish Study Bible*, ed. Adele Berlin and Marc Zvi Brettler (New York: Oxford University Press, 2004).
9. Marc Zvi Brettler, *How to Read the Bible* (Philadelphia: Jewish Publication Society, 2005), 279–83.
10. On the role of biblical theology as connecting the biblical text and a community that regards that text as sacred, see, e.g., Otto Eissfeldt, "The History of Israelite-Jewish Religion and Old Testament Theology," in *The Flowering of Old Testament Theology: A Reader in Twentieth-Century Old Testament Theology, 1930–1990*, ed. Ben C. Ollenburger et al. (Winona Lake, IN: Eisenbrauns, 1992), 20–29, esp. p. 28.
11. *ABD* 5.1017–56.
12. Ibid., 1017.

13. For differing conceptions of the Mishnah as oral law, see Jacob Neusner, *Introduction to Rabbinic Literature*, ABRL (New York: Doubleday, 1994), 124–28. In greater detail, see Hindy Najman, *Seconding Sinai: The Development of Mosaic Discourse in Second Temple Judaism* (Leiden: Brill, 2003); Benjamin D. Sommer, "Unity and Plurality in Jewish Canons: The Case of the Oral and Written Torahs," in *One Scripture or Many? Canon from Biblical, Theological, and Philosophical Perspectives*, ed. Christine Helmer and Christof Landmesser (Oxford: Oxford University Press, 2004), 108–50.

14. Brettler, *How to Read the Bible*, 279–83.

15. Ibid., 280.

16. On the use of this term, see Sid Z. Leiman, *The Canonization of Hebrew Scripture: The Talmudic and Midrashic Evidence* (Hamden, CT: Archon, 1976), 57.

17. The canonization of the Bible remains a complex issue; see *The Canon Debate*, ed. Lee Martin McDonald and James A. Sanders (Peabody, MA: Hendrickson, 2002).

18. On the structure of the Jewish Bible, see Marc Zvi Brettler, "The Canonization of the Bible," in *The Jewish Study Bible*, 2072–77, esp. the comparative chart on p. 2076.

19. Meira Polliack, "Medieval Karaism," in *The Oxford Handbook of Jewish Studies*, ed. M. Goodman (Oxford: Oxford University Press, 2002), 295–326. For more details, see Polliack, *Karaite Judaism: A Guide to Its History and Literary Sources* (Leiden: Brill, 2003).

20. On the secondary status of the oral law, see David Weiss Halivni, *Peshat and Derash: Plain and Applied Meaning in Rabbinic Exegesis* (New York: Oxford University Press, 1991), 152.

21. By this I mean, e.g., the pentateuchal sources. I am not here referring to versions of the text that might be preserved in the Septuagint or Dead Sea Scrolls. As a Jew, the Hebrew Masoretic text is of paramount importance, though as a scholar I certainly emend texts with ancient versions (sometimes based on conjecture).

22. The term "holistic reading" is emphasized especially in the works of the Jewish Bible scholar Moshe Greenberg. The interest in combining both synchronic and diachronic approaches, however, is not uniquely Jewish. See, e.g., Eep Talstra, *Solomon's Prayer: Synchrony and Diachrony in the Composition of 1 Kings 8:14–61* (Kampen: Kok Pharaos, 1993); and Talstra, *Synchronic or Diachronic? A Debate on Method in Old Testament Exegesis*, OTS 34 (Leiden: Brill, 1995).

23. See the essays on "The Jewish Interpretation of the Bible," in *The Jewish Study Bible*, 1829–1919.

24. Simon Rawidowicz, *Studies in Jewish Thought* (Philadelphia: Jewish Publication Society, 1974), 45.

25. Gershom Scholem, *The Messianic Idea in Judaism* (New York: Schocken, 1971), 289.

26. The best survey of different methods used to approach the Hebrew Bible is John Barton, *Reading the Old Testament: Method in Biblical Study* (Louisville, KY: Westminster John Knox, 1996).

27. On the extreme interpretations found in midrashic literature, see James L. Kugel, "Two Introductions to Midrash," in *Midrash and Literature*, ed. Geoffrey H. Hartman and Sanford Budick (New Haven, CT: Yale University Press, 1986), 77–103.

28. For a compelling defense of the documentary hypothesis, see Ernest Nicholson, *The Pentateuch in the Twentieth Century: The Legacy of Julius Wellhausen* (Oxford: Oxford University Press, 1998).

29. This was the thesis of his dictionary article "Biblical Theology, Contemporary," *IDB* 1.418–32; reprinted in Krister Stendahl, *Meanings: The Bible as Document and as Guide* (Philadelphia: Fortress, 1984), 11–44.

30. Gerhard F. Hasel, "The Future of Old Testament Theology: Prospects and Trends," in *The Flowering of Old Testament Theology*, 378, but see also the more positive assessment in James Barr, *The Concept of Biblical Theology: An Old Testament Perspective* (Minneapolis: Fortress, 1999), 196–205.

31. On the last issue, see A. Brenner and F. van Dijk-Hemmes, *On Gendering Texts: Female and Male Voices in the Hebrew Bible* (Leiden: Brill, 1996).

32. I am speaking here from a Jewish perspective. Although rabbinic texts are often emended and textual criticism is practiced to some degree with rabbinic texts even in the traditional Jewish world, this is not the case with the Bible. It is difficult to imagine that

Ronald S. Hendel, *The Text of Genesis 1–11: Textual Studies and Critical Edition* (New York: Oxford University Press, 1998), which offers an eclectic text of Genesis 1–11, would be well received by the traditional Jewish community.

33. Though she uses different images, a similar point about relativizing biblical material is made in Tamar Ross, *Expanding the Palace of Torah: Orthodoxy and Feminism* (Waltham, MA: Brandeis University Press, 2004), 196.

34. This term, along with "creative historiography," was coined in Isaac Heinemann, *The Ways of Aggadah* (Jerusalem: Magnes Press, 1949) (Hebrew).

35. *Mekilta De-Rabbi Ishmael*, trans. Jacob Z. Lauterbach (Philadelphia: Jewish Publication Society, 1976), 3.17.

36. In actuality, two of the letters of this verse are printed larger than the other letters, but the traditional reasons given do not include highlighting the importance of this verse as a whole.

37. By using this criterion, for example, a Jew could justify printing Ps. 51:7 ("Indeed I was born with iniquity; with sin my mother conceived me"), a verse that to the best of my knowledge is never found in the liturgy, in a 3-point font, effectively ignoring it, while printing v. 17, "O LORD, open my lips, and let my mouth declare your praise," which is used to open the standard statutory prayer (the *amidah*) and recited three times a day, in a bold 36-point font.

38. This term, reflecting the Hebrew, is preferable to the postbiblical term "Ten Commandments," especially in a Jewish context, since Judaism views "I the LORD am your God," which is not a commandment, as the beginning of this work.

39. See Michael Fishbane, "Torah and Tradition," in *Tradition and Theology in the Old Testament*, ed. Douglas A. Knight (Philadelphia: Fortress, 1977), 279–80.

40. See Ephraim E. Urbach, *The Sages: Their Concepts and Beliefs* (Jerusalem: Magnes, 1975), 420–523.

41. Bernard Grossfeld, *The Targum Onqelos to Exodus* (Wilmington, DE: Michael Glazier, 1988), 54. Grossfeld's translation italicizes additions in the Targum, not found in the Hebrew. Targum Neofiti 1 has a similar addition; pseudo-Jonathan does not.

42. See Grossfeld, *Targum Onqelos*, 55, n. 2; and Moshe Weinfeld, *Deuteronomy 1–11*, AB 5 (New York: Doubleday, 1991), 299.

43. See Lee I. Levine, *The Ancient Synagogue* (New Haven, CT: Yale University Press, 2000), 502.

44. For some similar notions that emphasize the community rather than the divine, see Moshe Halbertal, *People of the Book: Canon, Meaning, and Authority* (Cambridge, MA: Harvard University Press, 1997).

45. This is, of course, just the reverse of how the great German biblical scholar Julius Wellhausen viewed biblical religion, which reached its zenith early, as reflected in the pentateuchal sources JE, and subsequently devolved, necessitating the development of Christianity.

Chapter 3

1. Dr. Charles B. Copher was the third African American to receive the PhD in Old Testament, which he earned at Boston University in 1947. See his *Black Biblical Studies: An Anthology of Charles B. Copher: Biblical and Theological Issues on the Black Presence in the Bible* (Chicago: Black Light Fellowship, 1993); and *The Recovery of Black Presence: An Interdisciplinary Exploration*, ed. Randall C. Bailey and Jacquelyn Grant (Nashville: Abingdon, 1995).

2. Latta R. Thomas, *Biblical Faith and the Black American* (Valley Forge, PA: Judson, 1976), 13.

3. Ibid., 143.

4. James H. Cone, *A Black Theology of Liberation* (Philadelphia: J. B. Lippincott, 1970), 66.

5. Traci C. West, *Disruptive Christian Ethics: When Racism and Women's Lives Matter* (Louisville, KY: Westminster John Knox, 2006), xvi.

6. *Livingkind* is a concept that Taliba Sikudhani Olugbala uses to indicate all living things— from humans to animals to plants and microorganisms, including "inanimate" components

of Earth (cited in Layli Phillips, *Womanism: On Its Own* [New York: Routledge & Kegan Paul, 2006], xxii).

7. Martin Luther King Jr., *Stride toward Freedom* (New York: Harper & Brothers, 1958), 136.
8. James H. Cone, *God of the Oppressed* (New York: Seabury, 1975), 81–82.
9. "In the thirty-three year period from 1883 to 1915, the annual toll of Negroes lynched never fell below 50 but once—in 1914, when the number was 49. In nine of these years the figures rose to more than a hundred" (Thomas F. Gossett, *Race: The History of an Idea in America* [Dallas: Southern Methodist Univ. Press, 1963], 269). Stewart Burns observes, "More than four thousand black citizens, almost all male, had been lynched since Reconstruction. Nearly a century after slavery's abolition, lynching was still the core of a violent system of social control that terrorized African Americans in the Deep South" (*To the Mountain Top* [Chapel Hill: Univ. of North Carolina Press, 2004], 10).
10. Wilson Harris, *Selected Essays of Wilson Harris*, ed. A. J. M. Bundy (New York: Routledge & Kegan Paul, 1999), 157–59.
11. For a detailed analytical discussion, see my chapter "Racism and Economics: The Perspective of Oliver C. Cox," in *Katie's Canon: Womanism and the Soul of the Black Community* (New York: Continuum, 1995), 144–61.

Chapter 4

1. From the *Santa Biblia* (the Reina Valera edition of 1602).
2. Based on Rom. 7:15.
3. The Apostolic Network is a late twentieth-century Christian organization that fosters evangelistic and programmatic work with a particular focus on family ministry. Led by "apostles," its ministry has a strongly biblical orientation and helps Christian groups organize under the Apostolic Network. Its loose organization differs from a denomination yet has a strong hierarchical ladder marked by differing levels of apostolic privileges and responsibilities.
4. There are numerous other references in the Torah with this affirmation from God (e.g., Lev. 19:33–34; Deut. 5:15).
5. I strongly encourage the reader to read the biblical texts of the examples and let my questions and comments play with the reader's templates and matrixes.
6. Insights into our template and matrix metaphors come from many places. I am grateful to Thomas Thangaraj, *Relating to People of Other Religions* (Nashville: Abingdon, 1997) and Wesley Ariarajah, *Not without My Neighbour* (Geneva: WCC Publications, 1999).
7. Analects of Confucius, bk. 14, chap. 36.
8. Delores Williams, *Sisters in the Wilderness* (Maryknoll, NY: Orbis, 1993).
9. Among others, see the works of Ivone Gebara, *Out of the Depths* (Minneapolis: Fortress, 2002); Elsa Tamez, *Bible of the Oppressed* (Maryknoll, NY: Orbis, 1982).
10. For a discussion on Spiritism in the Caribbean, see Carlos F. Cardoza-Orlandi, "Vodou, Santería, and Spiritism," in the *Encyclopedia of Women and Religion in North America*, ed. Rosemary Skinner Keller and Rosemary Radford Ruether (Bloomington: Indiana Univ. Press, 2005), 732–38.
11. Walter Mignolo defines pluritopic hermeneutics in the following way: "Contrary to the monotopic understanding of philosophical hermeneutics, colonial semiosis presupposes more than one tradition and, therefore, demands a diatopic or pluritopic hermeneutic, a concept I borrow from Raimundo Pannikar" (*The Darker Side of the Renaissance: Literacy, Territoriality and Colonization* [Ann Arbor: Univ. of Michigan Press, 1995], 11). In other words, multiple interpretations of the text and our social locations need to be embraced, though they will not always be coherent. When interpretations collide, biblical authority does not call for an exclusion of one at the expense of others but enjoins us to be patient and to live faithfully in the complexity of the tensions of embodied biblical interpretations.

Chapter 5

1. Augustine, *Confessions* 12.14.17 (author's translation).
2. *Mishnah Avot* 5.22.
3. The image is cited by Thomas Cranmer (1549) in his first Book of Homilies for the newly reformed Church of England. See his "A Fruitful Exhortation to the Reading and Knowl-

edge of Holy Scripture," in *Sermons or Homilies Appointed to Be Read in Church in the Time of Queen Elizabeth of Famous Memory* (New York: T. & J. Swords, 1815), 5–6.

4. George Steiner, *Real Presences* (Cambridge: Cambridge University Press, 1986), 19.

5. The notion of charity toward the text is developed by Moshe Halbertal, *People of the Book: Canon, Meaning, and Authority* (Cambridge, MA: Harvard University Press, 1997). While we have different immediate frames of religious reference (his is Orthodox Judaism), our views are broadly compatible.

6. See Ellen F. Davis, "Critical Traditioning: Seeking an Inner Biblical Hermeneutic," in *The Art of Reading Scripture*, ed. Ellen F. Davis and Richard B. Hays (Grand Rapids: Eerdmans, 2003), 163–80.

7. "A good poem reminds us of love because it cannot be written or read in distraction" (Wendell Berry, "The Responsibility of the Poet," in Berry, *What Are People For?* [New York: North Point Press], 90).

8. On the notion of "productive uncertainty," see Ellen F. Davis, "Beginning with Ruth: An Essay on Translating," in *Scrolls of Love: Reading Ruth and the Song of Songs*, ed. Peter S. Hawkins and Lesleigh Cushing Stahlberg (New York: Fordham Univ. Press, 2006), 9–19.

9. Dante, *Paradiso*, XXXIII:145 (trans. John D. Sinclair, *The Divine Comedy of Dante Alighieri* [New York: Oxford University Press], 3.484).

Chapter 6

1. See *Constitutions, Bylaws, and Continuing Resolutions: Evangelical Lutheran Church in America* (1987), 2.03: "This church accepts the canonical Scriptures of the Old and New Testaments as the inspired Word of God and the authoritative source and norm of its proclamation, faith, and life." I believe that there is no peculiarly Lutheran understanding of the Bible, though Lutherans will, in the practice of interpretation, commonly reflect certain characteristic emphases (e.g., law and gospel). Obviously, not all Lutherans agree on matters relating to the authority of the Bible.

2. The "answer" to this point is "Often, but not always!" I recall in particular a kind of semi-legalism that pervaded the practice of our faith, standing in no little tension with traditional Lutheran emphases.

3. And not, say, by arguments on its behalf, though such reflections are, finally, important in spelling out what is entailed in speaking of biblical authority.

4. For an analysis of the characteristics of the current context that have problemized issues relating to the authority of the Bible, see Terence Fretheim and Karlfried Froehlich, *The Bible as Word of God in a Postmodern Age* (Minneapolis: Fortress, 1998; repr., Eugene, OR: Wipf & Stock, 2002), 81–87. I would emphasize even more strongly today that the Bible's own content creates major problems for contemporary views of its authority (e.g., its violence).

5. This is not the context for carrying out that discussion. But an example of a question to be explored would be, "Does God always get God's will done by working in and through human beings?"

6. See Terence E. Fretheim, "Is the Biblical Portrayal of God Always Trustworthy?" in Fretheim and Froehlich, *The Bible as Word of God*, 97–111.

7. For an earlier discussion, see Terence E. Fretheim, "Some Reflections on Brueggemann's God," in *God in the Fray: A Tribute to Walter Brueggemann*, ed. Tod Linafelt and Timothy K. Beal (Minneapolis: Fortress, 1998), 36–37.

8. New Testament examples would include Peter's sermon in Acts 2:14–36 and the passion narratives.

9. Most interpreters implicitly acknowledge these differences of value, seen primarily in their usage of the texts. For example, Psalm 23 has greater value than Paul's advice to Timothy to take a little wine for the sake of his stomach (1 Tim. 5:23), as do the Ten Commandments compared to the command not to wear clothing made of two different materials (Lev. 19:19; Deut. 22:11).

10. A time-honored rule of thumb, championed by Augustine, for interpreting and adjudicating texts is: *Let Scripture interpret Scripture*. That is, readers are to interpret difficult texts in view of other, clearer texts. This interpretive process is helpful, but has often proceeded in

a harmonistic way so that the difficult issues are, finally, explained away. Theological diversity in the Bible should be allowed to stand. Such an approach also tends to flatten out Scripture by not recognizing the evaluative pattern in Scripture already noted: Scripture may interpret itself *against* itself in view of a diversity of perspectives on any number of issues, even theological issues. We have learned to work this way with such social-order issues as slavery and patriarchy, lifting up the larger scriptural message about freedom and equality (e.g., Gal. 3:28) and, rather than engaging in harmonizing efforts, have determined that certain texts take priority over others. Because the Bible does not have a single point of view on a wide range of matters, a certain amount of picking and choosing will be *inevitable* in forging a biblically based perspective, recognized or not.

11. Darrell Jodock makes the point clearly: "Voices claiming the Bible as their authority advocate widely differing views" on a considerable range of ethical and theological matters (*The Church's Bible: Its Contemporary Authority* [Minneapolis: Fortress, 1989], ix). "Scriptural authority is not foundational. . . . [D]isagreements about the Bible are as much the symptoms as they are the causes of disunity" (ibid., 5). I wonder whether they are not more symptom than cause.

12. Among efforts I have made to come to terms with this issue, see: "'I Was Only a Little Angry': Divine Violence in the Prophets," *Interpretation* 58 (2004): 365–75; and my "God and Violence in the Old Testament," *Word & World* 24 (2004): 18–28.

13. This article is closely related to another essay of mine, "The Authority of the Bible and Churchly Debates Regarding Sexuality," *Word & World* 26 (2006): 365–75. The literature on biblical authority is immense, including Walter Brueggemann, *The Book That Breathes New Life: Scriptural Authority and Biblical Theology* (Minneapolis: Fortress, 2005); N. T. Wright, *Last Word: Beyond the Bible Wars to a New Understanding of the Authority of Scripture* (San Francisco: Harper, 2005); Alan G. Padgett and Patrick R. Keifert, eds., *Is It All True? The Bible and the Question of Truth* (Grand Rapids: Eerdmans, 2006); Peter Enns, *Inspiration and Incarnation: Evangelicals and the Problem of the Old Testament* (Grand Rapids: Baker, 2005). An especially helpful discussion of biblical authority is that of Jodock, *The Church's Bible*.

Chapter 7

1. Of course, these theologians also hedged the notion of knowing God with many precautions.

2. The translation is feeble, but *treiben* is impossible to translate into English.

3. Thus Luther's remark about James, that it was much straw and little gold, was comparative, not qualitative.

4. It should be noted that these arguments are almost always historically bogus.

5. This effort was brought to a halt by the Thirty Years' War, which dispersed the German university faculties.

6. For any given thing, there is the "material cause," the "effective cause," the "formal cause," and the "final cause" (see below). Of them, only "effective causes" are what modernity calls "causes."

7. The question of natural theology was important for these theologians, but it can be elided here.

8. Note the refrain of the Old Testament that the Spirit of the Lord "falls" on someone, who in consequence "prophesies," and the claim of the New Testament that the apostolic preaching is given by the Spirit.

9. I have myself provided some of these latter proposals.

10. It may be noted that this is now the official Catholic position; see Vatican II's *Dei Verbum*.

11. Why persons who do not believe the church's gospel bother to study Scripture at all (or as they call it "biblical literature") is one of those puzzles brought on by the present disestablishment of the church.

12. A title invented by the secular academy, which suits neither the Jews' nor the Christians' relation to the Tanakh.

13. Pastoral consumers of "contemporary" music might ask themselves what its rhythms emulate. The rock band on the podium may be in itself a repudiation of Scripture's authority.

14. In Reformation language, the *norma normans non normata*.
15. Strictly, the primary text of sermons in a communion that follows a lectionary should be the Old Testament selection.

Chapter 8

1. Editor's note: One of the most significant biblical interpreters of the second century CE, Marcion of Pontus, maintained that the only canonical writings were the Pauline epistles (without the Pastorals) and a shortened version of the Gospel of Luke.

Chapter 9

1. See Sigmund Freud, "The Unconscious," *The Freud Reader*, ed. Peter Gay (New York: Norton, 1989), 572–83.
2. See Claude Levi-Strauss, *Elementary Structures of Kinship*, trans. James Harle Bell et al. (Boston: Beacon, 1969); Mary Douglas, *Purity and Danger: An Analysis of Concepts of Pollution and Taboo* (London and New York: Routledge, 2002); Clifford Geertz, *Interpretation of Cultures: Selected Essays* (New York: Basic Books, 1973).
3. Ludwig Wittgenstein, *Philosophical Investigations* (Cambridge: Blackwell, 1997).
4. John Calvin, *Institutes of the Christian Religion*, ed. John T. McNeill, trans. Ford Lewis Battles, Library of Christian Classics (Philadelphia: Westminster, 1960), 1.6.1.
5. See Hans Frei's description of this hermeneutical approach in *The Eclipse of the Biblical Narrative* (New Haven, CT: Yale Univ. Press, 1974). There are several places where Frei describes this hermeneutic in general. With regard to Calvin, see pp. 18–26. In the latter case, Frei notes that "the text fitly rendered what it talked about in two ways for Calvin. It was in the first place a proper (literal or figurative) rather than allegorical description of the world or reality it narrated. But in the second place it rendered that reality itself to the reader, making the reality accessible to him through its narrative web. . . . Through the coincidence or even identity between a world being depicted and its reality being rendered to the reader . . . , the reader or hearer in turn becomes part of that depicted reality and thus has to take a personal or life stance toward it. For Calvin . . . not the act of recital or preaching of a text, but the cumulative pattern constituting the biblical narrative . . . is the setting forth of the reality which simultaneously constitutes its effective rendering to the reader by the Spirit. . . . It is the effective rendering of God and his real world to the reader by way of the text's appropriate depiction of the intercourse of that God and that world, engaging the reader's mind, heart, and activity" (pp. 24–25).

Chapter 10

1. The clearest example of how Wesley read a text in this way is his interpretation of passages that contain language used in a doctrine of predestination.
2. Richard T. De George, *The Nature and Limits of Authority* (Lawrence: Univ. Press of Kansas, 1985).
3. This idea and sometimes the exact phrase have a long history. In the controversy about infallibility, the area of the Bible's authority is sometimes argued to extend to other matters, such as history and science, but that extension is predicated on the need to safeguard the Bible's reliability about salvation.

Chapter 11

1. This language comes from the Confession of 1967 and is oft-quoted in Presbyterian circles to speak of the witness of Scripture. "The one sufficient revelation of God is Jesus Christ, the Word of God incarnate, to whom the Holy Spirit bears unique and authoritative witness through the Holy Scriptures" (*The Constitution of the Presbyterian Church (U.S.A.)*, Part I, *Book of Confessions*, 9.27).
2. Alex Ross, "Learning the Score: Why Brahms Belongs in the Classroom," *New Yorker*, September 4, 2006, 88. The book Ross discusses is Maxine Greene's *Releasing the Imagination: Essays on Education, the Arts, and Social Change* (San Francisco: Jossey-Bass, 1995, 2000).

3. Francine Prose, *"Middlemarch*: Juvenile Pleasure, Grown-up Insight," *All Things Considered*, September 7, 2006. Text available at http://www.npr.org/templates/story/story.php?storyId=5776481.
4. John Calvin, *Institutes of the Christian Religion*, ed. John T. McNeill, trans. Ford Lewis Battles, Library of Christian Classics (Philadelphia: Westminster, 1960), 1.6.1.
5. I am indebted to Beverly Gaventa for directing me to this poem. She includes it in her essay on the role of joy in Reformed biblical interpretation, "To Glorify God and Enjoy God Forever: A Place for Joy in Reformed Readings of Scripture," in *Reformed Theology: Identity and Ecumenicity II: Biblical Interpretation in the Reformed Tradition*, ed. Michael Welker and Wallace M. Alston Jr. (Grand Rapids: Eerdmans, forthcoming).
6. Brian K. Blount, "The Last Word on Authority," in Walter Brueggemann, William C. Placher, and Brian K. Blount, *Struggling with Scripture* (Louisville, KY: Westminster John Knox, 2002), 68.
7. NJPS translation, slightly modified, with my emphasis added.
8. For more on the dynamics of divine presence and absence in Ezekiel, see John Kutsko, *Between Heaven and Earth: Divine Presence and Absence in the Book of Ezekiel*, Biblical and Judaic Studies 7 (Winona Lake, IN: Eisenbrauns, 2000).
9. Angela Russell Christman, *"What Did Ezekiel See?" Christian Exegesis of Ezekiel's Vision of the Chariot from Irenaeus to Gregory the Great*, Bible in Ancient Christianity 4 (Leiden; Boston: Brill, 2005), 63–98.
10. "I prefer to talk about those who *benefit from* authority rather than those who are *subject to* authority" (Sarah Heaner Lancaster, *Women and the Authority of Scripture: A Narrative Approach* [Harrisburg, PA: Trinity Press International, 2002], 162–63).

Chapter 12

1. Pope Pius XII expressed this relationship between the sacred text and the incarnation in his encyclical *Divino Afflante Spiritu*, par. 20: "For as the substantial Word of God became like to men in all things, 'except sin' (Heb 4:15), so the words of God, expressed in human language, are made like to human speech in every respect except error." The Second Vatican Council expressed the same sentiment in its Dogmatic Constitution on Divine Revelation, *Dei Verbum*, par. 13: "For the words of God, expressed in human language, have become like unto human speech, just as the Word of the eternal Father, when he took on himself the flesh of human weakness, became like unto human beings." The *Catechism of the Catholic Church* (New York: Catholic Book, 1994), number 101, repeats this quotation from the Council. For the text of the *Divino Afflante Spiritu* and *Dei Verbum*, see *The Scripture Documents: An Anthology of Official Catholic Teachings*, ed. and trans. Dean P. Béchard, S.J. (Collegeville, MN: Liturgical Press, 2002).
2. In addition to the Second Vatican Council's Dogmatic Constitution on Divine Revelation, *Dei Verbum*, see the suggestive study of Sandra M. Schneiders, *The Revelatory Text: Interpreting the New Testament as Sacred Scripture* (New York: HarperCollins, 1991).
3. *Dei Verbum*, par. 2.
4. On the concept of inspiration, see Paul J. Achtemeier, *The Inspiration of Scripture: Problems and Proposals* (Philadelphia: Westminster, 1980); Raymond E. Collins, *Introduction to the New Testament* (Garden City, NY: Doubleday, 1983), 317–55; and Luis Alonso Schökel, *The Inspired Word: Scripture in the Light of Language and Literature* (New York: Herder & Herder, 1965).
5. Schneiders (*The Revelatory Text*, 44) notes that revelation and inspiration are closely related to each other because both "are concerned with God's relation to the content of the Bible." She then notes that inerrancy, authority, and normativity "concern the relation of the content to the readers."
6. *Dei Verbum*, par. 11.
7. *Dei Verbum*, par. 11, expresses the salvific purpose of divine revelation: "Therefore, since everything asserted by the inspired authors or sacred writers should be regarded as asserted by the Holy Spirit, it follows that we must acknowledge the Books of Scripture as teaching firmly, faithfully, and without error the truth that God wished to be recorded in the sacred writings *for the sake of our salvation*" (emphasis added).

8. On the canon, see Bruce M. Metzger, *The Canon of the New Testament: Its Origin, Development, and Significance* (Oxford: Clarendon Press, 1987); Collins, *Introduction to the New Testament*, 1–40.

9. The Muratorian Fragment, discovered and named after Lodovico Antonio Muratori, provides a list of books recognized as authoritative by the end of the second century. The list already included the Gospels, the Acts of the Apostles, the Pauline Letters, Jude, two letters of John, and Revelation. The final shape of the canon was set forth in the *Thirty-ninth Festal Letter* of Athanasius in 367 CE.

10. Schökel, *The Inspired Word*, 53.

11. "The Interpretation of the Bible in the Church," in Joseph A. Fitzmyer, *The Biblical Commission's Document "The Interpretation of the Bible in the Church": Text and Commentary*, Subsidia biblica 18 (Rome: Editrice Pontificio Istituto Biblico, 1995), 104.

12. Ibid., 37.

13. Gerald O'Collins, S. J., *Christology: A Biblical, Historical, and Systematic Study of Jesus* (Oxford: Oxford University Press, 1995), 187.

Chapter 13

1. This chapter is written in tribute to James Luther Mays, who, as teacher and scholar, has modeled for me and many others "the ministry of exegesis."

2. E.g., the "Westminster Larger Catechism," 5: "The Scriptures principally teach, what man is to believe concerning God, and what duty God requires of man" (*The Constitution of the Presbyterian Church (U.S.A.)*, Part I, *Book of Confessions* [Louisville, KY: Office of the General Assembly, 2002], 7.115), henceforth referenced as *BC*.

3. In what follows, emphasis will be placed on how these considerations are informed by biblical witnesses themselves and are represented in Reformed theological tradition. Of course, in each case there is much more that could and should be said. See, e.g., Paul J. Achtemeier, *The Inspiration and Authority of Scripture* (Peabody, MA: Hendrickson, 1999); David L. Bartlett, *The Shape of Scriptural Authority* (Philadelphia: Fortress, 1983); Robert Gnuse, *The Authority of the Bible: Theories of Inspiration, Revelation and the Canon of Scripture* (Mahwah, NJ: Paulist, 1985); and idem, "Authority of the Bible," *DBI* 1.87–91.

4. E.g., Job 12:7–12; 28; Pss. 8; 119:89–91; Prov. 8:22–36; Matt. 6:25–34; cf. Sir. 1:1–10.

5. E.g., Isa. 1:2–3; Jer. 24:7; Ezek. 12:2–3; John 1:10–13; Rom. 1:18–23. Cf. John Calvin, *Institutes* 1.5.1–15 (Calvin: *Institutes of the Christian Religion*, ed. John T. McNeill, trans. Ford Lewis Battles, Library of Christian Classics [Philadelphia: Westminster, 1960], 1.51–69).

6. Deut. 29:4 [3] (author's trans.); cf. Ps. 95:7–10; Eccl. 8:16–17; Isa. 6:9–13; Jer. 5:20–29; 31:33–34; Mark 8:14–21; 1 Cor. 1:20–21.

7. E.g., Deut. 4:15–19; Isa. 40:12–23; Jer. 10:1–16; Acts 17:16–31; Rom. 1:24–25.

8. E.g., Deut. 8:11–20; 32:28–35; 2 Kgs. 18:28–35; Ps. 53:1–4 [2–5]; Isa. 10:5–19; Amos 6:1–8; Jonah 4; Matt. 5:43–48; Luke 18:9–14. Cf. Calvin, *Institutes* 1.5.5; 1.14.1; 2.2.11 (trans. Battles, 1.56–58, 159–61, 268–70); also *John Calvin's Sermons on the Ten Commandments*, trans. and ed. Benjamin W. Farley (Grand Rapids: Baker, 1980), 65–80.

9. E.g., Pss. 19; 100; Jer. 9:23–24; 2 Tim. 3:16–17. Cf. Calvin, *Institutes* 2.2.12–17 (trans. Battles, vol. 1:270–77).

10. Calvin, *Institutes* I.6.3 (trans. Battles, vol. 1:72). Cf. the "Westminster Confession of Faith," 1.1 (*BC*, 6.001).

11. See, e.g., Calvin, *Institutes* 1.13.7 (trans. Battles, vol. 1:129): "Certainly, when God's word is set before us in Scripture it would be the height of absurdity to imagine a merely fleeting and vanishing utterance. . . . Rather, 'Word' means the everlasting Wisdom, residing with God, from which both all oracles and all prophecies go forth." Cf. also "The Second Helvetic Confession" (*BC*, 5.001): "We believe and confess the canonical Scriptures of the holy prophets and apostles of both Testaments to be the true Word of God, and to have sufficient authority of themselves, not of men. For God himself spoke to the fathers, prophets, apostles, and still speaks to us through the Holy Scriptures."

12. E.g., the prologue to Sirach; 1 Macc. 12:9; Matt. 5:17–20; Rom. 1:2; 3:2; 2 Pet. 1:20–21; Philo, *De vita contemplativa* 28; *Mishnah Yadaim* 3.5.
13. Calvin, *Institutes* 1.7.1; 4.8.9 (trans. Battles, vol. 1:74–75, 2:1155). Cf. "The Scots Confession," 19 (*BC*, 3.19): "We affirm, therefore, that those who say the Scriptures have no other authority save that which they have received from the Kirk are blasphemous against God and injurious to the true Kirk, which always hears and obeys the voice of her own Spouse and Pastor, but takes not upon her to be mistress over the same."
14. E.g., Deut. 18:18–22; 2 Sam. 7:4; 1 Kgs. 13:1, 5, 9; Jer. 1:2, 4; Ezek. 33:1; 34:1; John 3:34; Acts 4:31; Heb. 1:1. Cf. Walter Klassen, "Inspiration of the Bible," *DBI* 1.543–45, with bibliography.
15. Cf. Isa. 55:10–11; Jer. 1:9–10; 1 Pet. 1:23.
16. Cf., e.g., Babylonian Talmud, *Berakot* 31b; *Yebamot* 71a. Augustine and especially Calvin explain divine communication through the limited medium of human language as condescension or "accommodation," e.g., *Institutes* 1.17.13; 2.16.2 (trans. Battles, vol. 1:227, 504–5). Cf. Ford Lewis Battles, "God Was Accommodating Himself to Human Capacity," *Interpretation* 31 (1977): 19–38.
17. Karl Barth, *Church Dogmatics: The Doctrine of the Word of God*, I/2, trans. G. T. Thomson and Harold Knight (Edinburgh: T. & T. Clark, 1994), 463. See also one of Barth's seminal contributions to "incarnational" hermeneutics, *The Word of God and the Word of Man*, trans. Douglas Horton (New York: Harper & Brothers, 1957).
18. Babylonian Talmud, *'Erubin* 13b.
19. Cf. Calvin, *Institutes* 2.10–11; "The Westminster Larger Catechism," Questions 31–35 (*BC*, 7.141–45).
20. Gen. 1; Deut. 4:9–14; 9:10; 18:18–19; John 1:1–5, 14; Heb. 1:1; cf. Sir. 24:8–12.
21. E.g., Num. 12:1–9; Jer. 28; 1 Cor. 6:1–11; cf. *Mishnah 'Abot* 5.17–18.
22. E.g., Exod. 19–20; 34; Deut. 5; 34:10–12; Josh. 1:1–9; Ezra 7; Mal. 4:4 [3:22]; *Mishnah 'Abot* 1.1. "Torah" itself is a unifying and prioritizing concept, encompassing already in its written, pentateuchal form a great variety of literary components and thematic contents.
23. E.g., Exod. 3:7–4:17; 33:12–34:9; Num. 11:1–15; Deut. 3:23–27. Cf. also Gen. 18:22–23; Pss. 4; 74; Jer. 12:1–4. On the attribution of Job to Moses, see Babylonian Talmud, *Baba Bathra* 14b.
24. E.g., Matt. 23:1–36; John 7:40–52; Acts 15:1–21; 1 Cor. 11:17–34; Gal. 2.
25. E.g., Matt. 5:17–20; John 7:14–24; Gal. 3:6–14; James 2:14–26. As a unifying and prioritizing concept of the New Testament, the lordship of "Jesus Christ" is a counterpart to "Torah" in Jewish Scriptures (see n. 22 above), but there is no unanimous or common "Christology" among the New Testament witnesses.
26. *De doctrina* I.1 (*Teaching Christianity/De Doctrina Christiana*, trans. Edmund Hill, O.P., ed. John E. Rotelle, O.S.A., The Works of Saint Augustine: A Translation for the 21st Century I/11 [Hyde Park, NY: New City Press, 1996], 106).
27. Though Augustine does not make specific use of the image in this context, his accountable interpreter resembles the prophetic watchman or "sentinel" depicted in Ezek. 3:16–21 and 33:1–9.
28. *De doctrina* III.2–5, 38 (trans. Hill, 169–70, 186). Cf. Calvin, *Institutes* 4.17.23–25 (trans. Battles, vol. 2:1388–92); and, with somewhat different emphasis, "The Westminster Confession of Faith," 1.9 (*BC*, 6.009): "The infallible rule of interpretation of Scripture, is the Scripture itself; and therefore, when there is a question about the true and full sense of any scripture (which is not manifold, but one), it may be searched and known by other places that speak more clearly."
29. *De doctrina* I.40–41 (trans. Hill, 124). Christian teaching and preaching are specifically treated in *De doctrina* book IV.
30. See Irene Lancaster, *Deconstructing the Bible: Abraham ibn Ezra's Introduction to the Torah* (London: RoutledgeCurzon, 2003).
31. For a largely negative and, I think, severely limited view of "rationalist biblical criticism," see Roy A. Harrisville and Walter Sundberg, *The Bible in Modern Culture: Theology and Historical-Critical Method from Spinoza to Käsemann* (Grand Rapids: Eerdmans, 1995), esp.

pp. 25–31. Two particularly influential perspectives on the impact of the Enlightenment are those of Hans Frei, *The Eclipse of Biblical Narrative: A Study of Eighteenth and Nineteenth Century Hermeneutics* (New Haven, CT: Yale University Press, 1974); and Stephen Toulmin, *Cosmopolis: The Hidden Agenda of Modernity* (Chicago: University of Chicago Press, 1990).

32. Ibn Ezra's incisive identification of human rationality as the true angelic agent of interpretation occurs in the context of his critique of "those who fabricate from their minds mystical explanations" in preference to a text's "plain meaning and the normal function [of the wording]" (Lancaster, *Deconstructing the Bible*, 158–59). For Calvin's critiques of theological interpretation based on allegorical excesses, see, e.g., *Institutes* 1.13.22; 2.5.19; 4.17.15 (trans. Battles 1.147–48, 339–40; 2.1376–78).

33. E.g., "The Shorter Catechism" (*BC*, 7.090): "That the Word may become effectual to salvation we must attend thereunto with diligence, preparation, and prayer; receive it with faith and love; lay it up in our hearts; and practice it in our lives."

34. E.g., Gen. 12:1–3; Exod. 3:1–12; Deut. 26:16–19; Jer. 1:1–10; Matt. 28:16–20; Acts 9:1–22. On "hearing" and "doing" as interrelated responses to God's commanding presence, see Exod. 19:8; 24:3; Deut. 6:1–9; James 1:22–25; 2:14–26.

35. *De doctrina* I.20–30 (trans. Hill, 114–19). Cf. Lev. 19:18; Deut. 6:4–5; Matt. 22:34–40; Mark 12:28–34; Luke 10:25–28; John 13:34–35; 1 Tim. 1:5.

36. E.g., Deut. 10:12–22; Mic. 6:6–8; Matt. 7:12; John 21:15–19.

Chapter 14

1. See www.etext.virginia.edu/journals/tr/ and www.etext.lib.virginia.edu/journals/jsrforum/

2. David Weiss Halivni, *Peshat and Derash: Plain and Applied Meaning in Rabbinic Exegesis* (Oxford: Oxford University Press, 1990); and Halivni, *Revelation Restored: Divine Writ and Critical Responses* (Boulder, CO: Westview Press, 1997).

3. "Some give another reason why the dots are inserted. Ezra reasoned thus: If Elijah comes and asks, 'Why have you written these words?' [why have you included these suspect passages?], I shall answer, 'That is why I dotted these passages.' And if he says to me, 'You have done well in having written them,' I shall erase the dots over them" (*Bamidbar Rabbah* III.13).

4. Michael Fishbane, *Biblical Interpretation in Ancient Israel* (Oxford: Oxford University Press, 1985), 322.

5. In similar fashion, Tikvah Frymer-Kensky examines ways in which verses of the Five Books of Moses reinterpret other verses, for example, those in which Moses himself restates God's words. She suggests that the written Torah problematizes any notion that individual verses have the status of revealed text independently of their relation to the whole of the written Torah. See, for example, Frymer-Kensky, "Revelation Revealed, The Doubt of Torah," *Textual Reasonings, Jewish Philosophy, and Text Study at the End of the Twentieth Century*, ed. Peter Ochs and Nancy Levene (Grand Rapids: Eerdmans, 2002), 68–75.

6. Halivni, *Revelation Restored*, 2. The Babylonian Talmud (*Taanit* 28b), for example, observes that the traditional day for mourning the beginning of the destruction of the Temple, the seventeenth day of Tammuz, contradicts the text of Jer. 52:6, which identifies the day as the ninth of Tammuz. The Jerusalem Talmud (*Taanit* 68c) calls the difference a result of "an error in calculation" within the biblical text, not the traditional practice. Another example is Lev. 16:23, which the Babylonian Talmud (*Yoma* 32a) suggests is out of order and should be 16:28. Another is an apparent "interweaving of sections" of Exod. 22:8, 24 (according to Babylonian Talmud, *Baba Kama* 107a). Another is the apparent "emendations of the scribes," who, according to the midrash *Bereshit Rabbah* 49:7, wrote "Abraham stood before the Lord" (Gen. 18:22, which actually has the divine presence standing before Abraham). For many more examples, see Halivni, *Revelation Restored*, 36–44.

7. David Weiss Halivni, *The Book and the Sword: A Life of Learning in the Shadow of Destruction* (New York: Farrar, Straus & Giroux, 1996), 164.

A sensitive survivor—and particularly one who has the opportunity or the leisure to pursue intellectual activity—must work . . . under the influence of mutually contradictory forces. . . . The Shoah signifies that whatever one considered the pattern of life one should choose—the ideal standard—collapsed. . . . Something must be changed. . . . On the other hand, the person who has survived, and has been wounded so deeply, needs that support, that holding-on-to, which only tradition can provide. "Though he slay me, yet I will trust in Him" (Job 13:15). . . . That mankind could sink so low and inflict this kind of violence upon children: one must react to this spiritually. And at the same time, one must seek spiritual solace. . . .

On the one hand, . . . not criticizing the past is being like those who justify. . . . On the other hand, if you acknowledge the wrong [in God and tradition that is!], then you run the risk of cutting off the branch on which you rest. . . . Therefore the struggle this person has is the struggle to do both: to find a way of criticizing tradition, but of holding steadfastly to it. Criticizing affirms that something went wrong—badly wrong, deeply wrong. Yet there must be something to come home to. . . . Personally, I found this balance in the critical study of Jewish texts, in a combination of criticism and belief in the divine origin of the text.

8. *The Book and the Sword*, 164.
9. *Revelation Restored*, 82–85.
10. Steven Kepnes, *The Text as Thou: Martin Buber's Dialogical Hermeneutics and Narrative Theology* (Bloomington: Indiana University Press, 1992).
11. Cited in Michael Fishbane, "Extra-Biblical Exegesis: The Sense of Not-Reading in Rabbinic Midrash," in *The Return to Scripture in Judaism and Christianity: Essays in Postcritical Scriptural Interpretation*, ed. Peter Ochs (New York: Paulist, 1993), 182–83.

Chapter 15

1. Peter DeVries, *The Blood of the Lamb* (Boston: Little, Brown, 1961; New York: Penguin Books, 1987). The parenthetical references in this paragraph are to the Penguin edition.
2. Roderick Jellema, *Peter DeVries* (Grand Rapids: Eerdmans, 1966), uses the notion of "reverse pilgrimage" as a unifying theme for his perceptive study of DeVries.
3. Peter DeVries, *The Mackeral Plaza* (Boston: Little, Brown, 1958), 259.
4. There were resources in the tradition of Dutch Calvinism to find a path between obscurantist piety and worldly sophistication, notably John Calvin himself, Herman Bavinck, and others. On Calvin, see Kathryn Greene-McCreight, "'We Are Companions of the Patriarchs' or Scripture Absorbs Calvin's World," in *Theology and Scriptural Imagination*, ed. L. Gregory Jones and James J. Buckley (Oxford: Blackwell, 1998), 51–62. For later Dutch Calvinist resources, see Herman Bavinck, *Our Reasonable Faith: A Survey of Christian Doctrine*, trans. Henry Zylstra (Grand Rapids: Baker, 1956), and G. C. Berkhouwer, *Holy Scripture*, trans. Jack C. Rogers (Grand Rapids: Eerdmans, 1975).
5. They are and remain human words, of course, but in those human words God somehow speaks. "Docetic" views of Scripture and mechanical and artificial accounts of its inspiration never held any attraction for me. Docetism played an important role in the christological controversies of the early church; it denied the real humanity of Jesus, insisting that he only seemed to be human. Analogously, "docetic" views of Scripture minimize the significance of the real humanity of the words of Scripture. Mechanical views of inspiration (that God simply dictated the words to the human writers, for example) seem to me to be "docetic." Whether my father intended it so or not, I took this simple remark to be a permission to consider as carefully as I could the human words, in the confidence that such attention was the best way to hear the Word of God.
6. David Kelsey, *The Uses of Scripture in Recent Theology* (Philadelphia: Fortress, 1975), 89–119. "Part of what it means to call a community of persons 'church' . . . is that use of 'Scriptures' is essential to the preservation and shaping of their self-identity [and] part of what it means to call certain writings 'Scripture' is that . . . they ought to be used in the common life of the church to nourish and reform it" (p. 98). Of course, as Kelsey also made plain, to say that Scripture ought to be used "somehow" does not say precisely how

Scripture should be used to shape the church's faith and life. The agreement *that* Scripture has authority does not entail agreement about *how* Scripture should function as authoritative.

7. I tried it myself when I was asked at my ordination exam, "Did the serpent speak?" It was a scene worthy of Peter DeVries. I patiently (or pretentiously) explained that that sort of question is not appropriate to the narrative of Genesis 3. It is not the sort of history an Enlightenment historian would write, and it should neither be defended nor judged on the basis of what it is not. When I had finished, my examiner asked, "But did the serpent speak?" I summarized my earlier response and included my father's line, "If you ask the wrong question, you get the wrong answer." Then he asked again, "Did the serpent speak or not?" I replied that if I were forced to make a historical judgment, I would guess that there was no speaking serpent. My examiner thought it was the wrong answer. The exam prompted a little "skirmish for the Scripture" in the Christian Reformed Church that I have examined in "Notes on a Controversy about the Bible," *Reformed Journal* (May 1977): 9–12.

8. It is not the sort of question, however, that, given a little time and effort, we can figure out and set aside as solved. It is more a mystery than a puzzle. The formation of a community and its moral life by the reading of its Scripture is a mystery that transcends our puzzling over it, eludes our efforts at mastery of it, and evokes not just curiosity but wonder. That mystery is admitted and celebrated when Christians point toward the Spirit of God as the One who both inspires Scripture and illuminates it. The mystery should keep methodological reflection humble, but it does not eliminate the need for it. The Spirit did not simply overrule the human authors of Scripture. They spoke and wrote with their own voices. And the Spirit does not simply overrule the human readers of Scripture. We hear and interpret with our own ears. And as there were many prophets who claimed to speak a word from the Lord, so there are many interpreters who claim to hear a word from God in Scripture. The community that gathers around Scripture needs to think hard and humbly about *how* Scripture has authority for the moral life.

9. This section condenses a proposal offered more fully in Allen Verhey, *Remembering Jesus: Christian Community, Scripture, and the Moral Life* (Grand Rapids: Eerdmans, 2002), 49–76.

10. Alasdair MacIntyre, *After Virtue: A Study in Moral Theory* (Notre Dame, IN: Univ. of Notre Dame Press, 1981), 175.

11. For the notion of remembrance as the "good" of reading Scripture, I am indebted to Stanley Hauerwas, "The Moral Authority of Scripture: The Ethics and Politics of Remembering," in *A Community of Character* (Notre Dame, IN: Univ. of Notre Dame Press, 1981), 53–71. See also James M. Gustafson, *Treasure in Earthen Vessels* (New York: Harper & Row, 1961), 71–78.

12. See Luke Timothy Johnson, *Living Jesus: Learning the Heart of the Gospel* (San Francisco: HarperSanFrancisco, 1999), 3–11.

13. See Stephen E. Fowl and L. Gregory Jones, *Reading in Communion: Scripture and Ethics in Christian Life* (Grand Rapids: Eerdmans, 1991), 31–33. The church sets these writings apart as "holy" Bible, as canon. To read any text as canonical is to read it in Christian community and in the light of that "whole." The canon itself reminds its readers that texts have genre, authors, and audience, that they involve a process of tradition, that they have social and historical location.

14. Our practice here is frequently better than our theology. Our theology tends to construe God's relation to Scripture and to us through Scripture simply as "revealer." Then the content of Scripture can simply be identified with revelation, and the theological task becomes simply to systematize and republish timeless biblical ideas, doctrines, principles, or rules. In the practice of reading Scripture in Christian community, however, we learn to construe God's relation to Scripture and to us through Scripture as "sanctifier." Then what one understands when one understands Scripture in remembrance is the creative and re-creative power of God to renew life, to transform identities, to create a people and a world for God's own glory and for their flourishing. See further Allen Verhey, *The Great Reversal: Ethics and the New Testament* (Grand Rapids: Eerdmans, 1984), 180–81; David

Kelsey, "The Bible and Christian Theology," *Journal of the American Academy of Religion* 68, 3 (1980): 385–402. Sanctification, it may be said, invites and welcomes attention not only to the learned biblical scholars but also to the saints as the best interpreters.

15. Dietrich Bonhoeffer, *No Rusty Swords*, trans. E. H. Robertson and John Bowden (New York: Harper & Row, 1965), 185; see also 308–25. See Fowl and Jones, *Reading in Communion*, 42.

16. On discernment, see especially James M. Gustafson, "Moral Discernment in the Christian Life," in *Norm and Context in the Christian Life*, ed. Gene H. Outka and Paul Ramsey (New York: Charles Scribner's Sons, 1968), 17–36.

17. Consider also the observation of Nicholas Lash, "When Did the Theologians Lose Interest in Theology?" in *Theology and Dialogue: Essays in Conversation with George Lindbeck*, ed. Bruce D. Marshall (Notre Dame, IN: Univ. of Notre Dame Press, 1990), 131–47. "In the self assured world of modernity, people seek to make sense of the Scriptures, instead of hoping, with the aid of the Scriptures, to make some sense of themselves" (ibid., 143).

18. Margaret Farley, "Feminist Consciousness and the Interpretation of Scripture," in *Feminist Interpretation of the Bible*, ed. Letty M. Russell (Philadelphia: Westminster, 1985), 41–51, esp. 42–44. She cites Paul Ricoeur, *Essays in Biblical Interpretation*, ed. Lewis S. Mudge (Philadelphia: Fortress, 1980), 95. Talk of the "authority" of Scripture is sometimes used to end discussion as though we could beat those who speak from some other experience or from some other source of moral wisdom into silence and submission. Discernment, or the perception of what is fitting, may not demand that people violate what they know in other ways. It may not demand that they violate, for example, either the experience of oppression or the assured results of science or the rational standards of justice. Of course, there can be disagreements—and discussion—about how to read and interpret one's experience or the "assured results" of science or some minimal notion of justice, as there can be disagreement—and discussion—about how to read and interpret Scripture. On the relevance of other sources, see further Verhey, *The Great Reversal*, 187–96.

19. In Matthew the law holds (Matt. 5:17–20; 23:23), and Jesus is its best interpreter (9:9–13; 12:1–8).

Chapter 16

1. See, e.g., Pontifical Biblical Commission, "The Interpretation of the Bible in the Church," IV.A.3.

2. Pope Paul VI promulgated *Dei Verbum* in 1965. The PBC presented "The Interpretation of the Bible in the Church" to Pope John Paul II in 1993.

3. See also Seung Ai Yang, "Biblical Imperatives for the Mission of the Church for the Multicultural Society," in *The National Federation of Priests' Councils Annual Convention Proceedings* 11.3 (2000): 21–28. Some of its sections are included in this chapter.

4. For a nuanced discussion of the transformative function of biblical authority, see William C. Placher, "The Nature of Biblical Authority: Issues and Models from Recent Theology," in *Conservative, Moderate, Liberal: The Biblical Authority Debate*, ed. Charles R. Blaisdell (St. Louis: CBP Press, 1990), 8–19.

5. The term "revelatory text" comes from Sandra M. Schneiders, *The Revelatory Text: Interpreting the New Testament as Sacred Scripture*, 2nd ed. (Collegeville, MN: Liturgical Press, 1999). Because of its brilliant and clear delineation of the complexity of biblical hermeneutics, this book has become a classic resource in the field.

6. Schneiders, *The Revelatory Text*, 55.

7. *Deus Caritas Est* was promulgated on December 25, 2005.

8. The English translations herein are mine, unless otherwise indicated.

9. For other examples of the verb *qnh* denoting "to create," see Gen. 14:19, 22; Prov. 8:22.

Contributors

[handwritten annotations: "Male / female", "Jew / Christian", "White / Hispanic", "Catholic / Protest"]

Marc Zvi Brettler is the Dora Golding Professor of Biblical Studies and former chair of the Department of Near Eastern and Judaic Studies at Brandeis University. He is actively involved in many aspects of Jewish communal life and is coeditor of the *Jewish Study Bible*, winner of a National Jewish Book Award, *How to Read the Bible*, the award winner in the Judaism category of the Best Books 2006 Book Awards, and several other books and articles on biblical historiography, Hebrew grammar, gender in the Bible, and biblical metaphors.

Michael Joseph Brown is Associate Professor of New Testament and Christian Origins in the Candler School of Theology and the Graduate Division of Religion at Emory University and chair of biblical studies. He is an ordained minister in the African Methodist Episcopal Church and the author of *What They Don't Tell You: A Survivor's Guide to Biblical Studies* (Westminster John Knox, 2000) and *Blackening of the Bible: The Aims of African American Biblical Scholarship* (Trinity, 2004).

Katie G. Cannon is the Annie Scales Rogers Professor of Christian Ethics at Union Theological Seminary and Presbyterian School of Christian Education. As a front-runner in Womanist Theology and Ethics, Cannon lectures frequently on a wide range of justice issues related to living with integrity in situations of oppression. She is the author of *Teaching Preaching: Isaac R. Clark and Black Sacred Rhetoric* (Continuum, 2002); *Katie's Canon: Womanism and the Soul of the Black Community* (Continuum, 1995); and *Black Womanist Ethics* (Scholars Press, 1988).

Carlos F. Cardoza-Orlandi is Associate Professor of World Christianity at Columbia Theological Seminary. His writing and teaching are in the areas of mission studies and interreligious and intercultural studies in the third world, particularly in Latin America and the Caribbean. He is the author of *Mission: An Essential Guide* (Abingdon, 2002). He is currently the chair of the

155

Governing Board of the Hispanic Summer Program, Inc. and a member of the Iglesia Cristiana (Discípulos de Cristo) El Aposento Alto in Atlanta, Georgia.

Ellen F. Davis is Professor of Bible and Practical Theology at Duke Divinity School. A lay Episcopalian, she teaches and preaches on topics relating to the church's use of Scripture. Her publications include *Getting Involved with God: Rediscovering the Old Testament* (Cowley, 2002) and *Wondrous Depth: Preaching the Old Testament* (Westminster John Knox, 2005). She has long been involved in interreligious dialogue and has recently begun to develop theological education programs for the church in Southern Sudan.

Terence E. Fretheim is the Elva B. Lovell Professor of Old Testament at Luther Seminary. He is an ordained minister of the Evangelical Lutheran Church in America. His most recent works include *God and World in the Old Testament: A Relational Theology of Creation* (Abingdon, 2005) and *Abraham: Journeys of Family and Faith* (University of South Carolina Press, 2007).

Robert W. Jenson taught at Luther College and Lutheran Theological Seminary at Gettysburg and is now a private scholar resident in Princeton. Co-founder of the Center for Catholic and Evangelical Theology, he is a Lutheran clergyman who is much at home in the Anglican communion. Much of his understanding of biblical authority can be found in his *Systematic Theology* (Oxford University Press, 1997–1999).

Luke Timothy Johnson is the Robert W. Woodruff Professor of New Testament and Christian Origins at the Candler School of Theology at Emory University. A former Benedictine monk, he is a Roman Catholic layperson whose recent works include *The Creed: What Christians Believe and Why It Matters* (Doubleday, 2003) and *Hebrews: A Commentary* (New Testament Library; Westminster John Knox, 2006).

Serene Jones is the Titus Street Professor of Systematic Theology at Yale Divinity School. She is the author of *Feminist Theory and Christian Theology: Cartographies of Grace* (Fortress, 2000) and *Calvin and the Rhetoric of Piety* (Westminster John Knox, 1995). With Amy Plantinga Pauw she has edited *Feminist and Womanist Essays in Reformed Dogmatics* (Westminster John Knox, 2006). Ordained in both the Christian Church (Disciples of Christ) and the United Church of Christ, Jones is a founding member of the Initiative on Religion and Politics at Yale and an active participant in the Women, Gender, and Sexuality Program.

Sarah Heaner Lancaster is Professor of Theology in the Bishop Hazen G. Werner Chair of Theology at Methodist Theological School in Ohio. She is also an ordained elder in the North Texas Conference of The United Methodist Church. Her recent works include *Women and the Authority of Scripture: A Narrative Approach* (Trinity Press International, 2002).

Jacqueline E. Lapsley is Associate Professor of Old Testament at Princeton Theological Seminary, a member of the Presbyterian Church (U.S.A.), and is active in her local congregation as an elder. Her recent works include *Whispering the Word: Hearing Women's Stories in the Old Testament* (Westminster John Knox, 2005).

Frank J. Matera is the Andrews-Kelly-Ryan Professor of Biblical Studies at the Catholic University of America in Washington, D.C. A Roman Catholic priest, he is a past president of the Catholic Biblical Association of America. His publications include *New Testament Ethics: The Legacies of Jesus and Paul* (Westminster John Knox, 1996), *New Testament Christology* (Westminster John Knox, 1999), and *New Testament Theology: Exploring Diversity and Unity* (Westminster John Knox, 2007).

S. Dean McBride Jr. is the Cyrus H. McCormick Professor of Hebrew and Old Testament Interpretation at Union Theological Seminary and Presbyterian School of Christian Education. Before joining the faculty of Union Seminary in 1984, he taught for twenty years at a number of other institutions, including Pomona College, Yale University, and Garrett-Evangelical Theological Seminary. He is a member of the Revised Standard Version Bible translation committee and serves on the editorial board of the commentary series Hermeneia. Recent publications include the introduction and notes to the book of Deuteronomy in the revised edition of the HarperCollins Study Bible.

Peter Ochs is the Edgar M. Bronfman Professor of Modern Jewish Thought in the University of Virginia Department of Religious Studies. Cofounder of the Society for Scriptural Reasoning, his books include *Peirce, Pragmatism, and the Logic of Scripture* (Cambridge University, 1998), *Textual Reasonings* (coeditor) (Eerdmans, 2002), and *Another Reformation: Postliberal Christianity and the Jews* (Brazos Press, 2008).

Allen Verhey is Professor of Christian Ethics at Duke Divinity School. Before joining the faculty at Duke, he taught at Hope College for nearly thirty years. He is ordained as a minister of the Reformed Church of America. He is the author of *Remembering Jesus: Christian Community, Scripture, and the Moral Life* (Eerdmans, 2002) and *Reading the Bible in the Strange World of Medicine* (Eerdmans, 2003).

Seung Ai Yang, a Roman Catholic, is Associate Professor of Sacred Scripture at the St. Paul Seminary School of Divinity of the University of St. Thomas. She has served on the Committee on Race and Ethnicity of the Association of Theological Schools for six years and as chair for two years. Her recent publications include *Off the Menu: Asian and Asian North American Women's Theology and Religion* (Westminster John Knox, 2007), which she coedited with Rita Nakashima Brock, Jung Ha Kim, and Kwok Pui-lan.